Holding On To Heaven While Your Marriage Goes Through Hell

By Connie Neal

Holding on to Heaven While Your Marriage Goes Through Hell

Mun Gode Press

Copyright © 2012 by Connie Neal

No portion of this book may be reproduced, stored in a retrieval system, or transmitted in any form or by any means—electronic, mechanical, photocopy, recording, or any other—except for brief quotations in printed reviews, without the prior written permission of the publisher.

Unless otherwise noted, Scripture quotations are from the Holy Bible: New International Version®. Copyright © 1973, 1978, 1984 by International Bible Society. Used by permission of Zondervan Publishing House. All rights reserved.

Scripture quotations noted NASB are taken from the New American Standard Bible ®, Copyright The Lockman Foundation 1960, 1962, 1963, 1968, 1971, 1973, 1975, 1977. Used by permission.

Scripture quotations noted KJV are taken from the King James Version.

Library of Congress Cataloging-in-Publication Data

Neal, C. W. (Connie W.), 1958-

Holding on to heaven while your marriage goes through hell / Connie Neal.

p. cm. ISBN-13: 978-1468155648

ISBN-10: 1468155644

CIP

TABLE OF CONTENTS

Reviews ii

Dedication i

Introduction i

CHAPTER ONE: Holding on to Heaven While Your Spouse Goes through Hell 1

    Setting Your Mind Above, Where Christ Is, and Grasping His Hand in the Storms of Life Below 1

CHAPTER TWO: The Humanly Impossible Calling of a Christian Spouse 19

    Lord, I Don't Know If I CAN Love My Spouse through This! 19

CHAPTER THREE: Following God's Guidance While Your Marriage Goes through Hell 52

    Lord, How Am I Supposed to Know What to Do in This Situation? 52

CHAPTER FOUR: Setting Relational Boundaries 79

    Where Does My Spouse's Life End & Mine Begin? 79

CHAPTER FIVE: God's Purpose in Pain and the Sanctifying Power of Suffering 103

    God, Why Are You Allowing This to Happen? 103

CHAPTER SIX: Tending a Jointly Owned Spiritual Garden 128

    Lord, How Can I Deal with My Spouse's Problems & Pain That Intertwine with My Life? 128

CHAPTER SEVEN: Do Your Spouse Good and Not Evil All the Days of Your Life 155

    Lord, How Can I Be a Blessing to My Spouse While He or She Is So Troubled? 155

CHAPTER EIGHT: Combating Hell Head-On 188

Holding on to Heaven While Your Marriage Goes Through Hell

How Can I Bring the Power of Heaven against the Forces of Hell on Behalf of My Spouse? 188

CHAPTER NINE: Staying True to God When Your Spouse Gets Off Track 209

Lord, What Should I Do If My Spouse is Drunk, Disobedient, or Putting Me in Danger? 209

CHAPTER TEN: Keep Your Balance 232

Practical Advice from Those Who've Been Through Hell and Survived 232

CHAPTER ELEVEN: Do You Take This Man? Do You Take This Woman? 249

Lord, I Said, "For Better or for Worse," But How Far Does That Promise Go? 249

CHAPTER TWELVE: Putting the Past Behind You 267

Lord, Will We Ever Really Get Over What Happened and What It Did to Us? 267

Acknowledgments 286

Other books by Connie Neal: 288

Speaking Engagements 289

REVIEWS IN PRAISE OF HOLDING ON TO HEAVEN WHILE YOUR MARRIAGE GOES THROUGH HELL

"*I LOVE THIS BOOK! Through Connie's own experience, she is qualified to comfort others with the comfort she has received from God. This book is a dose of reality, a dose of truth, and a dose of hope. And hope in God does not disappoint.*" **Jan Dravecky, wife of cancer-survivor and baseball great Dave Dravecky; Author of A Joy I'd Never Known**

"*This book shows a married couple how to go through tough times without faltering in their faith, and how to be a source of spiritual strength for each other. Men, if you're going through tough times that impact your marriage or fighting some spiritual battle, do yourself a favor, read this book and give your wife a copy.*" **Coach Bill McCartney, founder of Promise Keepers, Author of Sold Out,, and Ashes to Glory**

"*Connie Neal has been of personal encouragement to me as I seek to support my husband in his ministry and to continually strengthen our marriage. She has written a powerful book with deeply moving true stories. If you follow the practical and biblical instruction, you will make a dramatic difference in your marriage.*" **Lyndi McCartney, wife of Promise Keepers founder Bill McCartney, Contributor to Sold Out**

"*When I first met Connie Neal, I saw a woman who was keeping her faith while her world shattered around her. After persevering, her faith was rewarded; her imperiled marriage turned around. What Connie shares will encourage, train, and equip other married couples to make it through the "worst" and live together to see better days and years.*" **Stephen Arterburn, founder and chairman of New Life Ministries, co-author of Every Man's Battle: Winning the War on Sexual Temptation One Victory at a Time**

The following quotes are Amazon.com reviews of a previous version of this book. While this version is adapted to speak a broader audience the content is basically the same so I trust the reviews apply. ~ C W N

5/5 stars: What to do when there is nothing you can do. By A. Customer

"I recently finished reading this book (devouring it is more of an apt description). My husband is, as I write, "going through hell", and I am clinging tenaciously to my God, because He is my only hope. All around me, I am being persuaded to "let him go", "get rid of him", etc., - the world's answers to all problems - discard & recycle. Jesus very graciously led me to Connie Neal's book. At last, here in written form were the feelings of my heart - what about all the promises I made to You, Lord, & the promises You made to me? I loved this book and have re-read it now several times over these past couple of months. I am doing all that Connie suggests that she and the others she wrote about who have experienced first-hand the anguish of storms and trials in their marriages did when there was nothing they could do other than turn to God. I am so grateful for the honesty and obedience of all these Christians who have exposed the most awful times of their lives for the encouragement of ME."

5/5 stars: Thy will, not my will. By Lisa Simpson

This book made God's plan for marriage so clear. It provided a much needed contrast to what the world says marriage is.

5/5 stars: What an Incredibly Honest Book!! By A. Customer

Connie Neal is one of the best artists I have had the privilege of reading! Her work on this book and research into the lives of real people in real situations is filled with honesty. Makes me know the feelings, thoughts I had as I journeyed with my husband through cancer were normal, and that I was not a fledgling Christian because of my weakness. Keep writing, Connie!!!!!!

5/5 stars: Inspiring! By A Customer

This book has given me hope. Please tell Connie Neal that I really appreciate her writing this book. Even though sometimes I feel like giving up on my marriage, I am trusting God for our future. Thanks again for a real inspirational book!

5/5 stars: Life Altering Literature By A. Customer

"I saw this book in the store, and it kept calling my name, for many reasons ... but it seemed a reasonable choice, at the time I was looking for ways to help my husband through some difficult times

Once I began reading the book, I found it to be a help to me spiritually. It covered all the bases of my relationship with God and my spouse. I knew I was being ministered to through this book.

I look at things so differently now... not just because of the author's practical applications of God's Word, (which was truly enlightening), but the sheer ability to motivate me to change and place myself in a position to seek God more in regards to my marriage, and His total purpose for marriage."

5/5 stars: Fantastic!!! By friendlynfun

"This is one of the best books that I have read. It is right on the money with where your hope comes from in a marriage crisis – Jesus Christ! It avoids making false promises, stating that our hope is in God, and that is where we hang our hats. It is written and supported by Biblical truths, which is the only hope in time of crisis!"

5/5 stars: This is a book all women should read. By A. Customer

"I believe every woman (married or not) should read this book and keep it in her library. Personally, I want to share the book with others but I am reluctant to loan my copy so I have purchased copies to give away. YES! I believe it is that good. I never realized so many women go through similar things with their husbands. This book covers whatever the problems are or might be. Connie Neal has been there and she spoke with and received input from other women who have been there – their husbands may have been unfaithful, or abusive, or had cancer, or walked out, or committed a crime. But whatever his personal hell the wife goes through the crisis too. Bill McCartney founder of Promise Keepers said: 'This book shows a wife how to go through tough times with her husband without faltering in her own faith, and how to be a source of spiritual strength for him. Men, if you're going through tough times or fighting some spiritual battle, do yourself a favor; give your wife this book." That last sentence is what happened to me. My husband spotted this book several months ago and got it for me. I didn't know at the time how much I was going to need it. But God did. So my recommendation is, get the book and read it. Then keep it in your library. I pray you never need it, but if you do you will have it and if you don't I still believe it will help to read it – maybe it will help you to help another woman going through a crisis with her husband.'"

Dedication

This book is dedicated to the courageous wives and husbands who are holding on to heaven while their marriage goes through hell. May God grant them all the strength and wisdom they will need; may He help them develop perseverance and increase their hope. May they be encouraged not to grow weary in well doing so that, in due season, they and their families will reap the good rewards God intends for them.

Introduction

This book is intensely spiritual, personal, and practical. Every one of the stories I tell here are true. They are not fictionalized, nor are they compilations of bits and pieces of several stories. In some cases, those who shared their stories asked that I keep their identities a secret. In these cases, I changed minor details so that they are not recognizable.

I chose to use real stories because I have seen how God has used the sharing of my personal story to encourage others. Knowing you are listening to someone who has been there gives greater credence to what is said. This is as it should be. God tells us to comfort others with the comfort we have received from Him. In these pages, I share the real comfort God has given real husbands and wives, along with practical solutions, wisdom, and advice. I hope and pray that you are encouraged and helped so you will become one of us; who has come through a difficult season of marriage victoriously and will go on to comfort others with assurance of God's love and redeeming power.

I first crafted this book in 1998 (eight years removed from our ordeal). At that time the publisher required me to address it only to wives. Now that I am publishing directly, I have expanded the reading audience to include husbands and wives. I decided not to make the reading tedious by saying "him or her" repeatedly throughout. The message of this book applies to husbands and wives, so despite the gender of the pronouns, please freely apply the message to your needs. The only distinctions would be where Scripture specifically assigns differing roles and responsibilities to husbands and wives. I trust that if you are a man whose wife's problems are causing your marriage to go through hell, you will be able to apply the contents of this book to your situation. Whether you are a husband or wife reading this, I pray you will find help here to get through this difficult time in your marriage and go on to enjoy the good years ahead of you.

We celebrated our 32 wedding anniversary in the summer of 2011 and look forward to many more. Our years of marital "hell" are more than two decades behind us. We will never forget what we went through together but the pain is gone and the joy remains. We also never want to forget those things we learned that might help you and your spouse make it through to the happy years ahead. Our prayers go with you on this journey.

CHAPTER ONE: HOLDING ON TO HEAVEN WHILE YOUR SPOUSE GOES THROUGH HELL

SETTING YOUR MIND ABOVE, WHERE CHRIST IS, AND GRASPING HIS HAND IN THE STORMS OF LIFE BELOW

They stood together, seemingly alone in the path of the approaching storm. They stood on an immovable rock that protruded out into the ocean. The turbulent wind ripped at their clothes; the waves crashed about them with unbridled fury. Heavy clouds advanced from off shore like a lumbering herd of dark misshapen animals, picking up speed, pounding earth and sea with each thundering hoof-beat. The menacing force and strange shapes bore down on them with the apparent concentration of a mad bull, aroused to do battle.

Lightning broke through the darkness, like the talons of a concealed predatory bird readying itself to fall upon its helpless prey. Its great shadowy wings beat the air above their heads, each flash of its talons coming nearer and nearer. They held to one another but did not take a step to run away. The man's arms enveloped the woman standing before him, as if trying to spare her the ravages to come, his head bowed over hers, a mingled symbol of shame and prayer. She buried her face in the crook of his neck and heard his sobs, escaping rhythmically with heavy measured heaves of breath. She had no more power to stop the tumult within him than to halt the tempest bearing down on them from without.

The leaves of the nearby trees escaped their branches and raced away. The storm was at hand. The claws of lightning lunged at them again and again, barely missing them. Dirty leaves and broken palms raced past, skittering across the ground as if whispering a warning. The woman turned to face the storm, pressing her back against the man's chest, as if their solidarity was their only means of preservation. His arms never left her, sliding down to hold her securely around the middle. His hands spreading out, as if to protect the child she carried within her. He lifted his head, placing his chin firmly on her shoulder. Her long hair, whipped by fierce winds, lashed at him as the first icy rains spat down on them. They stood resolutely. They would face the storm together.

I viewed this scene from far above. It was only as I came out of sleep that I realized it had been a dream, and that the man and woman I had seen caught in the storm were my husband, Patrick, and me. While still in that land between sleeping and waking, a familiar voice spoke to me. *"One thing you must never forget,"* He said, *"I am not sending the storm to destroy you."* That's when I shook myself awake and sat halfway up in bed. I pulled the worn comforter up around my neck to warm me. I couldn't tell if the chill I felt was real or a remnant of the vivid dream.

I recounted the dream to myself, although I didn't think I could forget it if I tried. I looked over at Patrick, sleeping beside me, unaware, and wondered if I should awaken him. I wondered what the dream might mean and if it was from the Lord. While the setting had been surreal, I found it telling that the depiction of Patrick and me was precisely as we were at that time, even with me being visibly pregnant. I slipped back down under the covers and lay there quietly for a time, but the baby within me was not so quiet. This child didn't kick as my daughter had done when I carried her five years earlier. This child stretched until it found the boundary of a rib to press against. I wondered if my troubling dream had awakened this little one or if the trials I had borne secretly during my pregnancy would have a negative effect on my baby's development. I lay perfectly still, watching the movement within my womb, ever amazed at life in motion. This child was intimately connected to me, and yet it was growing in its own way: moving, living, reaching outward by its own power which I could do nothing to control.

There was so much intimately connected to my life that I could not control and the thought of it chilled me even more than the lingering cold of the winter morning. I pulled the covers up to my neck and gazed at Patrick, still lost in sleep. I wondered how many times in the nine years we had been married I had stayed awake, thinking, planning, praying, sometimes merely directing God as to the proper thing He should do to set the world to rights, while my husband slept. I wondered how many times I had studied his sleeping face, ever perplexed as to why he seemed just out of reach to me. Now that I understood, the understanding was of little consolation.

I had first realized how troubled he was several months earlier. It was more than just his usual retreats into silence. He had grown pale and tense. For the first time in his Christian life he had begun fasting and praying, seeking God about something he did not share with me. Something was obviously wrong with him. Everyone close to us, including those who worked with us on the staff of our church, could tell. Some showed concern and asked me what was wrong with him, but I didn't know. I asked, but he offered no reasonable explanation for his gravity. I didn't press. I knew he would share with me when he was ready.

I was the one who was not ready: not ready to see into the depths of the pain that others had only viewed on the surface; not ready to see the reality of the hell he was going through. It was August of 1988 when he had come to me, asked me to sit beside him, looked into my eyes, and said, *"There is something I have to tell you, although I would rather die, but that wouldn't be fair to you."*

He seemed to be half talking to himself, as if still trying to convince himself that he really should tell me whatever it was that was so troubling.

He went on, "I've been seriously contemplating suicide, but I couldn't bring myself to do that to you, and to Casey [our daughter]. I've met with a counselor who persuaded me to share this with you because I really do love you."

I don't remember if I said anything with words at that point, but in my heart—and perhaps through some look or gesture—I wanted him to know that I loved him and I *would* love him no matter what he had to tell me.

He haltingly proceeded to tell me that he had been unfaithful to me and that this was not the first time. I was in absolute shock. This seemed unbelievable. *How could he have been such a loving husband and done what he had just said? How could I not have known?*

He tried to explain his inner battles, the shame, the self-loathing, the repentance, and the inner resolutions he had made to himself that it would never happen again. He had wanted to tell me at times, but we were both youth ministers, known in our community as Christian leaders. He had not dared, fearing it would mar the reputation of our church. He had sought to spare me the humiliation that would surely come, especially in light of the public confession of sexual sin that had brought down the national Christian leaders Jimmy Swaggart and Jim Bakker. He explained his reasons for not telling me, but the more he had sought to act the part expected of him in public, the more his private life had spiraled deeper into sin, taking him further and further away from the dictates of his own Christian beliefs. A split took place within him; he was unwilling to let go of what he knew to be right while he recklessly gave himself over to do what he believed to be absolutely wrong. His private self was diverging further and further from his public persona. Even the man he allowed me to know became a torn and double-minded man, until finally he came to the breaking point. Knowing that he could not go on with this double life any longer, he reached a crisis. That was when he began to fast and pray as to which direction his life would take: Would he give in to hopelessness that beckoned him toward suicide or would he turn to find another way out?

That was when he sought help from a counselor. The man urged him to tell me and give me the chance—at least—to understand, perhaps to stand by him and help him. I assured him that he had made the right choice in telling me.

He continued, *"I couldn't go on living a lie, even if no one ever found me out. It was destroying me. But something real has to happen. Jesus said he came to set the captives free. I want to be free. But if he can't free me, I don't want to play the game. I'd rather die."*

In that moment, I think my shock had numbed me to his offense against me as his wife. My reaction to that would come shortly and with force. However, at the moment Patrick dared to allow me to see into the depths of him, even the dark recesses of his soul, I recall my deep concern for him, and for the genuine anguish he had risked sharing with me.

I responded with confidence that God could free him, indeed would free him if we took Him at his Word. I didn't want to play some Christian game either. If God could not really come through for my husband to free him not only from the penalty of sin but also from its power, then what good was faith in such a God? If His power was not accessible to us at our point of need, if His goodness was only theoretical, if His promises were not to be trusted, what good was any of it? But I believed that God is ever powerful, good, and true. I believed that He would prove Himself to us through these trials. My confidence in God, as He is revealed in the Bible, gave me the courage and strength to hold on.

I saw the darkness of my husband's condition, and the torment he was going through. This was part of his life he had never revealed before. But I also saw that it could be the beginning of a beautiful story of love and redemption. I determined right then that I was not about to close the book on our relationship before I saw God unfold the rest of the story in a way that displayed His glory.

Over the next five months my confidence in God was severely tested. I came to realize that there was deep brokenness within my husband underlying the sin he had committed. Forgiving the sin was far easier than accepting the reality that I could not heal his brokenness. I loved him with all my heart, but I came to see that my love was not enough. I could not control his behavior, much less his desires. I could not fix him. I couldn't even make God fix him. My love lacked the power to do what needed to be done within him. It would take God's love and power to free him and heal him. The best I could do was to love him, stand by him, pray, and follow God's lead.

I had the dream on the morning of January 15, 1989—five months after Patrick first confessed to me. Our counselors had helped us stabilize our marriage; Patrick had kept his word and remained faithful to me during that time. He seemed to be doing better at handling his temptations and the waves of shame and remorse that sometimes threatened to overwhelm him. The next step was for us to tell our pastor, who was also our boss at the church where we were both youth ministers.

When I awakened Patrick that morning and told him of the dream, he thought it meant it was time for us to tell our pastor. He also thought it meant that things would get far worse before they got better. To him the storm in the dream was God's way of warning us that the reaction we would get to our revelation would be fierce and that it would hit both of us. We prayed and asked the Lord to give us the courage to face the coming storm together.

We did tell our pastor that morning. And the storm hit! Patrick was fired; I was dismissed from my position immediately and later forced to resign. Pat had to make a public confession. There I was, five months pregnant, trying to help my husband get his life right, and we were both hit with the full force of the storm. We lost both our incomes, and our insurance, which meant we could no longer afford counseling. Our four-year-old daughter could no longer attend the church-run pre-school because her tuition had been part of our employment package. The public humiliation we endured caused us to feel isolated from those who could have been a source of support. We ended up going through inpatient treatment, having to sell our home, and basically seeing every part of our lives devastated in some way.

As we were going through all of this, we held on to the assurance God had given us through the impression that had come after my dream, "*I am not sending the storm to destroy you!*" And God's promise in this regard proved true. As I stood by my husband, while holding on to heaven, we weathered the storm even though our marriage went through hell. Everything I believed God could do and would do proved true. He gave Patrick power over sin, although neither of us will ever again underestimate the corruption of the flesh (in every human being), which must be put to death daily that Christ may live in us. Our relationship today – twenty-two years later – is secure, loving, fun, and relaxed once again. It also has an added dimension I find hard to describe. It's as if what we hoped for was the menu, and what we are experiencing now is the feast itself. Everything that was blown away in the storm has been given back to us, only better than before. That child within me the morning I had the dream just graduated from college with a BA in Christian Theology. As a child he was full of boundless energy and a keen sense of humor. He was not hurt by the trauma of the burdens I secretly bore while carrying him; rather it is as if God made him more naturally happy than anyone in the family. In him, God gave us a living spark of joy and laughter, a continual reminder to Patrick and me that God brings laughter after the sorrow has passed. Our two daughters, the one who was four at the time and the one who was born because we stayed together have grown into amazing young women. Looking back, we are all tremendously grateful that we held on to the LORD while our marriage went through hell. The pain of the events I will share with you has faded but valuable lessons remain, and that is good— very good.

WHAT'S YOUR STORY?
No two stories are alike. I don't know how your story reads to this point. I don't know if you or your spouse is a Christian or not, or if you're open to God's word. Whatever your story, or how you read it, God can pick it up at this point and turn it into a story of love and redemption. As surely as I live and breathe the fulfillment of God's promises today, I also believe that God's promises and their fulfillment are available to you and to your spouse as well. I urge you to stand firm in hope, securing yourself firmly to the promises of God. Stand by your spouse while reaching out to God. Don't close the book on your spouse or your marriage until you have seen what God can do.

You picked up this book because your marriage is going through something troubling, disturbing, and something that causes you to want to find help. It may be some kind of affliction, problem, disease, addiction, or circumstances that are putting your marriage through "hell" in one form or another. I do not know what kind of storms are brewing over your heads. I do know that God did not send the storm to destroy you.

THE VIEW FROM ABOVE

Once while I was flying from Denver to Sacramento, I had an experience that is instructive. At the time, thunderstorms were forecast for the region. As is usual whenever I go to Colorado, I prayed that I wouldn't get caught in a thunderstorm. My sense of relief grew as we climbed through the clouds. The more time that passed as the plane proceeded heavenward without turbulence, the greater my sense of relief. The sunlight came shining into my window, the skies shone blue and bright in cloudless brilliance. The brightness was such that I could not comfortably look out and up. But I love to look out the window whenever I fly, so I looked down and back toward the place from whence we had come. There far below was an astounding sight, one that took me by surprise.

It was a thunderstorm, but such as I had never seen—even in pictures—because of the perspective from which I was viewing it. The plane must have been flying at more than twenty thousand feet through clear blue, cloudless skies. The clouds of the thunderstorm were so far below me that it seemed they were part of the ground. I was seeing them from so far above, and from such a distance away that I had a side view. It let me see the white tops of the clouds that faced heavenward and the dark gray underside that seemed to weight them down toward the ground. Lightning seemed to explode across the whole bank of clouds, only occasionally breaking out to stab the earth. From where I sat, the scene appeared silent and beautiful. Only those beneath could hear the echoing thunder that accompanied the lightning.

A Bible verse sprang to mind that says, *"And God raised us up with Christ and seated us with him in the heavenly realms . . ."(Ephesians 2:6).* Now I could picture what that was like! Sometime later the Lord revealed the following lessons from the sight I had been privileged to see. The storm represents the problems, trials, troubles, sorrow, peril, and suffering that come and go in our lives. God lives far above our storms, even beyond our universe. James calls God the *"Father of the heavenly lights, who does not change like shifting shadows"(see James 1:17)*. God remains as he was, is, and always will be. His light cannot be diminished by clouds that hover and circle over the earth. He is light and the ultimate source of light. He is unchangeable. His steadfast love, His good intentions toward all who live on earth, His unapproachable brightness and shining goodness are always a reality, even when the storms of life rage over us. God does not change, even though our view of God often changes depending on what storms overshadow our lives.

God must surely look upon the storms in our lives from His position in the heavenly places, and we look at God from earth, with our view of His goodness and love obscured by the storms. The difficulties, troubles, and suffering we endure can obscure His light from our point of view. While we see only the dark underside of our situation, God can see the entire storm, upper and undersides; He sees from whence it comes and where it will go. He can see the overall beauty and greater purpose that storm may serve. While we can only trust that there is some greater purpose, the reality of our lives is shaken as if by thunder, and we may fear for our survival as one who fears that lightning may strike at any moment. And yet, the Bible tells us that God is not unfeeling toward those who dwell on earth. He sees every storm and says to those who have ears to hear, *"You must never forget; I am not sending the storm to destroy you."*

Scripture tells us, *"Set your hearts on things above, where Christ is seated at the right hand of God. Set your minds on things above, not on earthly things" (Colossians 3:1-2)*. I obey this admonition by calling to mind the nature and power of God that stands eternal, far above the difficulties that come and go from our lives. I see "setting my mind above" as reminding myself that God is always there, and that He is always good. While we cannot know what storms may come, we can find reassurance if we know the heart of the one who promises to see us through life's storms. While we do not share God's foreknowledge of what will happen or how close the lightning will strike, we can trust that God knows what we do not. We can also trust that He will cause *"all things to work together for good to those who love him and are called according to his purpose"* (Romans 8:28).

Setting our minds on things above doesn't mean that we escape the reality of difficulties that come in the normal course of life any more than me recalling the memory of seeing the thunderstorm from heavenly places would keep me from getting wet if I stood outside during a storm today. The value of setting our minds above is that it gives us courage to do what is right in God's eyes when life is difficult and circumstances are threatening. Knowing God is over all and sovereign, gives us courage to go through whatever He allows into our lives and our marriage. However, when we go through those difficulties, they have real effect and we feel the force of them. This shouldn't surprise us.

The reality of the view I had from where I was seated in "heavenly places" in the airplane did not diminish the reality of the violence of the storm as it was experienced on the ground. Just the day before, I heard that a man had been killed by lightening in the same area. Just knowing that God's love and good intentions shine brightly above while you are in the storm below does not mean that the storm is not dangerous to you when you are in it. The storms of life are dangerous; that is why we must not only know God as the One who is above; we must also know God as one who is with us in the storm. We must not only set our minds above, we must reach out to grasp God's outstretched hand to save us when our lives, loved ones, and marriage are in real trouble.

THE ONE WHO IS WITH YOU IN THE STORMS

Surely, Christ is seated at the right hand of God the Father. However, it is also true — and vitally important that you know – that Jesus Christ is the One who came down from heaven to be with us in the storms of life. He did not just come and go. He preserved his place with us when he promised his disciples, *"And surely I am with you always, to the very end of the age (Matthew 28:20)."* He made this promise after his resurrection. Then he ascended into the heavens until the clouds obscured him from their view. Though they could not see him, the book of Acts shows how his followers maintained a close relationship with their living Lord. The Lord spoke to them; he worked with them by performing signs and wonders; he led them according to the need of the moment. They knew Jesus as the risen and ascended Christ, but they also knew him personally as one to whom they could turn whenever they were troubled and threatened by the storms of life.

When you are going through some trying circumstance with your spouse, it is important to trust in God's unchangeable goodness and love. However, the troubles that overcome you in the storms of life have the potential of blocking your view of God even though He remains sovereign in heaven. We must never forget that while God is eternal in the heavens, He has also made himself available to be with us always. As surely as you must "set your mind above" in complete trust that God's love toward you and God's nature are unchanging, you must also trust that Jesus is with you. Trust that he will lift you up in practical ways when the storms of life threaten to take you under.

Think of Jesus' disciples who were out on the Sea of Galilee when Jesus came walking across the surface of the waters. Remember how Peter called out,

> *'Lord, if it's you, tell me to come to you on the water.'*

> *[When Jesus said,] 'Come,' Peter got down out of the boat, walked on the water and came toward Jesus. But when he saw the wind, he was afraid and, beginning to sink, cried out, 'Lord, save me!'*

> *Immediately Jesus reached out his hand and caught him. 'You of little faith,' he said, 'why did you doubt?'*
>
> *And when they climbed into the boat, the wind died down. Then those who were in the boat worshiped Jesus, saying, 'Truly you are the Son of God.'* (Matthew 14:28-33)

This wasn't a major storm, but it was a walk of faith under extraordinary circumstances. And when Peter saw the windswept waves, he was afraid. When I chose to step out and walk by faith in our turbulent marriage while we were being hit by our storm, I was afraid. I was terribly afraid at times, which is only human. When you step out into whatever storm your marriage is going through, you too will have times when the real circumstances will terrify you. Peter didn't *spiritually* begin to sink; his body plunged down under the icy waters in the middle of the night, wet and cold. In this *real* situation he cried out, "Lord, save me!" Then Jesus reached out his hand and caught him. Jesus didn't just lift him in some *spiritual* sense. He lifted him up out of the waters in which he might have drowned and put him safely in the boat. There were times my leap of faith preceded a plunge toward the depths, times I had to cry out, "*Jesus, save me!*" At these times Jesus may have marveled at me, "Oh, you of little faith. Why did you doubt?" But when I was swept away in the icy reality of my husband's situation – and it sometimes threatened to drown me too – I knew Jesus was right there with me. I knew enough to call out to him; and when I did, he caught me. He moved in some real way to lift me up out of the threatening circumstances. He provided safety in some tangible form.

If you are Christ's disciple, if you have opened your heart to Jesus and received the promised Holy Spirit, Jesus **IS** with you. He still has the power to take your hand in real ways and lift you up to a place of safety. You can call out to him on your spouse's behalf as well. If you do not have this kind of close and personal relationship with Jesus, if God is only known to you as one who is far off and not nearby, I urge you to stop right now and ask Jesus to come into your life. Seek to draw near to Him and invite Him to draw near to you, that he might give you a strong hand of assistance while your marriage is going through hell.

YOUR UNIQUE POTENTIAL TO HELP YOUR SPOUSE

You probably picked up this book because your marriage has hit a rough patch. You may be concerned to help your husband or wife, to solve the problems or make things better between you. That is as God intended from the start when He ordained that a husband should love his wife and protect her, and that a wife would be a helpmate to her husband. While you want to help your spouse, you probably also know that you may not have the power to do so directly. How frustrating it is to realize that you cannot reach out and heal him or her with a touch of your hand when they are sick; you cannot wave a magic wand and turn debts into assets; you cannot break the power of sin in their life even when it threatens all you hold dear; you cannot make their boss appreciate them or cause them to be selected for a prime position within their chosen career field; you cannot bring your spouse out of depression; nor can you undo the damage from their childhood or a hundred other things you might want to do for your spouse or your marriage.

While you do not have the power in yourself to do any of these things that might help your spouse and your marriage, God has given you unique potential to help your husband or wife through your marital position. Your unique, God-ordained position in your spouse's life puts you in the place where you can be a conduit for God's love and power to flow through you to him or her.

God has given you a position of tremendous influence in your spouse's life. However, judging from Eve's example (when she disobeyed God and ate the forbidden fruit), we see that a wife also has the keen potential to make matters worse if she turns away from obedience to God while influencing her husband. We also see from Abraham's example (when he said his wife was his sister and she was taken into a harem) that a husband's choices can put his wife in danger. Therefore, if you would fulfill your purpose to be a true blessing to your spouse you must have an open and obedient relationship with the living God.

WHAT DOES IT MATTER?

You may wonder, as I have wondered at times, whether it really matters that you stand by your spouse when your marriage is going through hell. Indeed, it does. It matters because it is your place alone to be your spouse's life-mate and support. This is a created purpose which you accepted with a solemn vow before God when you entered into marriage. Who can say what is forfeited in the spiritual realm if a husband or wife does not volunteer before God to help their spouse by the power of God working through them?

You may wonder if it really matters that you effectively hold on to heaven, seeking to hear and obey God's word. Indeed, it does. Jesus told a story that shows what makes the difference between survival and destruction in life. He said a foolish man built his house on the sand, while a wise man built his house on a firm foundation made of rock. Then identical storms hit both dwellings, but the outcome was not the same. One survived, the other was destroyed. Jesus explained what made the difference, saying,

> *Therefore everyone who hears these words of mine and puts them into practice is like a wise man who built his house on the rock. The rain came down, the streams rose, and the winds blew and beat against that house; yet it did not fall, because it had its foundation on the rock. But everyone who hears these words of mine and does not put them into practice is like a foolish man who built his house on sand. The rain came down, the streams rose,*

> *and the winds blew and beat against that house, and it fell with a great crash (Matthew 7:24-27).*

This parable is not addressed toward husbands and wives with regard to their stormy marriage. However, the operative principle is that your willingness to hear and obey God's word will make the difference between survival and destruction when the storms of life hit. You cannot control whether or not your spouse is hearing and obeying God's word. It's a waste of energy if you focus your attention there. However, if you are in the storm together which we are in marriage – like it or not – we can infer from this parable that our determination to hear and obey God's word can make the difference between survival and being swept away. You can determine that you will hear and obey God's principles with regard to your spouse, marriage, and the life you share. That will make a difference! That is at the heart of what matters with regard to the outcome of your lives and your marriage.

Your determination to keep holding on to heaven while your marriage goes through hell also matters because God intended marriage to be a living representation of Christ's love for his church. I don't think this just means the idea of marriage. God wants to redeem each marriage so that it becomes a living picture of Christ's love for the church: love that forgives, love that causes each marriage partner to lay down his or her life for the other, love that bears all things, believes all things, endures all things, love that never fails. This can only be done by the supernatural power of God working in and through the lives of individual husbands and wives who yield in obedience to God. When you treat your marriage as a divine assignment and allow God's Spirit to flow through you, God can make your marriage a living testimony of Christ's love in real life.

Therefore, I believe your determination to stand by your spouse in whatever storm you're facing, while holding on to heaven, truly matters in spiritual and practical ways. It matters to your children and the future of your family, obviously. It matters to those who look to you in curiosity to see if your faith makes a difference where it matters most—in real life.

LIVING PROOF

I have seen living proof that God can actually do this in real lives. I have seen—miraculously—how my faith affected my husband and how God's power flowed through me to him. Beyond my personal experience, I have found numerous other husbands and wives from varied backgrounds and situations who are living proof that God can work through a spouse who will hold on to heaven while seeking to help their marriage or spouse. I will share these stories with you. Some had Christian spouses; others had spouses who wanted nothing to do with God. It is not who these people are or how spiritual their spouses were at the beginning of the story that seemed to dictate the outcome. It was not their denominational affiliation, education, race, social standing, or income level that caused them to survive the storms with their spouses. What made the difference for all of them, and for me, was that we determined to stand by our spouses when they were hurting, and we did our best to hear and obey God's word in the midst of life's storms that hit our marriages hard. The truths apply across the board when a husband seeks God on behalf of his wife and marriage or when a wife seeks God on behalf of her husband and marriage. Either partner can be the initial opening for God to accomplish His work.

Since these are the common denominators for seeing God's good purpose worked out in our lives and marriages, I will do my best to intertwine what I know of God's word with regard to these issues and what I know of real-life stories where husbands and wives stood by their spouses during difficult times. I will present God's instructions regarding how you can help your spouse in spiritual and practical ways. I will share with you the teachings of God's word that helped me and my husband survive. I will try to show you in simple, biblical, and practical ways how to have a close personal relationship with God that includes both setting your mind above and grasping Jesus' hand in the storms of life.

I cannot offer a specific plan of action for each person who will read this book and make it applicable to the varied situations each one's marriage may face. However, I do aim to help you discern what you should do to test all your decisions by biblical principles. When you know what God says is right and wrong in general terms and determine to do what God says is right, you begin moving in the right direction. Beyond this, I will do my best to help you develop a personal relationship with God where you can get direction from Him for your situation. Jesus said, *"My sheep listen to my voice; I know them, and they follow me" (John 10:27).* If I can help you draw close enough to God to hear His voice, then God Himself can guide you to do what is right in your particular situation and give you the power you lack.

The stories I share, I share in the hope that you will see God's faithfulness in action, His overcoming power, abounding love, forgiveness, and redemption. I pray you become convinced that God can do the same for you and your marriage that he has done for others whose testimonies I share in these pages. I pray you will come to see how God can change you and your spouse for the better, bless you, free you, enlighten you, and lift you both up while you stand firm in the midst of the storms, come hell or high water, while relentlessly holding on to heaven.

My prayer is that you, too, will determine to keep holding on to heaven while your marriage goes through hell; and, in so doing, you will see God's kingdom come, God's will be done, on earth— and in your marriage—as it is in heaven.

CHAPTER TWO: THE HUMANLY IMPOSSIBLE CALLING OF A CHRISTIAN SPOUSE

LORD, I DON'T KNOW IF I CAN LOVE MY SPOUSE THROUGH THIS!

Sometimes we want to do whatever we can to help our spouse, but there's nothing we can do. Sometimes we are willing to do God's will with regard to a troubled marriage but find ourselves unable. There are times when we are willing to do anything in our power, but the power is lacking and our best efforts are ineffective. When we try with all we've got and find it's not enough, we end up exhausted, disappointed, frustrated, and confused. At such times you may think *I'm trying to do what the Bible says, so why am I getting nowhere? I'm giving this all I've got, but this situation is impossible!*

These questions become especially urgent if your spouse's struggles are severe. This isn't just a doctrinal issue to be tossed around academically in a college classroom or at Bible study. When your marriage is in trouble and the possible ramifications threaten your whole family and future, God's word needs to work in real life.

It does work in real life; just not in the way we human beings tend to expect it to work. I've known the frustration of trying to be a good Christian wife in a crisis. I've tried to be kind, tenderhearted, and affectionate, *"loving each other and forgiving each other"* just like the Bible verse I memorized decades ago told me I should. But I discovered that what I easily memorized proved humanly impossible for me to do in the situations in which I found myself. It was only after coming to the point where I realized that I was powerless—and wondered why God's word wasn't working—that I discovered another way.

When trying hard and giving it all that was within me didn't work, I gave up trying in my own strength and learned to live completely dependent on God. (This wasn't some noble act on my part. I was wiped out and completely exhausted.) But when I gave up striving in my own strength, God empowered me to become the kind of wife I wanted to be. He's changed me in ways I thought were impossible. They were impossible for me, but God did the impossible in and through me. I will do my best to show you how he can do the same for you and through you.

When God calls wives to love and respect our husbands and to aspire to do them good; or when the Bible tells husbands to love their wives like Christ loves the church, God isn't aiming to frustrate us. There is a way to do what seems impossible and God wants us to find it. These are scriptural truths that will work for you as surely as they worked for me and others. The life God calls us to live is both impossible for us apart from God and entirely possible with God. This chapter will show you how to have the kind of relationship with God that allows you to live out that which is seemingly impossible.

Jesus tells us about this kind of life in his parable of the vine and the branches. He said,

> *"I am the true vine, and my Father is the gardener. . . . Remain in me, and I will remain in you. No branch can bear fruit by itself; it must remain in the vine. Neither can you bear fruit unless you remain in me. ... I am the vine; you are the branches. If a man remains in me and I in*

him, he will bear much fruit; apart from me you can do nothing" (John 15:1, 4-5).

In this context, it makes sense that the same branch that would find it impossible to bear fruit apart from the vine will bear much fruit if it remains connected to the vine. The branch has no other purpose than to bear fruit, but the source of its ability to produce such fruit is entirely in the vine, and in the care of the gardener. So too, those of us who find it impossible to live out some aspect of Christian life have the capacity to do so if we remain rightly connected to Jesus, dependent on our Father in heaven who watches over us and tends to our lives.

Remaining completely dependent on God for the outcome of our lives and to produce in us that which He commands goes against our culture and our upbringing. Remaining completely dependent on God is incompatible with the belief that God helps those who help themselves. Rather it is more compatible with the belief that God helps those who recognize that they cannot help themselves and therefore depend entirely on Him.

Your mind may recoil at such a thought with questions like:

Wait! Don't I have to DO something?

Don't I have to work to make my life conform to God's commands?

Don't I keep doing my best and pray that it's blessed, and then Jesus takes care of the rest?

You may think, *Surely God doesn't intend me to do nothing when I see so much that needs to be done! Especially when I see clearly all the things my spouse should be doing. I have to figure out some way to get him to do them.*

These questions and thoughts confuse the inner preliminary dependence on God with the secondary result, the outward fruit of godly attitudes and actions that will be produced by such dependence.

Just as the goal of the gardener is to produce glorious fruit, your goal is to enjoy the outward changes in real life that will be accomplished by some things you do, things your spouse does, and things God does on your behalf. However, the **doing** is a separate matter altogether, which will be addressed in the next chapter. You have done plenty, and perhaps you know the frustration of doing all you can and not seeing it achieve the results you want. If you learn to remain completely dependent on God and connected to Jesus, you will end up doing the things God commands; but that will flow from Jesus Christ himself and not be put on by you. When the doing flows from your inner life and right relationship with Jesus it will be both effective and enjoyable.

This jumping ahead to try to **do** what needs to be done and to force the outcome is the cause of much fruitless effort, exhaustion, and frustration. This comes from a misunderstanding of how we are to live out the Christian life. The Bible says, *"So then,* **just as you received** *Christ Jesus as Lord,* **continue** *to live in him, rooted and built up in him, strengthened in the faith as you were taught, and overflowing with thankfulness"* (Colossians 2:6-7, emphasis mine). How did you receive Christ Jesus as Lord? Was it by grace, through faith, and not of works so that you have nothing in which to boast? Indeed! We tend to understand and accept that we are completely dependent on the grace of God when we receive Jesus as Savior. We put our trust entirely in the finished work of Jesus on the cross and the love of God freely bestowed on us as a gift.

However, when it comes to living the Christian life, we tend to think that is something we do in our own strength, perhaps to pay God back for the free gift of salvation. Most people struggle to accept that we are to **continue** to live in Christ, **just as we**

<mark>received him—by grace, through faith, and not by our works or self-effort.</mark> Those who live by allowing God's power to flow through them as they continually depend on Him are an enigma. The people I interviewed who lived as victorious Christians in impossible situations, exhibiting miraculous strength, all have this same baffling dependence on God. People see their lives and say, *"That is IMPOSSIBLE! I know him and her! And what's happening in their marriage (as one or both depend entirely on God) must be the work of God!* Yes, that's the reaction God wants. That is how the Father is glorified through your life.

Some receive Jesus Christ by faith then make the mistake of thinking that once they have received Jesus Christ as their Lord by grace, through faith, they must now stay in his love and good graces by works. They say to themselves, *I'm completely dependent on God for eternal life, but I have to work hard at living as God says I should.* They employ their best human efforts to obey God's commands, fearing that God will cut them off or sever their relationship if they fail to obey all that he commands.

This is the same mistake made by the church in Galatia, to whom Paul wrote,

> *I would like to learn just one thing from you: Did you receive the Spirit by observing the law, or by believing what you heard? Are you so foolish? After beginning with the Spirit, are you now trying to attain your goal by human effort?"* (Galatians 3:2-3).

I ask you to consider the same questions. The way you answer those questions makes the difference between whether or not you will live so as to see God do the impossible things he wants to do through you, in your marriage, and in every other facet of life.

Let me contrast these two spiritual dispositions using real life examples of women who wanted God to help them deal with impossible challenges regarding their husbands. Notice how our first example, Cindy, continued to live by grace, through faith, and remained completely dependent on God to deal with her husband's impossible situation:

CINDY

Cindy married Roy while he was in prison serving a life sentence. In 1976 he had been involved in a drug deal that went bad. Roy's friend shot and killed two men while Roy waited in the car. Under California law, Roy was found guilty of all the crimes, including two counts of felony murder. Cindy was a nominal Christian when she met Roy through her roommate, who was visiting Roy's friend in the same prison. This was a season when Cindy was breaking away from parental authority. She knew her parents wouldn't approve of her visiting a convicted murderer, especially since Cindy is white and Roy is black. So, as her feelings for Roy grew, Cindy kept their relationship a secret from her family.

Cindy would visit him often. Soon they were falling in love. Despite the obvious barriers to a life together, they decided to get married. This did little to change their routine, except for the added privilege of conjugal visits. When Cindy became pregnant, she decided to break the news to her parents. Can you imagine that scene? *I have good news and bad news. The good news is I'm pregnant and I'm not going to be an unwed mother. The bad news, the baby's father is serving a life sentence for murder.* I don't think her parents wanted to run right out and throw a baby shower! They were predictably upset, but they didn't kick Cindy out of the family.

Roy worried terribly that Cindy would divorce him. This drove him to attend a chapel service. He didn't want to let on that he was troubled; he knew he had to be tough to survive in prison. But when the minister invited the men to come forward to receive prayer, Roy wanted the man to pray that Cindy wouldn't divorce him. The minister broke into tears when he prayed for Roy and told him, *"Whatever your request is, God will answer it."* Roy tried to hold back the tears, but he couldn't. Roy gave his life to Jesus Christ that night, wholeheartedly!

Roy began devouring the Bible and encouraged Cindy to do the same. God took hold of that man. When he called his God-fearing mother to tell her he got saved, she asked, *"Did you get it good, Son?"*

"Oh yes, Mama!" Roy said. *"I got it real good!*

From that day forward Roy and Cindy grew closer and closer to the Lord. They went to church separately, read the Bible, repented of their sins, and prayed for Roy to be released. Year after year, the parole board declined Roy's request for parole. Birthday after birthday for their little girl, her daddy could not be there to celebrate with them at home. Even though Cindy and Roy could not have what they wanted most, they both remained entirely dependent on God.

They could not change the circumstances, but God changed them through the circumstances. Roy learned to be content where he was, discovering that God can give a man freedom even though he is physically locked in a prison. Roy settled down, seeking to be a witness for Jesus Christ where he was. Cindy kept visiting, but now they would read God's word together, encourage each other to keep the faith, and share what the Lord was doing in their respective homes.

Cindy believed that God would set Roy free. All along—even when they had to wait three years for a new parole hearing—Cindy encouraged him that every day he spent in prison would be worth it on the day he finally got to come home. Cindy says it was during these years that they both learned to live above their circumstances. They lived by faith because reality was too bleak. They remained completely dependent on God because they knew the outcome was completely out of their control.

Instead of trying to change things outwardly, they focused on changing the state of their faith. Cindy took Polaroid pictures of Roy (this was before digital photography and Photoshop software). Then she took pictures of every room in their home, where Roy had never been. She cut out the pictures of Roy and pasted "him" into every room of their home. Cindy gave these pictures of what they were hoping for to Roy to post on the wall of his cell, where she had never been. They believed that Jesus could set the prisoners free – even though Roy was guilty as charged. If he got out they knew it would only be by God's grace.

After more than twelve years of marriage, the parole board granted Roy a release date. With time off for good behavior, his release was set for a certain day. They held their breath right up until the day because many prisoners had their release order revoked on the day they were supposed to be set free. Cindy bought Roy a new suit so he could walk out of those doors in style rather than in the standard-issue jeans and denim shirt. The morning arrived. Roy took off his prison garb for the last time and put on his new suit. Cindy stood in the waiting area looking down the barred corridor as Roy walked through gate after gate. Roy Davis walked tall, his Bible under his arm, tears streaming down his face. He kept repeating, *"This is impossible! This is unbelievable!"*

As the staff said good-bye to Roy, they said it with admiration. Cindy and Roy drove past the yard filled with inmates separated from them by high fences and barbed wire. The men waved and shouted, *"Good-bye, man! We love you! We'll miss you!"* Roy Davis had been in prison nineteen years, five months, and four days.

There was so much Roy was looking forward to: hearing a dog bark, eating peach pie, going home. Most of all he wanted to go home. But first he wanted to stop at the Christian bookstore to buy a Bible for a friend he had led to Christ in prison. Cindy's friends, people from church, and their daughter's Christian friends all shared in the joy of his miraculous release. On their way to the bookstore, a huge banner hung across the freeway overpass. It read: **WELCOME HOME ROY DAVIS**. The parking lot of the bookstore was filled with brothers and sisters in Christ whom Roy had never met, well-wishers, and those who had fervently prayed for his release. When they got home they ate peach pie and made the dog bark. Roy was home! He was sitting in the places Cindy had pictured him in, but this time he was sitting there for real. That night, Roy's ten-year-old daughter – who had waited her entire life for Daddy to come home – fell asleep in the shelter of his arms.

Roy turned to God because he was worried that Cindy would leave him. Instead, she kept the faith, turned her life completely over to the Lord, believed the best, prayed relentlessly, encouraged him, and lived to see God do that which she knew was beyond her ability to do. People sometimes ask if reality pales in comparison to their dreams of his release.

"*No!*" Cindy says. "*It's better than we ever dreamed possible.*"

God went beyond their hopes that Roy would be out of prison. Shortly after his release Cindy became pregnant again and gave birth to a son, Israel. God had given Roy a fresh start to be a godly father from the very beginning to the youngest of his children. Roy accepted a job as all-around handy-man, janitor, and groundskeeper for their church. When he received the job, he showed his love, humility, and appreciation by washing the feet of the pastors. Everyone who saw Roy Davis around the church saw the Lord Jesus flowing through him. It wasn't long before the pastors promoted Roy. He had compassion for the men still in prison and wanted to minister the gospel to them. Roy's pastors affirmed this desire. At first, Cindy hesitated. She wanted to forget all about prison. But the Lord asked her, "*If you don't have compassion on prisoners, who will?*" With that, she yielded to what she sensed as God's particular will for them and joined Roy in ministering to prisoners. God not only did the impossible *for* her; he was doing it *in* her too.

On the twenty-year anniversary of the day Roy Davis went to prison in leg irons and handcuffs, Roy, Cindy, and the ministry team they led went back into the same prison where Roy had been incarcerated. Ordinarily, an ex-felon still on parole is not allowed to associate with inmates in any way. But Jesus Christ sent Roy back on a mission and arranged for the government to give him unprecedented privileges. Roy wore a suit, and the joy of the Lord was all over him. As they greeted the prisoners, many of whom Roy knew, an old black man beamed brightly, *"Roy Davis! You look like a million dollars and ain't none of it spent!"* One of the correctional officers recognized him. As she greeted him, she said *"Davis, I see you came back to show the men that there's hope, that there's light at the end of the tunnel."*

"No, ma'am," Roy said. *"I came to show them that there can be light* in *the tunnel."* When their clearance came through, the gates clanged open and Cindy passed through metal bars that had previously separated her from her husband. For the first time, she was allowed to see beyond the visiting area, to see the tiny cell where Roy had lived all those years. After Roy preached, men lined up for prayer. They were so hungry for hope. Roy and Cindy had hope to spare. They knew that when we depend entirely on God, He can do the impossible, in us and through us.

JAN DRAVECKY
Now consider another friend of mine, Jan Dravecky. She is an example of someone who began with the Spirit but fell into a pattern of trying to live out her Christian life by human effort. Jan was a strong woman even before she became a Christian. Then she became a strong Christian. Her husband, Dave, was a major league baseball player, first for the San Diego Padres and later for the San Francisco Giants. Jan felt especially suited for the

demands of being married to a major league ball player. Her independent nature, strong mind, and ability to handle almost anything—without her husband being there to help her while he was on the road—gave her a sense of pride.

Jan and Dave both committed their lives to Jesus Christ and were baptized in 1981. Jan tried to be a "good witness" by doing good deeds, helping others, and being a good wife. Dave and Jan thought that God might use their high visibility to allow them to share their faith publicly. Jan is a naturally gifted speaker and supposed that someday God might use her in that area.

In September of 1988, Dave was diagnosed as having a tumor in his left arm—his pitching arm. On their tenth wedding anniversary, Dave underwent surgery to remove the tumor. The prognosis was that Dave would probably never pitch again. When Dave became weak, Jan gathered up all her strength to be strong for both of them. She also immediately began to plan what they should do and what Dave's next career moves should be. But God had a miracle in store for them. Even though the doctors said Dave would be lucky to play catch in the backyard with their son, just six weeks after the operation Dave was able to go through his pitching motion. By July of 1989 he was pitching in the minor leagues; and on August 10, 1989 Dave made a truly miraculous comeback to pitch a major league game for the San Francisco Giants at Candlestick Park.

A media-frenzy began with all the hoopla over the Dave's comeback. Jan took responsibility for handling it. When the mail poured in, Jan volunteered to answer each of the thousands of letters. Then, just five days after the comeback game, Dave was pitching in Montreal when the bone in his pitching arm snapped. That effectively ended his pitching career, but he stayed on the team and Jan stayed in high gear. Dave broke his arm a second time at the World Series, as the players rushed the mound in a victory celebration. As media interest soared, Jan took on more and more.

It's as if she kept saying, *"Don't worry God, I can handle this!"* Then more came, and more and more and more, until she couldn't possibly handle it. The cancer came back, they moved, Dave retired from baseball while Jan was still trying to answer all the mail, cook all the meals, keep Dave happy, take care of their kids, handle the media, help Dave write a book, and smile for the cameras. It's what she thought she had to do to obey God's commands and be a "good Christian wife." But her strength eventually gave out. Even though she was entirely willing to be the kind of wife God wanted her to be and to do whatever Dave needed her to do, whatever the kids needed her to do, what the church expected her to do, she came to realize that it was impossible for her to keep it up.

Jan started having panic attacks; she collapsed while at CBS studios on book tour with Dave; she went into clinical depression and was unable to get out of bed. Dave underwent further surgery and radiation treatment. Jan did her best to be strong. She made herself get out of bed to tape a testimony for the Billy Graham crusade. In June 1991, Dave's arm and shoulder had to be amputated. All through this process, Jan thought she was supposed to make herself stronger, to hold on tighter. When she finally lost her grip, she thought all was lost. But that was when she discovered that God Himself was holding on to her. Metaphorically speaking, she thought her branch was supposed to hold up the vine and make fruit at the same time. When she realized she had misunderstood, she was exhausted but also greatly relieved.

Her utter exhaustion was a turning point for Jan. She learned to let go and completely depend on God to keep her. She and Dave have since gone on to create a fruitful ministry to others who are facing crises because of cancer, amputation, or other debilitating illnesses. Much of Jan's ministry happens when she shares how she collapsed by trying to do for God the things He wanted to do for and through her. In letting go and depending completely on God, she discovered a joy previously unknown to her. By learning to depend completely on God, she ended up being the kind of Christian wife she could not be by force of human strength alone.

DRAMATICALLY DIFFERENT APPROACHES

Cindy and Jan both ended up seeing God do His will in and through them in a way that helped their husbands and made them into the kind of wives they knew God wanted them to be. However, the difference in the way they approached the challenge initially can be instructive for you and helpful to your marriage.

Cindy recognized her complete dependence on God from the start. She didn't expend her energies in fruitless efforts trying to manage the situation and control the outcome. She directed her mind and activities toward developing a closer union with Jesus, dwelling on God's word, and affirming God's steadfast love to her own wavering heart. She knew her situation was impossible for her to change directly, so she focused on developing her connection with Jesus. Then she asked her Father in heaven to do that which she could not do. She had confidence that God would answer her prayer because Jesus promised, *"If you remain in me and my words remain in you, ask whatever you wish, and it will be given you"* (John 15:7). Then she waited and watched for God to fulfill His Word. As she did, God changed her, changed Roy, changed their circumstances and blessed their marriage. God did, and continues to do, the impossible in and through their lives. Over many years God even promoted Roy to become a pastor at their church.

Jan Dravecky's approach was to begin in the Spirit by faith alone, but she fell into a lifestyle common among Christians. She tried to live out her Christian life in her own strength. She believed it was her responsibility to do all God commanded and all that needed to be done around her. She feared God might cut her off from His love if she didn't do enough. Therefore, she exhausted herself and collapsed. That's when she ended up spiritually where Cindy started out—completely dependent on God alone.

Both Cindy and Jan reached the state of complete dependence on God by recognizing their emptiness and powerlessness. Cindy did so from the beginning, while Jan had to arrive at that point after exhausting her own strength and self-effort. This prepared them both to experience God's fullness flowing through their lives with full force. It was in this state of complete dependence on God, not relying on their own power, strength, or ability, that God did for them that which was impossible for them to do on their own.

Try thinking of this metaphorically as you might think of a garden hose. If you look at a hose disconnected from a water source, it is completely empty. Perhaps there is a small reserve of water previously stored up, but otherwise there is nothing in and of the hose that can flow out. However, if you take that empty hose and connect it to a water source, its state of being empty makes it well suited to be a conduit through which water can flow freely for as long as it is connected. Anything added to the inside of the hose, any clog or obstruction, will not help the flow. It will slow or temporarily impede the full flow of the water it was created to dispense.

Our relationship with God bears a similarity to the empty garden hose. If we are disconnected from God, we are completely empty and have nothing in ourselves that can do the impossible things God intends to do through us. This does not mean that God does not intend those things to happen. In fact, we were designed by God to be filled with His Holy Spirit. God's wants us to allow Him to flow through us in all His strength, goodness, righteousness, power, wisdom, and grace. Cindy was like the empty hose. Her recognition of her powerlessness to affect the outcome of her husband's situation predisposed her to allow God to flow through her fully. Jan was also connected to Jesus, but her belief that she had to do everything God wanted her to do in her own strength was like a clog. Her self-sufficiency impeded the flow of what God wanted to do through her. The pressure built up until her self-sufficiency burst away and dissolved. Then, when she was empty of dependence on her own human strength and wisdom, God was able to flow through her and do for her and Dave that which she had been trying to do on her own.

A MISCONCEPTION THAT MAKES A DIFFERENCE

The difference between how Cindy and Jan responded to their husbands' situations shows a differing understanding of their relationship with God. This can be explained by two differing views of Jesus' parable of the vine and the branch. How you interpret the lesson of this parable will make the difference between whether you try to do the impossible for God and become frustrated or whether you remain completely dependent on God in your inner life so that He does the seemingly impossible through you.

What seems like a slight nuance in the translation of one verse can make a major difference in whether or not you will experience the abiding fruitfulness and joy that Jesus promises. So, please follow this closely. It will pay off for you although it requires careful attention. Some versions of the Bible quote Jesus in John 15:10 to say, *"As the Father has loved me, so have I loved you. Now remain in my love.* **If you obey** *my commands, you will remain in my love, just as I have* **obeyed** *my Father's commands and remain in his love" (John 15:7-10, emphasis mine).*

But the King James Version and New International Version translate this verse with a crucial word-swap. The KJV quotes Jesus to say: *"If ye* **keep** *my commandments, ye shall abide in my love; even as I have kept my Father's commandments, and abide in his love."* The NIV translates it, *"If you* **keep** *my commands, you* will remain in my love, just as I have **kept** my Father's commands and remain in his love." So what is the difference between "obey" or "keep"? And what does it mean to you?

One might take the first version to imply that the only way we stay in God's love is to obey His commands. If you don't obey, you're cut off and don't get any of the privileges or the joyful outcome assured to those who do obey. The person who believes this meaning might sound something like this while thinking: *If I obey the Bible I can stay in God's love. He will keep on loving me if I keep obeying Him. And if I can keep on obeying His commands, I will eventually have joy.* There is a major problem with this line of thinking: No one can continually obey God's commands. We may try our best to obey, but all of us fall short of God's expectations when we try in our own human strength. So we try, we fail, and we get frustrated because we cannot do what we are willing to do and what we know God wants us to do. One might conclude, *Well, Jesus said I would abide in his love if I obey his commands. But I couldn't quite obey his commands fully. Does that mean God has cut me off from His love? Do I have to obey all His commands before He will love me again? Do I have to obey all His commands before I can have joy? If so, I'm never going to make it.* One might get discouraged and conclude: *There's nothing I can do! That confirms it! I must not be abiding in Jesus. Does that mean I've been cut off? Am I hopeless?*

That's the line of reasoning that goes along with trying to fulfill God's purpose without God's power. Its effects are described in the Book of Romans chapter seven as a circular life of frustration in which you don't do what you know is right but you do the very things you hate and you know God hates. It's what the Bible calls the *"works of the flesh";* but such works don't empower you to live a godly life. Instead of works of the flesh, God wants you to experience the fruit of the Holy Spirit. These are love, joy, peace, patience, kindness, goodness, faithfulness, gentleness, and self-control—all qualities that would help you deal with your spouse and whatever difficulties your marriage is going through. So what's the problem? How does someone whose heart is set to live out the will of God end up frustrated and powerless to do what she agrees to be right? Well, it starts with a misunderstanding of what Jesus meant when he said, *"If you **keep** my commandments, you will abide in my love."* Or the other way it has been translated, *"If you **obey** my commands, you will remain in my love."(John 15:10)*

WHAT'S THE DIFFERENCE BETWEEN KEEP AND OBEY?

I noticed that the people I interviewed who were miraculous overcomers with regard to their marital challenges all had a common characteristic. They espoused a view of God's word that was one of relentless belief— even when they were unable to live out what they believed God promised and required. They seemed to watch over God's word expectantly. In my life this is one of the few characteristics I could single out as giving me strength when our marital difficulties were so trying. I wanted to understand what Jesus meant by, "If you keep (or obey) my commandments, you will remain in my love." So I checked the original Greek language for the word *translated "obey" in one version of John 15:10 and "keep" in another translation*. Did it really mean God's love is contingent on us continually obeying God's commands or something else? I believe that what I found explains the difference between how Cindy approached her husband's situation and how Jan initially approached her husband's crisis.

The New Testament was originally written in Greek. The original word that has been translated variously as "keep" or "obey" is the word **Tereo**. So understanding the intent of the original language will help us understand the meaning of this verse. There is a Greek word that can be translated in English as "keep" that means "to do" or "to obey." Jesus used this word to say, "Has not Moses given you the law? Yet not one of you *keeps* the law." This is the Greek word *POIEO*, which means *"to do."* This is the word I would have expected to be used if remaining in Jesus' love were dependent on what we *do* to *obey* God's commands. However, the actual Greek word used in Jesus' statement, *"If you **keep** my commandments, you will abide in my love,"* (John 15:10) is not *POIEO* (to do); rather it is *TEREO*, which means "to watch over, preserve, keep." It is the same word used of the keeping power of God the Father and Christ, which God exercises over His people. It is the word used by Jude to describe "keeping the faith." It also can be used to mean "to observe, or give heed to [God's commands]." So the emphasis in the verse in its original form is on what takes place in the inner being: believing, keeping our faith, observing, or watching over God's commands as true. In this sense, keeping His commands is something that occurs in the mind (by believing and relentlessly agreeing with God's word) and in the will (choosing to observe God's commands).

God could have chosen to use either word to make His meaning clear; but He chose NOT to use *POIEO*, "to do." Instead, He chose the word that meant to watch over, observe, preserve, and give heed to, *Tereo*. Let's listen to how the internal reasoning might go with this understanding of what it takes to abide in Jesus' love.

INTERNAL REASONING
Jesus himself said that not one of those to whom Moses gave the commands keeps the law. And the Bible also says that "There is no one righteous, not even one; there is no one who understands, no one who seeks God" (Romans 3:10-11). He knows we are incapable of continually obeying His commands on our own. Jesus isn't saying that God will only continue loving me if I obey him. Jesus will not cut me off from his love if I do not perfectly obey God's commands. So, it doesn't make sense that I would be separated from God's love every time I sin and be back in His love when I begin to obey again. That would be salvation by works. And yet, Jesus does seem to be saying that we can expect to obey his commands. But could it be that just as the fruit grows from a

branch that remains connected to the vine, outward obedience grows from "keeping God's commands" in the inner being. It comes by refusing to let go of God's word even if we are powerless "to do" all God commands apart from Jesus abiding in us and his life flowing through us?

This is the only explanation I have found that both makes sense of God's word and provides a way to live out the kind of life that I am powerless to live on my own. It is this understanding of "abiding in Christ" that can bring about God's outcome in our marital relationship too.

Trying to stay in God's love by continuously obeying presents a serious danger. Like Jan, we may become frustrated if we continually experience defeat in trying to do in our own strength that which only God can do. We may get discouraged when we occasionally fall short and disconnect completely, becoming altogether unfruitful.

Since Jesus told us to remain in him, there must be some danger that we might not remain rightly connected to Jesus. Remaining in Jesus is **NOT** about what you do in your outer life (although that will be affected eventually). It's about how you observe, watch over, and see God's word in your inner life. Let's look at the difference in how the one who remains in Jesus and abides – completely dependent on God for the outcome—differs from the one who disconnects.

Those who "remain in Jesus" see God's word with eyes of faith. Hebrews 11:1 tells us, *"Now, faith is the assurance of things hoped for, the conviction of things not seen" (Hebrews 11:1 NASB).* One who keeps the faith keeps God's word in their mind (abiding in him or her). They watch over God's word expecting Him to perform it, instead of just watching over life's circumstances and trying to affect the outcome. If there is a marked difference between what they are experiencing and what God says they can expect, they look for God to bring His Word into reality. They are assured that God intends His Word to be proved true—with or without their help. Jan and Cindy both remained in Jesus because they both continued to watch over God's word with eyes of faith. Jan's initial misunderstanding of what she had TO DO didn't cut her off from God's supply or God Himself. It just caused her to exhaust herself needlessly.

The one who disconnects from Jesus is the one who lets go of God's word and stops watching over it with the expectation that God will somehow prove it true. They may try it for a while but conclude that since it didn't immediately work for them, God can't really mean what is recorded in the Bible. They stop expecting God's word to be fulfilled and stop seeing it as living and active. This kind of disconnected religion is exemplified in the life of cartoon character Homer Simpson.

HOMER SIMPSON'S CYCLE OF SPIRITUAL FAILURE

Whether or not you watch **The Simpsons**, you're probably familiar with the longest-running American cartoon family on prime time television. By any estimation, the dad, Homer Simpson, is not a role model many would want to follow—especially a Christian. And yet I see a cycle in Homer Simpson's life that is common among Christians who get frustrated trying to live up to God's word without having the power to do so.

In one episode, Bart Simpson, the troublesome fourth-grader in the family, asked his dad, *"Homer, what religion are you?"*

Homer replied, *"Oh, you know, that one with all those well-meaning rules that don't work out in real life. What's it called? Oh yeah, Christianity."*

While many Christians won't even admit to watching **The Simpsons**, many may live as if they share Homer's view of Christianity. They agree that the sentiments and commands presented in the Bible are well-meaning, but they have given up believing they can live their lives in obedience to the Bible. Just because it is humanly impossible to fulfill God's commands apart from Jesus Christ, they never quite got the hang of allowing God to do through them what they could not do themselves. So they just stopped keeping the faith. They stopped believing that God really intends for them to live up to those impossible standards. And if they don't keep on believing God's commands are intended to be the living fruit of the Christian life, they stop clinging to Jesus and depending on Him to fulfill His commands and promises in their lives.

WHERE ARE YOU?

My goal in this chapter is to help you remain rightly connected with God so you can respond to your marital difficulties with the love and power of the Holy Spirit. To do this, you need to identify your current spiritual disposition. Don't worry about what you are supposed to do at this point. The fruit-bearing action is the result of "abiding in the vine" or remaining completely dependent on God. The abiding takes place in your inner life, not initially in your outward actions. Take a look at these three patterns of relating to God. Once you see which one best describes your spiritual disposition, you'll be able to make any needed adjustments to get rightly aligned with God.

HOMER'S CYCLE OF SPIRITUAL FRUSTRATION

Here is a cycle that represents someone with a spiritual disposition like Homer Simpson's:

HOMER'S CYCLE OF SPIRITUAL FRUSTRATION

Here is the text copy of the cycle that represents someone with a spiritual disposition like Homer's:

1. God's commands are clearly written.

2. I tried to live that way.

3. I'll try again to obey. But I don't know...

4. Repeated failure and frustration

5. How can God demand what I can't do?

6. I don't have the power. I can't do this.

7. God's word must not mean what it says.

8. I am powerless! There's no way...

9. Start the cycle over again.

There are only so many times a reasonable person can go through that cycle before being worn down by the dissonance it creates. A host of uncomfortable thoughts and emotions arise as one goes through this cycle: anger at God, confusion, fear, guilt, a sense of condemnation, and instability. When we can't make God's word work in our lives and when we entertain the idea that God's well-meaning rules were never meant to work out in real life, we go on to wonder if the rest of God's word works either. Can we be sure of anything the Bible says? If we can't obey God's commands, even though we know what's right and want to do it, what's the point of trying? Anyone who falls into this cycle and doesn't find a way out will — at best — be a Christian in name only. He or she will not be fruitful, as Jesus says the Father intends, nor will their life bring glory to God. If this is your spiritual disposition, you will not be able to access the help God has available to help you work through your marital problems successfully until you find a better cycle.

THE CYCLE OF PERPETUAL WORKS AND FRUSTRATION

Here's a cycle that represents someone with the spiritual disposition of trying to stay in God's love by maintaining obedience to God's commands (like Jan started out):

THE CYCLE OF PERPETUAL WORKS AND FRUSTRATION

Here's the text version of the cycle that represents someone with the spiritual disposition of trying to stay in God's love by obedience and trying harder (like Jan started out):

1. I love the Lord.

2. Therefore, I will do all God commands me to do.

3. Problems or difficulties arise.

4. I'd better take care of this.

5. I can handle this. I'm a strong Christian. I can do this. God can help.

6. Stop praying and start working, doing whatever God needs me to do to control things.

7. Work harder; pray harder.

8. I'm working fervently, but growing anxious.

9. I'm exhausted — but have to keep going.

10. God, if I'm working so hard, why isn't this working?

11. I'm discouraged and confused.

12. I can't manage this. I'm powerless!

13. Back to the start of the cycle; I love the Lord...

Therefore I will do all God commands me to do. ...

This person can help their spouse in many ways. However, they probably exhaust themselves in the process. They may also grow resentful at all God and their spouse expect of them. These are the kind of people who tend to create conflict because they are so focused on the outcome that they attempt to manipulate others and control the situation. The person with this kind of spiritual disposition may come off as judgmental, but they are as hard on themselves as they are on others. Neither of these cycles will result in what you need to receive God's overcoming power while your marriage is going through hell. The next cycle is the best way to go. The good news is that you can start it any time you realize you are powerless apart from the power of God.

THE OVERCOMER'S CYCLE OF SPIRITUAL SUCCESS

Here is the cycle that represents someone with a spiritual disposition of completely depending on God and "keeping" his word (like Cindy did) from the start:

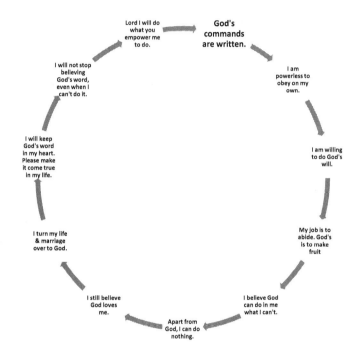

THE OVERCOMER'S CYCLE OF SPIRITUAL SUCCESS

Here is the text version of the cycle that represents someone with a spiritual disposition of completely depending on God and "keeping" his Word (like Cindy did from the start):

1. God's commands are clearly written.

2. I'm powerless to obey God's commands on my own.

3. I'm willing to do God's will, choosing to say, *"I can't do it in my own strength, nevertheless, not my will but God's will be done."*

4. God's part is to make the fruit. Mine is to abide. Instead of focusing on my emptiness, I choose to focus on Jesus' fullness.

5. Lord, I believe you can do in and through me what I can't do on my own. All things are possible for you.

6. Abba, Father, I still believe you love me, even though apart from You I can do nothing.

7. I surrender! I turn my life and my marriage over to your care.

8. I will keep your word in my heart as TRUTH. Please make it come true in my life because I can't.

9. I will not stop believing your word is true and your commands are right, even if I can't obey them fully in my own strength.

10. Lord, I will do whatever You empower me to do.

11. Go back to the start of the cycle, God's commands are clearly written.

THE POINT OF POWERLESSNESS

Notice that these patterns or cycles have one point in common: the point of **powerlessness**. It may be phrased in different ways, but the people in any of these cycles come to a place where they would be saying things like, *"This is impossible for me!"* Where one proceeds from that point of powerlessness is what makes all the difference in the spiritual and practical outcome. Cindy always realized she was powerless over their situation. Cindy started at a point of complete dependence on God. Jan went to work for God until she exhausted her own strength and collapsed into powerlessness. Then Jan turned to complete dependence on God. Homer's frustration over his repeated pattern of powerlessness disconnected from God and went into disbelief.

That point of powerlessness is the turning point of life. It is the point at which God can take over to do the impossible. When you realize that you are powerless, you can make the right choice that Cindy Davis and Jan Dravecky made. You can choose to depend entirely on God. You can choose to believe His Word. Just because you rightly conclude that you can't deal with whatever you're going through in your marriage doesn't mean that God can't. With God, all things are possible. Really!

Here is the simple progression you can make from any place on any of these cycles to immediately being rightly connected with Jesus and remaining in Him. Whenever you hear yourself say, *"I can't!"* follow that with, *"But God can!"* Then choose to turn your will and your life over to the care of God. These are the same principles that begin the 12 Step program used successfully by millions in Alcoholics Anonymous.

STEP ONE: admit you are **powerless** and your life has become unmanageable.

STEP TWO: come to believe that a power greater than you—who we know to be Jesus Christ—*could* restore you.

STEP THREE: make a **decision** to turn your life and your will over to the care of God.

One reason the 12-step program works is because it has tapped into the true application of what Jesus explained in the parable about a branch abiding in the vine.

Understand that your act of realigning yourself to abide in Jesus is not an act of human strength. It's using your will to **choose** to depend entirely on God at any moment. This can be done in any situation, even if your strength has been worn down by stress, heartbreak, or utter exhaustion with self or your spouse. It's saying, *"God, I can't handle this. I can't control the outcome but I turn it over to You."* You may have to make that choice countless times in the same day; but that is something you can choose as an act of your will.

As a human being, created in the image of God, you have been created with the capacity to choose. Even in the most desperate and debilitating circumstances (like those described by Viktor Frankl in his book *Man's Search for Meaning* about his experience in a Nazi concentration camp) you are able to choose the disposition of your inner being. You may not be able to choose your circumstances, but you can choose the way you view those circumstances, your life and the meaning of the whole. You can always choose to see yourself safely growing in the vine, with God the Father watching over you and caring for you as a competent gardener watches over his vineyard—even if there's no fruit yet. You can choose to believe that you are in the Lord's vineyard and that the promise of Isaiah applies to you where it says,

> *"Sing about a fruitful vineyard: I, the LORD, watch over it; I water it continually. I guard it day and night so that no one may harm it"* (Isaiah 27:2-3).

You can use your will to choose to believe that God's word is true — not just in theory but in real life. You can choose to turn your life, your spouse's, and your marriage life over to the care of God. This is all done in your mind and your will by an act of faith—

choosing to believe the best for your life and your spouse and that God's word is true even if you don't see the good outcome yet.

You actually do see part of God's word proved true: the part where Jesus says, *"Apart from me, you can do nothing."* You see that part and you can choose to believe the other part you cannot see yet. God's word also says, *"I can do everything through him who gives me strength" (Philippians 4:13).* You can choose to believe that Jesus – the true vine – is sufficient to produce fruit from your life. Even the difficulties in your marriage can eventually bring glory to God and joy to you—if you just hang in there.

God is the gardener. And what loving gardener doesn't want good fruit he can show off? God wants the fruit of your life to be glorious. If your response to your spouse or your spouse's situation is not such that it brings glory to God, then hang on until it does. God the Father will do the work of pruning you and Jesus will sustain you and flow through you to make it happen.

So, how do you remain in the right spiritual disposition? You do what the fruitful branch does. You don't focus on working to make fruit. Instead you simply abide in Jesus, receiving his life in you and resting and waiting for God to do His transforming work in and through you. If you want to do something, let that be to allow His word to abide in you more fully. Go to God's word. Let God's word abide in you and let its assurance flow into your innermost being: assurance of the Father's steadfast love, assurance of the love of Christ, assurance that NOTHING can separate you from the love of God that is in Christ Jesus your Lord. For it is written,

> *"For I am convinced that neither death nor life, neither angels nor demons, neither the present nor the future, nor any powers, neither height nor depth, nor anything else in all creation, will be able to separate us from the*

love of God that is in Christ Jesus our Lord" (Romans 8:38-39).

Then keep watching over God's word to see God make it come true in your life. Choose continually to pray after Jesus' example, *"Not my will, but your will be done, Father."* Then cling to Jesus in the expectation that He will watch over his word to perform it. Remain in this relationship of dependent reliance on God alone. As you are "hanging in there," make use of the promise Jesus gave to those who abide in him and have his word abiding in them. Ask the Father for whatever you wish and it shall be done **for** you!

This isn't a once and for all event. It's more like an inner pattern of mind, will, and spirit that you have to practice. If you have the wrong pattern set up as a ritual in your life, you will need to stop yourself any time you start going in circles of frustration. When you hear yourself say, *"I can't!"* remind yourself to say, *"But God can! And I choose to turn my life over to Him and depend on Him entirely to do that which I cannot do."* What does the Bible tell us about how we are transformed (in Romans 12:2)? It is by the **renewing of our minds**. As you continually renew your mind to agree with God's word, you will see God transform you. Then you can better deal with your spouse and the hell your marriage is going through.

There were times after my husband was unfaithful to me when I was deeply afraid he might be unfaithful again. My first response was to try to make sure that didn't happen. I tried to control him, to monitor his movements. I wanted to drive him to work and pick him up—even though he worked nights and that meant packing three small children into the car in the middle of the night. I checked the odometer to make sure he had only gone where he said he had gone. I knew the outcome I wanted and tried to achieve it by outward means. I also prayed that God would help make sure he was faithful to me—but in my mind God was my back-up! I was intent on making sure by my own efforts that he didn't go out on me again. In the end, I only exhausted myself. I realized that the kind of life and relationship I wanted wasn't something that could be forced by outward means. It had to come from the inside, starting in my husband's heart. Except by this time, his heart was already right in this regard. My fears, worry, and compulsion to monitor his life were **my problem**. My outward efforts did nothing to help; they only added stress to our relationship. They worked against the outward outcome I was trying to force.

I came to realize that I was absolutely powerless to make my husband remain faithful to me. That moment was very scary! But I was able to make the shift from *"I can't!"* to *"God can!"* to *"I make a decision to turn my life, my husband and our marriage over to the care of God."* Sometimes I had to go through this process many times in the course of one night. But as I continued to redirect my mind and my will to choose complete dependence on God, God took care of a situation over which I had no control. When I could not even control my fears, it brought me realize I was also powerless to control my husband's heart or his life. That inner *"I can't"* became *"God can!"* and led me to say, *"I choose to turn my fear and all my life over to your care, God."*

I also built up my inner person by allowing God's word to abide in me through songs, hymns, and spiritual songs. Every time I noticed myself worrying about the outcome of the situation I would redirect my attention to my connection to God. That was the best way to expedite the outcome I wanted. I turned every worry into a prayer (which meant that verse about praying without ceasing became second nature to me). Also, I would sing songs to remind me how God compensated for my lack. When I was not able to do something, I would sing, *"He's able! He's able! I know he is able! I know my Lord is able to carry me through."* When I felt like I was going under, I would sing, *"On Christ, the solid rock, I stand! All other ground is sinking sand."* When I didn't know what was going to happen, I sang, *"I know whom I have believed, and am persuaded that He is able, to keep that which I've committed unto Him ..."*

Then God worked miraculously in me, in my husband, and in our life together. It took time and we don't know exactly how it happened. It was an inner process that is still a mystery. We saw the results, but we do not understand how God did the wonderful things He did any more than I know how a baby grows from the loving union of husband and wife. One who watches for grapes to grow on a vine doesn't need to know exactly how the life of the vine flowing through the branch produces the fruit to taste the sweetness. And we don't know how God has renewed our marriage, restored our trust, and blessed us beyond expectations. We can't explain how God did the impossible that we could not do. But He did it and we're enjoying the fruit.

God can do the same for you and your marriage. Abide in Jesus. Depend entirely on God. Keep the faith. Enjoy the fruit!

CHAPTER THREE: FOLLOWING GOD'S GUIDANCE WHILE YOUR MARRIAGE GOES THROUGH HELL

LORD, HOW AM I SUPPOSED TO KNOW WHAT TO DO IN THIS SITUATION?

This chapter brings you good news! If you choose to believe what God's word says, you will be able to breathe a sigh of relief. You can get excited because God Himself is willing to guide you in whatever you are going through in your life and marriage. I'm not talking about just having a list of guidelines to follow; I'm talking about having God Himself—the One who loves you dearly and has good plans for your life—personally guide you as you make decisions regarding your current situation with your spouse and whatever your marriage is going through.

I have even better news than that. God is guiding you even when you don't know He is, even when you're complaining because this was not part of your plan! I heard a recurrent theme from every person with whom I discussed this topic. One said, *"I feel like we're stuck in the wilderness."* Another said, *"It felt like we were just wandering around out in the wilderness."* Jan Dravecky even refers to one season of their lives as *"our wilderness experience."* Others just express feelings like these: *"I feel so lost!" "We're so confused; we don't know which way to turn." "This is scary; we can't figure out where God is taking us."*

I know the feelings! And I have good news for everyone who's going through some sort of wilderness experience. The wilderness is the way to the Promised Land! I'm not going to get all biblical on you here. This isn't just academic. I'm telling you that this is what happened in my life and in the lives of those I interviewed. The times when I was complaining to God because He was taking me away from what I personally believed He had promised me turned out to be the times I was on the route to the fulfillment of those very promises—only better than I anticipated.

We all have a plan for our lives. As Christians, we probably consult God in the planning process and try to set our goals within the scope of what we believe to be our calling. Our spouses have their plans; and God has His. Sometimes one of the most upsetting results of our spouses going through something difficult is that it interrupts our plans. It seems to take us off track from where we expected to go. It threatens to keep us from getting what we expected—and getting to our goals in the way we expected to get there. That was certainly the case for me.

I was focused. I had clearly envisioned plans and goals that I believed God had given me the vision for in the first place. There was nothing I wanted so much as to serve God, to use my talents to His glory, to write, and to speak publicly—and I believed God had put these desires in my heart. I was aiming to get there by diligent ministry in the local church combined with persistent efforts sending out book proposals to publishers. My local ministry was flourishing, and though my proposals had not been accepted yet, I was confident that my diligence would pay off. My husband's crisis interrupted my plans in a big way when he confessed to infidelity.

Suddenly, I was out of ministry and removed from my position within the Christian community. Circumstances dictated that I had to go back to work in a secular job. Financial limitations and other influences that were beyond my control—which I fought against—

caused us to decide to move away from the town where we had been in ministry. That's when I entered my wilderness period. Patrick was experiencing his own kind of wilderness, but that had more to do with the inner battles he was waging. We were both confused, uncertain of which way to turn or what move to make next.

This wilderness experience continued for a few years. To me, it looked like I was not getting guidance from God. I wanted Him to show me how to get back to the plans I had in mind for myself and on the track I thought would take me to the fulfillment of my dreams. Instead I was in a new city away from the few trusted friends I had left, eight months pregnant, and staying home with a toddler and a seven-year-old. I thought I could not have been further from the plans I felt sure God told me He had for me. And this all happened because of my husband's problems and wrong choices.

I was convinced that God was not guiding me. In fact, I was crying out for Him to guide me and felt quite defeated as a Christian because I thought I was so far off track and God was not telling me how to get back on track. Then, I was asked to help a friend write some youth ministry training materials. It wasn't the kind of writing I hoped to do, but it would give me something meaningful to do using my expertise in youth ministry. And it would give us Christmas money.

That led to me assisting at the National Youth Workers' Convention. While there, I had an off-hand conversation with someone who was writing a book dealing with sexual addiction. I suggested a few things that should go in such a book. When he said the manuscript had already been turned in, I quipped, *"Well, I guess I'll just have to write my own book then."*

"You write?" he asked.

That connection led to me receiving numerous writing assignments— one after another—continually for the next three years. That led to a publishing contract of my own for my signature book, *Dancing in the Arms of God;* which led to ... which led to . . . which led me straight into the fulfillment of my dreams, and the fulfillment of the plans God had for me. My wilderness experience was a short-cut to the "Promised Land" that God had caused me to desire and had given me a vision for years earlier.

So, any time you feel like you're in the wilderness, if you are a child of God, I say, get happy! The wilderness is the way God takes his children to the promises He has for their lives. You might want to read the stories of the wilderness journeys of the children of Israel. They are in the Bible for our example. And there's plenty you can learn from reading them again with this correlation in mind.

One key lesson is that your time in the wilderness can be shortened considerably if you take God at His word, expect His guidance, and move out confidently to follow His guidance by faith. By the direct route, it only should have taken the children of Israel eleven days to get through the wilderness on foot (see Deuteronomy 1:2). Instead the whole generation wandered for forty years. Why the delay? The Bible says it was because of their unfaithfulness—their refusal to believe that God meant what He said and wanted them to apply it in everyday life. This dealt specifically with regard to following God's guidance in their lives. Yes, even though they lacked faith, God continued guiding them during their forty years in the wilderness. He kept protecting them and miraculously providing for their needs. But it didn't have to take nearly so long (see Deuteronomy 8:2-9). God is the same. He will do the same for you, but why waste time wandering aimlessly?

Decide (which you can do by a simple act of your will) to believe God's promises of guidance that are clearly stated in the Bible.

Get excited! God will guide you, and you can enjoy the adventure of following Him. I will show you how you can become confident in your decisions and be assured that you are walking by faith. That will allow you to go through this wilderness experience by the most direct route possible.

Consider these clear promises of God's guidance in the Bible:

(As you read them, check to see if you believe them with faith that these apply to you. If you have not previously received these with faith, choose to do so now. Ask yourself, *"What could I expect if these promises are true for me regarding my spouse and our current situation?"* Then choose to believe God for that.)

If any of you lacks wisdom, he should ask God, who gives generously to all without finding fault, and it will be given to him. But when he asks, he must believe and not doubt, because he who doubts is like a wave of the sea, blown and tossed by the wind. That man should not think he will receive anything from the Lord; he is a double-minded man, unstable in all he does. (James 1:5-8)

Trust in the LORD with all your heart and lean not on your own understanding; in all your ways acknowledge him, and he will make your paths straight. (Proverbs 3:5-6)

My sheep listen to my voice; I know them, and they follow me. I give them eternal life, and they shall never perish; no one can snatch them out of my hand (John 10:27-28).

(If you're wondering if John 10:27-28 applies to believers today, consider that this is the same verse we trust for eternal life. If you apply this as qualifying you to receive eternal life that means you also qualify to hear His voice and follow Him.)

Although the Lord gives you the bread of adversity and the water of affliction, your teachers will be hidden no more; with your own eyes you will see them. Whether you turn to the right or to the left, you will hear a voice behind you, saying, 'This is the way; walk in it.' (Isaiah 30:20-21)

There are other promises which you may want to search out on your own, but my point here is that Christians should expect to receive and be prepared to follow God's guidance in life. The emphasis of the Old Testament could be summed up as, *"Be careful to follow all the commands of the LORD your God, that you may possess this good land and pass it on as an inheritance to your descendants forever" (1 Chronicles 28:8b)*. However, the emphasis of the New Testament could be summed up in Jesus' call, *"Come, follow me."* This was not just for the disciples who walked with Jesus on earth but for all His servants. He said, *"Whoever serves me must follow me; and where I am, my servant also will be. My Father will honor the one who serves me" (John 12:26)*. Therefore, we can expect God's personal guidance.

Some people feel uncomfortable with this idea of receiving personal guidance from God. Don't let this scare you, even if it is unfamiliar. Having the living God as your guide is not cause for fear but a relief from fear. Pastor David George of Valley Springs Church in Roseville, California, tells a story that exemplifies this truth. He and his family had planned a day of skiing on December 26, 1996. They had made the plans far in advance, invited friends, and looked forward to a brief respite after the busy Christmas season. The day dawned gray and overcast, but they would not be daunted. They headed up to the mountains, despite the lousy weather forecast. They arrived at the ski resort to find the parking lot empty and covered with ice. It had been raining but they were determined to look on the bright side of this drizzly day.

Pastor George suggested that they think of how nice it would be to ski without having to battle the crowds that are usually there. Their attitudes remained undampened, although their clothing did not. It was sprinkling on the lower slopes, and overall this was not a good day for skiing—no matter how positive the skier's attitude.

They gave it a few hours and made the best of it. Around noontime, the group had grown tired of being so cold and wet and wanted to call it a day. Pastor George and his wife, Jayne, agreed but wanted to make one decent run from a higher elevation before going home. Both are confident skiers, so they eagerly headed for the ski lift and hopped on. They thought perhaps the weather would be better higher up the mountain.

Not so! The higher they rose, the more the wind whipped at them. They traded in the light rain for an icy rain, then for snow, then for much heavier snow. As the weather worsened, they looked forward and noticed that there were no other skiers on the chairs in front of them. They looked back and saw no other skiers on the chairs behind them. As they continued their ascent, the snow swirled in the wind so much so that they could not see the chair immediately in front of them. That's when the lift stopped; but the winds did not. They hung on to the immobilized lift, dangling there like a toy on a string with the wind whipping them about for twelve long minutes—one wind-whipped second at a time. From this position, their desire to make the best of a less than ideal situation seemed foolish. By the time the lift creaked to a start, they had said their prayers and were determined to jump off at the next possible moment.

They approached a platform where it looked possible to make their escape. The sign read in big letters: NO EXIT AT THIS POINT. They held on until they reached the top of the lift where they could get off, and then they jumped. They landed on the platform but had no idea where they were on the mountain or how to safely get down. The weather was getting progressively worse, they were chilled to the bone, their clothes and gloves were soaked, and they were scared.

They decided that their best course of action would be to sidestep down the mountain, hoping to spot a ski patrol. They made their way carefully downward. Eventually they spotted a small shack, which they hoped would be occupied. They made their way to it and were relieved to find a member of the ski patrol inside—dry and relaxed. He assured them that they were in a spot from which they could easily get down the mountain. He drew them a map, showing them that all they needed to do was to go outside, make their way to a clearing, then head downward. He told them they would need to be sure to veer to the right as they passed the first landmark because there was a pretty substantial cliff there, but once they rounded that curve they would be home free.

Under different conditions, this wouldn't have been a challenge for them; but they had been through a lot. They were not in any emotional or physical condition to just be handed a map and pointed in the right direction. They were able to persuade the man to keep his map and personally guide them down to safety. He kindly obliged and they gratefully thanked him. Then they followed him down the mountain. When they were reunited with their group, they were more than happy to call it a day. Pastor George used this illustration in a sermon to explain that when we've been through something tough or when we are in a crisis, we need more than a map from God telling us general directions. We need a personal guide.

This is a picture of what God does for us. In the Bible He has written out the map of the way we should go. But God also knows there are times when just looking at the map will not be enough—not because of any fault in the map but because of our fears and human frailty. There are times we need more than written guidance; we need God to guide us

The Pharisees were expert map-readers of Scripture, but they didn't follow God's guidance in life. They didn't even recognize Jesus as the promised Messiah, whose coming the Scripture foretold. Jesus told them,

> *The Father who sent me has himself testified concerning me. You have never heard his voice nor seen his form, nor does his word dwell in you, for you do not believe the one he sent. You diligently study the Scriptures because you think that by them you possess eternal life. These are the Scriptures that testify about me, yet you refuse to come to me to have life. (John 5:37-40)*

Another time Jesus told his disciples,

> *And I will ask the Father, and he will give you another Counselor to be with you forever—the Spirit of truth. The world cannot accept him, because it neither sees him nor knows him. But you know him, for he lives with you and will be in you. I will not leave you as orphans; I will come to you." (John 14:16-18)*

And again,

> *All this I have spoken while still with you. But the Counselor, the Holy Spirit, whom the Father will send in my name, will teach you all things and will remind you of everything I have said to you. Peace I leave with you; my peace I give you. I do not give to you as the world gives. Do not let your hearts be troubled and do not be afraid." (John 14:25-27)*

We do not have to be afraid because we have God's word that provides a map and we have God as our guide throughout life. We can also rest assured that God intends to guide us to somewhere very good. Keeping this in mind can encourage you when the road is rough. Just knowing that you are going somewhere good can change your attitude on the journey. Think of how kids approach a trip when they are on their way to an amusement park as compared to how they act while on their way somewhere boring. Just knowing that the destination is a good one seems to instill patience and endurance.

Sometimes I think we hesitate to follow God's guidance because we know exactly where we want to go in life and we don't trust that God will take us there. We may be so focused on life taking us where we want to go that we are convinced that wherever God would take us would be a disappointment. This misconception keeps us from following God to the best life possible. As I have followed God's leading, I have not ended up exactly where I wanted to go, but I have ended up with the kind of life I aspired to – only better. God has taken me places far beyond the limited life I could imagine before.

You may not see how what your marriage is going through has anything to do with God taking you toward a better life or a better relationship. But God's word promises that wherever He guides you in life His overall intention is to guide you toward a good end. When I was confused and unsure of what to do and which way to turn while Patrick was going through great perplexity, I took comfort in the promise,

> 'For I know the plans I have for you,' declares the LORD, 'plans to prosper you and not to harm you, plans to give you hope and a future. Then you will call upon me and come and pray to me, and I will listen to you. You will seek me and find me when you seek me with all your heart.' (Jeremiah 29:11-13)

Again we have the assurance of personal relationship and some insight into our destination. We may not know where God is leading us by circumstances beyond our control, but we can be sure that He knows where He is taking us and that His destination is somewhere very good. How differently would you respond to God's guidance if you believed this to be absolutely true?

If we are going to follow the pattern of overcoming faith given in the last chapter; that means remaining completely dependent on God and expecting Him to guide us. It also means we trust Him to superintend over directions our lives take that are not what we expect and are beyond our control.

Patrick and I were returning from Israel in May of 1986. I was very excited by every facet of the trip because our trip to the Holy Land was the fulfillment of a lifelong dream. On the flight home, I studied the map showing the flight path our plane was scheduled to take as we left the Middle East. I was somewhat confused and concerned when the pilot pointed out landmarks we were passing over that indicated our flight path had diverged from the one shown in the on-board magazine. When we arrived in New York, the television news reported that American military aircraft had received special clearance to take off from Britain so that they could bomb Libya. This was during the USA confrontation with Muammar Gaddafi. The pilot had diverted our plane around Libyan airspace for our protection, but he did not announce this change of plans so as not to alarm the passengers. Looking back on how God has directed our lives, I now can see times when God diverted our lives around dangerous situations. It was only when the danger had passed, and we could look back from a position of safety, that we realized God's providential care in what we thought was an unwelcome change of plans. You don't have to wait for God to guide you. God **is** guiding you even when you don't realize it, and He remains ever intent on guiding you somewhere very good.

God's guidance is already in effect. But God will always respect your free will. There are two ways of experiencing God's guidance: when He guides us without our knowledge and when He leads and calls us to choose to follow Him. These two often overlap and are apt to cause some confusion. I spent the entire last chapter trying to convince you that your primary goal in your spiritual life is to remain **completely dependent on God.** That translates into phrases such as *"I'm just resting in the Lord!"* and *"I'm waiting on God to take my life wherever he wants me to go."* Now, in this chapter I will show you what you are **to do** to **actively follow**

God's guidance. You may be thinking: Aren't these contradictory instructions? Which is it: Do I depend completely on God to get us through this or do I actively follow God's guidance? The answer is both—and simultaneously!

Stay with me here. You can understand this concept easily and I will show you how to apply it. Picture yourself approaching a high and rugged mountain range. Your destination is on the far side of those mountains, which are impossible to scale by ground transportation. Let the mountains represent whatever difficulties your marriage is going through. Let the destination represent being where God wants you to be in life, accomplishing the things God intends for you to accomplish, and "getting over" whatever mountainous situation you're facing together.

Linking in with the three kinds of spiritual dispositions depicted in the last chapter, a person with Homer Simpson's disposition would look at the mountains and conclude that God never meant for them to get over something that big. The person disposed to use all their human strength to obey God's commands would conclude that they had to obey God and get over those mountains. They would set out on foot, determined to get over the mountains or die trying. The third person, who recognized that God did call them to get over the mountains but that it was also humanly impossible, would look for an airport to see if there was a flight available to lift them over the mountains.

The third response is the one that represents being completely dependent on God. That is the response that prompts you to go from saying, "*I can't!*" to saying, "*But God can.*" Therefore, I will turn my life (and my marital situation) over to the care of God. Turning your life over to the care of God is done by an act of the will. You simply choose to put your life in God's keeping and trust Him entirely with the outcome of your situation. That concept was pictured in the last chapter by Jesus' parable of the branch being completely dependent on the vine for life, sustenance, and to produce a good outcome (i.e., fruit). In this chapter, the same spiritual dependence on God is represented by getting in the airplane so that you can get over mountains impossible to scale any other way.

Flying in an airplane is a matter of choice. You choose to fly, make reservations, and at the appointed time, put yourself completely in the airplane. There is no half-way about it! Your life is completely dependent on the ability of that airplane to get you off the ground and hold you suspended tens of thousands of feet above the ground, and if it cannot, your life is over. It takes faith to board an airplane, but the way you do it is by an act of your will.

Once you are in that airplane, you don't have **to do** anything to make sure the aircraft makes it to the destination. In fact, the pilot wouldn't let you help if you tried. The pilot is completely responsible and capable of flying you to your destination. Your part is to get in and stay in. The pilot's part is to fly the plane.

So, let's say that getting in the airplane represents saying yes to God's will for you, making yourself completely dependent on God, and trusting Him wholly with your life. You don't have to do anything other than stay committed to God's will and keep believing that God's word is true, that He really can get you over this, that He really does intend to help you deal with whatever He has allowed in your life and marriage. You don't have to help God at all. Your part is to trust Him completely.

This is a matter of your will. Your emotions are another matter altogether. Some people are relaxed when they fly. Others are a nervous wreck. How they **feel** about the flight doesn't make a difference in whether they make it to their destination, only how much they enjoy the ride! Passengers don't even have to carry their own baggage; they can hand it off to someone before they board or stow it away once they are inside. When the plane experiences turbulence, the passengers don't jump out. They sit down and buckle their seat belts.

Likewise, God would like everyone to trust Him enough that they could turn their lives over to Him and simply rest. That is all they need to do. However, if their confidence in the plane or in the pilot is incomplete, they may stay within God's will but enjoy their life less. As for their baggage, ==God says we are invited to cast all our cares and anxieties on Him. Any time we feel burdened or weighted down with anxieties, we can hand these cares and worries over to God in prayer.== And when we hit turbulence in the form of troubles, the natural response will be to draw closer to God until the troubles pass. This whole idea of being **in Christ** and being completely dependent on God is the basic disposition in which Christians should live their lives.

Let's take this metaphor to another level. We can agree that all the people who are in the plane are powerless to make the plane stay in the sky, they know that someone can, and they have put their lives completely into the care of the pilot and the plane until they land. In that sense they do not have **to do** anything. They can rest completely. The job of getting them to the destination will be done for them without any effort on their part.

However, within the plane there will come a time when the pilot's voice will come over the intercom and say, *"You are now free to move about the cabin."* Then the passengers will conduct a wide range of activities according to their personal choice.

So, too, you are completely dependent on God to guide your life, to protect you, and to lift you above the situation that would be impossible for you to scale by your own strength. However, within the confines of God's will, where you are completely dependent on God, you have tremendous freedom of choice. It is within this context that we are to actively follow God's guidance. This is how you are able to completely depend on God and simultaneously take personal responsibility for your life as you follow God's guidance. In this way these can be done concurrently without being contradictory.

Learning to follow God's guidance is a matter of following certain biblical principles and applying them as you make decisions. The best and most concise description of these principles I have found was written long ago in the Christian classic **A Christian's Secret of a Happy Life** by Hannah Whitall Smith.

> *But, these points having all been settled [these points being:*

1) You are willing to do God's will,

2) Your soul is completely surrendered to God,

3) Your purpose is set to obey the Lord in every area of your life,

4) You believe divine guidance is promised],

> *...we now question how God's guidance comes to us, and how we will be able to know His voice. He reveals His will to us in four ways: through the Scriptures, through providential circumstances, through the convictions of our own higher judgment, and through the inward impressions of the Holy Spirit on our minds. It is safe to say that God speaks where these four are in harmony. I present this as a foundation principle. His voice will always be in harmony with itself, no matter how many different ways He may speak. There may be many voices, but there can only be one message. If God tells me in one voice to do something or not to do something, He cannot possibly tell me the opposite in another voice. If the voices contradict the speakers cannot be the same. My rule for distinguishing the voice of God would be to bring*

> *it to the test and see whether the four points beginning this chapter are in agreement.*

I have followed similar principles for discerning God's will in my life. Now I will show you how to apply these with regard to your spouse and marriage, using this example. About a year and a half after both Patrick and I were dismissed from our youth ministry positions at our church, I had done all in my power to get reinstated because I did not want to move away from the area. However, there were some practical concerns that became apparent to us. We needed ongoing counseling to deal with our issues. We were unable to find qualified counselors in our area. Financially we were barely scraping by because of a depressed economy. And we had just found out that I was pregnant with our third child.

We considered these practical concerns within the context of our adherence to biblical principles. We knew that God held us responsible to pay our bills and provide for our family. We knew that God could give us good jobs and adequate provision right where we lived, and we had sought him in prayer to do so. We had been doing our best to meet our commitments and had not been able to keep up. So we asked God if he was trying to show us something.

Patrick was growing more and more convinced that the best thing we could do was to move back to southern California, where the economy was better and where we had contact with the Christian counselors who had helped us when we were at the worst point in our crisis. He explained this to me and I became upset. This was not the plan I had in mind. However, I agreed that what I wanted more than anything was to know that we were doing what God wanted us to do. So I agreed to pray with Patrick, asking God to guide us in this matter and to make His will clear for us. I was afraid but willing. We knew that if we were to move Patrick would need a good job (especially since I was pregnant and would have to quit my job when the baby came). We also knew that we needed counseling and did not have money or insurance to cover ongoing therapy. We had already prayed, so Patrick sought wise counsel from a few Christians we trusted. One of these was our counselor in southern California, with whom we had conferred off and on since we went through treatment. When Patrick told him we were thinking of moving there, he said, *"Great! I just got a new position doing clinical research dealing with your issues. If you move near the university where I'm doing research, I will counsel you—free of charge!—for as long as it takes."* That seemed providential.

The next step was to see if Patrick could get a job in that area with the kind of salary and benefit package that would warrant a move. He went to a job fair in southern California. There were numerous employers available to interview prospective managers. He interviewed with several firms. The one he liked best interviewed over two hundred applicants that day. Patrick was the only person they hired. Although they could have placed him at any of their numerous locations throughout southern California, they assigned him to a location five miles from our counselor's office. They offered him the salary we needed, full moving expenses, relocation costs, and a good benefit package, and they even agreed to cover my maternity and delivery costs. We took these as all the signs we needed. All four "voices" – Scriptures, 1providential circumstances, 2convictions of our own higher judgment, and 3inward impressions of the Holy Spirit – were saying the same thing. Even though I still felt sad and upset at the prospect of moving, I could choose to do so with confidence because I knew God was guiding us. And if He was guiding us, I knew that was the best place to go. This proved to be true.

I had another friend whose husband's problems caused them to lose their home and landed him in jail. She trusted God as she went through the heartbreaking process of selling the house where they had raised their family. She had to move to an apartment because she was living on a tiny salary while her husband was in jail. But she kept praying that God would watch over her and her children and protect them. She endured living in an apartment but never liked it in the least. After her husband got out of jail she began to feel an inner prompting that God knew she wanted a house and that he would give her one. Since there was nothing unbiblical about wanting a house, she prayed that God would guide her to "her" house if it was really the Holy Spirit leading her. Then she looked in the newspaper classified ads under **Houses for Rent**. She saw an ad that looked too good to be true. There was a house listed for rent at an amount that was within their meager budget and yet would accommodate their family. She called, went to look at it, and was amazed. It was a nicely appointed, well-kept home that satisfied my dear friend's longing to have a house again. She asked if the ad was a misprint because the price was several hundred dollars per month lower than the going rate. *"No,"* the kindly gentleman told her, *"we only want to get what it costs us to keep it, so it's not the money we're concerned with. We just want a nice family who will love it like we do and take good care of it."* My friend assured him that they were that family. Her husband came back with her, and they were accepted.

With a deal like that she was sure that it couldn't have been available long. No, it had not. It had come available at the same time she received the inner impression to look in the classifieds. The beautiful thing about this story that touches my heart is that this woman had wanted a house all along but did not discourage herself by looking in the classifieds every weekend. Instead, she remained content to live in the apartment until the Holy Spirit let her know that "her" house was ready. The family lived there knowing that God guided her to the home He had prepared for them.

GETTING PRACTICAL

Let's get practical with all this spiritual understanding. You are at the point where you earnestly desire to follow God's guidance. You're looking to follow Jesus and the leading of the Holy Spirit, not just God's rules and regulations. How do you do that?

START WITH SCRIPTURE

You must start at the point of God's written word in the Bible, even though you continue to trust the living Jesus who abides in and empowers you to keep God's word. All your basic decisions can be influenced by the principles given in the Bible. Therefore, you need to have a good understanding of what God's word says. This can be intimidating. The Bible consists of sixty-six books, some of which you may not have read or are not sure you understand. So how can you be confident that the principles that guide your decisions are in keeping with the whole of Scripture?

There is a way to simplify that. Jesus always did the will of the Father. Jesus kept the law on every point. So you don't have to wait until you can comprehend the whole of Scripture to start testing your decisions by it. All you have to do to make a good start is to get to know Jesus. If you know what Jesus is like—which you can do by a prayerful reading and study of the four gospels or even just the gospel of John—you can have a guide to follow in making decisions.

This form of basic decision making has been popularized in the book **In His Steps** by Charles Sheldon and more recently in a youth edition of the same book, titled **What Would Jesus Do?** The premise of this story is that an entire town was revolutionized by obeying the simple idea that *"Jesus has left us an example that we should follow in his steps."* The characters in the book's fictional town were challenged to ask themselves one question before making any decision then to follow through and do whatever the answer to that question dictated. The question was, *"What would Jesus do?"* This rule of guidance is so simple and profound that its application transformed lives. Perhaps it was a bit overdone in pop culture, but at its essence it is a good starting point to figure out what to do.

The other basic rule of scriptural guidance is the rule of love. This is summed up in the Golden Rule to love others as ourselves or to treat others as we would want them to treat us. As Jesus said,

> 'Love the Lord your God with all your heart and with all your soul and with all your mind.' This is the first and greatest commandment. And the second is like it: 'Love your neighbor as yourself. All the Law and the Prophets hang on these two commandments (Matthew 22:37-40).

Paul also affirmed this in greater detail in his letter to the Romans, saying:

> Let no debt remain outstanding, except the continuing debt to love one another, for he who loves his fellowman has fulfilled the law. The commandments, 'Do not commit adultery,' 'Do not murder,' 'Do not steal,' 'Do not covet,' and whatever other commandment there may be, are summed up in this one rule: 'Love your neighbor as yourself.' Love does no harm to its neighbor. Therefore love is the fulfillment of the law. (Romans 13:8-10)

So whenever you have to make a decision, start by asking yourself, *"What would Jesus do?"* Then check your actions by the Golden Rule.

LOOK FOR PRACTICAL ADVICE IN THE BIBLE & APPLY IT

Next, look to see if the Bible has any practical advice regarding the issues associated with the kind of decision you are trying to make. The Bible is full of practical advice and detailed instruction on the most important basic aspects of life. If you don't know how, learn to use a good concordance (which lists key words and tells you where they are in the Bible), or get a study Bible with help sections that will lead you from topic to topic, or check related topics at www.Biblegateway.com. The instruction given in God's word is given to teach us, to help us see when we are out of line, to correct us, and to train us to live the kind of lives God intends so that we *"may be thoroughly equipped for every good work" (2 Timothy 3:17)*. Let's not neglect such a rich source of sound guidance from the One who made us and knows how it's best for us to live.

I came to appreciate this more fully when I wrote a series of self-help books on family roles. I did one book on being a great wife and another on being a great husband. The premise was to show people how to apply biblical principles in their marriage. However, we directed the books to a general audience, so we did not quote Scripture and verse. I simply showed people how to set goals to do what God says we should in marriage. It was basic Bible application to everyday life, but without revealing the source. I later received a call from a woman who could not find these books in stock in her area. She was a dorm mom at the University of Texas and wanted more books to give to young couples as wedding gifts. In our conversation, she went on about how much wisdom there was in what I had written. She wanted to know how I gained such wisdom. When I told her that all I'd done was apply what the Bible says, she was shocked. She said she was an atheist and had no idea that the Bible contained such effective advice for everyday life. Her comments made me realize that we often take for granted the riches of wisdom we have at our fingertips within the Bible.

WALK IN THE LIGHT YOU HAVE

Once you have a sense of what is right and what the Bible says specifically about your situation, you come to the matter of obeying what the Bible says. You know what to do, but how do you carry that out? Answer: one step at a time. Psalm 119:105 says, *"Your word is a lamp to my feet and a light for my path."* This imagery comes from the life of a shepherd. The shepherds in ancient Palestine had to keep watch over their flocks day and night. There were many dangers that could be in their path, so they needed a form of illumination when they walked in the dark. At night they would strap a lamp to their ankle; that way, when they took a step they had a light for their path, step by step.

David writes here that God's word does the same thing for us. You are not promised that God's word will illuminate the entire journey all at once. It will illuminate the next step for you. You take that step by faith. Then when you have to make the next decision, God's word will give you enough illumination to know what step to take at that point. This is how one "walks by faith" in practice.

When you have to make a decision, ask yourself, *Is there one step that I could take now that is clear from God's word?* If there is, ask the Lord to give you the grace, courage, and strength to take that one step. When you walk in the light you have, God will give you more light, step by step. Don't get ahead of yourself; and certainly don't hesitate to take the step that is clearly right just because you don't know what might come along down the road.

KEEP WALKING

Don't wait for God to tell you every step to take! God gave you His written Word as guidance, along with your intelligence and free will. You don't need God to tell you personally to forgive someone. That's a given according to His written Word. Any time God's word plus common sense equals a specific action, don't expect God to lead you in some supernatural way. God always leads us toward forgiveness; it is our responsibility to continually walk in that. The same holds true for many other issues where Scripture clearly tells you what you should do. While you may need grace and strength to obey, you don't need a special revelation to know what you should do.

Also be careful not to misuse Scripture by taking an isolated verse or part of a verse out of context and using the words to try to support an action that is contrary to the whole of God's word. We can easily deceive ourselves, especially when we want something that contradicts God's word. Therefore, make sure your take on any isolated verse is tested by the Life of Jesus, the Golden Rule, other Bible verses and that which is accepted by orthodox Christianity. Never decide to go against Scripture because of some inner impression or supernatural "revelation." Impressions, spiritual influence, and even supernatural phenomenon can come from sources other than God. If the spiritual influence is of God and from the Holy Spirit, it will never contradict the Bible. For example, God will never tell you by an inward impression to divorce your husband apart from Scriptural grounds—however, your own heart might.

INWARD IMPRESSIONS
There are two common extremes regarding inward impressions as they relate to receiving God's guidance: One is to dismiss them out of hand and the other is to rely on them entirely. Those who dismiss them are missing out on one of the most beautiful privileges of walking with our living Lord Jesus Christ. Those who rely on them entirely risk going off into heretical teachings and also risk becoming immobilized in their Christian walk while waiting for "a word from the Lord." God expects us to continue walking in His Spirit by exercising the free will and common sense He gave us to go with His written revelation in the Bible.

What I see taught and exemplified in the New Testament church is a healthy balance between walking by faith while using our

God-given freedom of choice and being responsive to the inner witness of the Holy Spirit as it speaks to us. Let me explain how to keep this balance so that you can accomplish all that God has for you to do and enjoy the freedom God has given all His children.

Look at the life of the apostle Paul. After his miraculous conversion, he had no doubt that God certainly could speak to him. He knew God could stop him dead in his tracks and knock him off his horse if He had good reason to do so! But Paul did not go on to allow his spiritual life to be immobilized while waiting for miraculous revelations from God every day. He was a faithful member of his local church in Antioch, where he was one of the leaders. Scripture tells us,

> *While they were worshiping the Lord and fasting, the Holy Spirit said, 'Set apart for me Barnabas and Saul for the work to which I have called them.' So after they had fasted and prayed, they placed their hands on them and sent them off. The two of them, sent on their way by the Holy Spirit, went down to Seleucia and sailed from there to Cyprus.   (Acts 13:2-4)*

Paul knew his calling, his gifting, and what he wanted to do. He went where the Holy Spirit sent him, but he also had goals and desires that he allowed to influence his decisions of where he would go. Notice in the following passage how Paul was moving in the direction God had given him and setting his course as he thought best. He remained ready to change his course when God intervened to give him specific direction.

> *Paul and his companions traveled throughout the region of Phrygia and Galatia,* **having been kept by the Holy Spirit** *from preaching the word in the province of Asia. When they came to the border of Mysia,* **they tried to enter** *Bithynia, but the Spirit of Jesus* **would not allow** *them to. So they passed by Mysia and went down to*

> Troas. During the night Paul had a vision of a man of Macedonia standing and begging him, 'Come over to Macedonia and help us.' After Paul had seen the vision, we got ready at once to leave for Macedonia, **concluding that God had called us** to preach the gospel to them. (Acts 16:6-10 emphasis mine)

This is a beautiful picture of active trust in God's guidance. Paul felt free to proceed to do what he knew God had called him to do, trusting that, because he was in close fellowship with the Lord, if he started to go in the wrong direction, the Lord could keep him from going there or get a message to him of where he was to go. This kind of guidance only works when we are completely willing to go wherever the Lord tells us to go and do whatever He tells us to do. But once you've experienced this kind of adventurous faith life, you'll never want to live any other way!

Here's what this means for you. You are free to set goals and move out in any direction you like as long as you are staying within God's moral will. You are encouraged to pursue the specific calling God has put on your life (if you know what that is). You need to be open to hearing whatever God might say to you, through an inner impression, a verse of Scripture that seems to be highlighted to your mind, a dream, a word of encouragement or correction from other believers, or other supernatural means. You will always test the spiritual source by comparing any guidance received by that which is clearly written in the Bible. If you think God is the One impressing you to do something and you're not sure it's from the Lord, but it's in keeping with God's word and nobody will be hurt by it – go for it. What could it hurt to do what God's word says?

When you move out in the direction you think God wants you to go—whatever the source of that inspiration—you will next look to providential circumstances. Try to go there. Just like Paul and his companions tried to enter Bithynia. If God wants you to go somewhere else, he can use circumstances or other means to keep you from going where he doesn't want you to go.

However, if you feel "led of the Lord" to do a certain thing or to pursue a certain course of action, a "closed door" or adverse circumstances don't always mean it is not God's will for you. It may be that you are experiencing spiritual opposition from forces of wickedness. God can handle them! If you feel led of God in a certain way and you try but can't do it although the inner desire persists, pray that God will overcome any spiritual resistance that may be keeping you from what you believe He wants you to do. Then trust that God is in control. If He wants you to do that now, He can easily change the circumstances so that you can. Trust God. Another explanation might be that God is prompting you in this direction for the purpose of prayer but the fulfillment of what God is calling you to do will come at a later time. If a leading is truly from God, God will make a way for you to accomplish it in His time.

Here is the most beautiful aspect of God's guidance. When we are fully committed to allowing God to guide our lives, He guides us by the desires of our hearts. The heart that is not yielded to God is deceitful and will lead you astray from God's will. However, the yielded heart – where Jesus abides – is changed so that your desires, the deepest longings of your heart, spring from the heart of God Himself. He causes you to desire inwardly the very thing He wants to bless you with outwardly. Then as you eagerly pray for and pursue the desires of your heart, God delights to lead you to the fulfillment of that which you most desire.

The Bible says that God is at work within you both to will and to do of His good pleasure. When you are living in this kind of close relationship with God, looking to Him for guidance and actively following it, the prayer of David applies to you: *"May he give you the desire of your heart and make all your plans succeed"* (Psalm 37:4, paraphrased). At this point God can gladly make all your plans succeed because your plans have been inspired by the Spirit of God working in you and flowing through you.

What joy it is to live this way, even when—or perhaps especially when—your marriage is going through hell. If you practice following God's guidance and trusting that He *will* guide you, indeed *is* guiding you even when you don't know it, and that where God intends to guide you is very good, you can even enjoy a bumpy ride!

I close with this beautiful psalm that attests to the harmony of resting and doing, trusting God's guidance, and setting out to seek our heart's desires:

> *Trust in the LORD, and do good;*
>
> *Dwell in the land and cultivate faithfulness.*
>
> *Delight yourself in the LORD;*
>
> *And He will give you the desires of your heart.*
>
> *Commit your way to the LORD,*
>
> *Trust also in Him, and He will do it. (Psalm 37:3-5 NASB)*

CHAPTER FOUR: SETTING RELATIONAL BOUNDARIES

WHERE DOES MY SPOUSE'S LIFE END & MINE BEGIN?

"I still see two, not one."

This statement was meant as an indictment. I was supposed to lower my gaze and admit, *"Yes, I see myself as an individual, separate from my husband."* That was to be my confession. Then what was I to do? Apologize for being a person?

I could hardly believe I was in this situation. My husband, Patrick, and I sat together on one side of a large conference table in the church office. Up until a few weeks earlier we had often sat in this same room for staff prayer meetings. We had been youth ministers in this church for over a year and a half, Pat as youth pastor and me as an associate youth minister. That was before he confessed to sexual misconduct. When we told the pastor, Pat was fired immediately. I was told that my position was secure. "After all," the pastor said, *"Connie didn't sin. Why should she be fired?"* That was before meetings took place behind closed doors.

No one told me I was out. They just forbade me from doing my job, required me to clear out our office, stopped my pay and benefits when they stopped my husband's, and started discussing how to explain my dismissal to the congregation. I caught wind of these discussions when several of our volunteer youth workers came to me with questions. They were confused and rightly so.

The line of reasoning went something like this: *"Husband and wife are one flesh. So, when he fell, she was taken down with him."* Another variation said, *"Well, she had to know something when this was going on. She covered up for him. Yes, that's it; she's a co-conspirator."* Their position was not only untrue, it assaulted a vital truth of God's word—that each individual stands before God as such. A woman does not lose her identity when she weds. She is not part and parcel of her husband. Nor does it work the other way around.

I was shocked and deeply offended, not just because they were maneuvering to keep me out of my job and ministry. I was appalled at how they were twisting God's word. It was hard enough to get through the crisis of my husband's infidelity and public humiliation, but this went deeper. Their misuse of Scripture undermined God's word and, at that point in my life, God's word was all that stood secure. I determined to confront these issues with those who were promoting them.

I asked for the meeting. That is what brought us to this table where Pat and I sat across from our pastor, another pastor on our large church staff, and several key members of the governing board. I was hoping that what I'd heard second-hand was twisted. I hoped they would say, *"How absurd! Who could believe that a woman is guilty for her husband's sins? Who could make a case for dismissing you for something he did?"* But that's not what they said. Instead the kind gentleman who led our church board looked into my eyes and said, *"I still see two, not one. The Bible says that the two become one flesh. But when I look at you and listen to you, I still see two, not one."*

DANGERS OF FAULTY RELATIONAL BOUNDARIES

That was their indictment, and they let it stand. They had drawn the boundary lines of marriage with the wife being included in her husband's life, consumed by him. Therefore, their actions seemed justified—to them. They didn't mean to violate me as deeply as they did. They did so because they misread God's word and had drawn the relational boundaries contrary to God's design. Their faulty boundary map and its enforcement caused untold suffering and confusion. It didn't matter that I pointed out their misinterpretation of Scripture or that several other biblical passages made their position indefensible. They held to their faulty relational map and ended up trespassing against me without acknowledging it.

That's one of the major dangers of operating with faulty relational maps: If you don't know where the true boundary lines are, you trespass and don't see it. You are trespassed against, you feel violated, but you can't convince the person trespassing against you that a trespass occurred. The whole forgiveness process is made more difficult when one or both parties are operating with faulty relational maps.

It matters where you draw the relational boundary maps in your life. When you accept a faulty view of where your spouse's life ends and yours begins, you will continually cross lines that you don't even recognize. You will hurt and be hurt, offend and be offended, without realizing why. You may be doing your best, expending all your energy and merely trying to help, but the results will be more conflict, not peace. Faulty personal boundaries always lead to more conflict—especially in times of stress. If your marriage is going through deep waters, you don't need more conflict. You need to be in a healthy union with God and your spouse. You can't be in a healthy union with anyone if the boundary lines of where your life ends and others begin are out of line with God's design.

BENEFITS OF RELATIONAL BOUNDARIES IN KEEPING WITH GOD'S DESIGN

I never got my job back at that church, but I gained something of great value from the experience. I learned the danger of setting faulty relational boundaries and the importance of setting personal boundaries where God decreed them to be. What I learned in this regard helped me weather the crisis in a way that strengthened my relationship with God, enhanced my self-respect, and quite possibly saved our marriage. It also gave me guidelines to follow as I made difficult decisions.

Your situation is different from mine, but the boundary lines I encourage you to draw are based on God's word. God's guidance applies to you as well as me. I've discussed these issues with people across the country in all sorts of crisis situations in their marriages. What they tell me confirms what I learned: When your marriage is going through hell, your personal boundaries need to be set in accordance with the plan of your Father in heaven.

MODELS OF FAULTY BOUNDARY MAPS

Most faulty relational patterns can be illustrated by one of the following three boundary maps:

Faulty Boundary Map #1

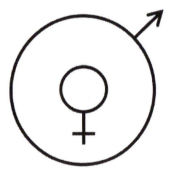

The first boundary map is the view the church board proposed, where the wife's life is consumed by her husband's. She has no life of her own apart from him. She asks him before she does anything and often uses the phrase *"I'd love to, but my husband won't let me."* She is consumed with trying to please her husband to the extent that she has few if any outside interests. She may live in fear of displeasing him. He promises to take care of her and she lets him. While doing so, she may become so dependent on her husband that she looks to him in matters where she should place her trust in God. This woman makes the mistake of letting her husband play God in her life.

In this kind of relationship the man may use abuse, threats, intimidation or legalism to keep his wife in line. He may be overly possessive, jealous or controlling even to the point of abuse. He may insist that she stay home, refrain from getting an education, have no independent interests and have no friendships he does not sanction.

FAULTY BOUNDARY MAP #2

The second relational map is the opposite of the first. Here the wife tries to control her husband. She sees it as her responsibility to take care of his every need. She thinks that she must direct him, telling him what to do, what to think, what to say. She usually feels superior and even brings God into her plans to get her husband to live the life she wants him to live. She may resort to manipulation, if necessary, giving or withholding sex, using emotional blackmail, or going behind his back to arrange something she thinks is good for him. She does not let him live his own life, whether directly or indirectly. She may be so busy tending to his life that she neglects her own. This woman makes the mistake of trying to play God in her husband's life.

Faulty Boundary Map #3

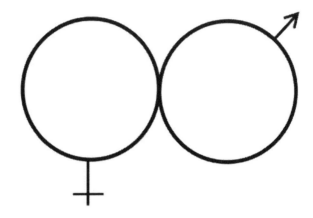

In the third faulty boundary map the husband and wife all but disconnect. They still live in the same house, are parents to the same kids, and share a mortgage payment but their personal lives are disconnected. They may not have sex or may go through the routine of having sex without intimacy. They live together alone. She doesn't want to know about his problems. She may say, "*I can't deal with this.*" or "*That's your problem, just leave me out of it. I don't want to know anything about it.*" She may fill her life with good things like community activities, extra work or outings with the kids, but if she has no real relationship with her husband, her boundaries are out of line. This woman makes the mistake of practically undoing the union God has ordained. The husband may pour himself into his work and get his social needs met outside of his marriage. Disconnecting happens little by little. It's usually a reaction to something the disconnecting party wants to avoid. If you and your spouse are disconnecting, get help to discover and deal with whatever is being avoided.

SETTING BOUNDARIES AS MARRIAGE BEGINS

When a marriage is just starting out, husband and wife have to adjust to each other. Each partner comes into the relationship with a view of how they want to make the marriage work. If he is trying to get her to live within the confines of his dreams, goals and plans without a life of her own (faulty boundary map #1) and she is trying to control and manipulate him to do what she wants (faulty boundary map #2), there will be ongoing conflict. If he's somewhat disconnected—not talking much, not sharing anything of himself, ignoring her—except when he wants something (faulty boundary map #3) and she's trying to make him love her, make him talk, make him pay attention, or share his secrets (faulty boundary map #2), there will be ongoing conflict. If he's trying to make her live solely for his interests (faulty boundary map #l) and she is trying to disconnect (faulty boundary map #3), contesting his claim on her, there will be ongoing conflict even if one partner is trying to avoid or resolve conflicts.

Living with continual conflict gets old. If the relational battlegrounds are not agreed upon and relational boundaries drawn, the conflict will continue. Many spouses who disconnect do so because they are tired of fighting the same battles. At some point in every marriage, the partners come to accept how they will relate to each other. The stronger or more forceful partner may appear to have won the battle. Their relational map is accepted by the other on a surface level, but the human spirit does not welcome being subdued by force. The wife who acquiesces to being consumed in her husband's life may be resentful and inwardly rebellious. The husband who allows his wife to rule over him may go along with her externally. However, he will most likely be driven underground to find some outlet where he can do what he wants. He may live a secret life as his way of proving that she really doesn't control him. In a marriage where the spouses seem to have agreed to disconnect, there is one person who first gravitated away and the other who finally gave up trying to get close. The one who is willing to accept a disconnected marriage may stay out of duty or fear of abandonment, but he or she is not satisfied. They will look for an opportunity to reconnect with their spouse—or if those attempts are repeatedly rebuffed they may resort to finding the kind of intimacy they are lacking with someone else.

A marriage can go along smoothly even though one partner has imposed his or her faulty design for the relational boundaries on the other—until a crisis hits. When a crisis hits and things are insecure, there is an opportunity to adjust the boundary lines. In your spouse's times of crisis or times of crisis in your marriage, you can watch closely and discover which type of faulty relational boundaries you are inclined toward.

This isn't a conscious decision. You don't say to yourself, *Aha! Now here's my chance.* You will just see yourself go in one of three directions. If you are inclined toward map #1 the wife will become clingy, desperate, and childishly dependent. If you're inclined toward map #2 the wife will take charge, seeking to rescue, cure, and control; while the husband abdicates responsibility and allows the wife to take control. If you're inclined toward map # 3 you will become distracted, disengaged, and distant; you'll occupy yourself elsewhere and go into a state of denial about your spouse's problems. All three of these patterns are out of line with God's ideal because they represent our human attempt to cope on our own, to manipulate through weakness, to control, or to escape. God calls us to stay, to allow his strength to flow through our points of weakness, to allow him to control the situation, and to wait on him instead of running away or playing God ourselves.

God uses times of trial to point out where our lives need to come into alignment with His design, to show us when we are trusting in our own devices instead of trusting Him. If the relational boundaries are out of line in your marriage, your stressful situation will make that apparent. When that happens, praise God! Seeing where your relational boundaries are out of line is the first step toward having your relationship aligned with God's design. That is what happened in my situation. It started as a crisis but created a learning experience that has reshaped my life, our marriage and ministry. Now, many years later, the war is over and the boundary lines redrawn in closer alignment with God's design. Our marriage relationship and family life is far healthier and happier.

GOD'S MAP FOR HEALTHY RELATIONAL BOUNDARIES IN MARRIAGE

Here is a diagram of what a healthy marriage relationship looks like:

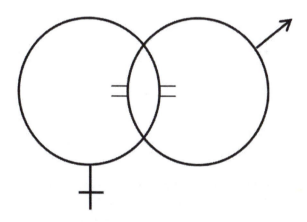

The Bible says that when a man and woman marry, they are joined together by God. Scripture repeatedly says, *"The two become one flesh."* A careful consideration of that statement makes it clear that they become one flesh as opposed to becoming one in soul and spirit. There is a mystical union; there is a sexual union that takes place so that the two are united physically. However, nowhere does the Bible say they become one person, one soul or one spirit. In physical terms, there is a holy devotion declaring that husband and wife are one flesh. Scripture even goes so far as to say the husband's body does not belong to him but to his wife and her body does not belong to her but to her husband (1 Corinthians 7:4). Their union is not only sanctioned by God but recognized by society as they unite legally—sharing finances, business dealings, and special privileges toward the spouse afforded to no one else. Their one flesh union may create children who are a shared responsibility for both parents. With the coming of children who share DNA of the father and mother, the husband and wife have become a single link with the next generation. They also share a home and a commitment to travel through life together until parted by death.

IT TAKES MORE THAN TWO

Marriage — at its best — is not a relationship between two people; it's a relationship between two people and God. During our wedding ceremony, the pastor cited Ecclesiastes 4:12: *"Though one may be overpowered, two can defend themselves. A cord of three strands is not easily broken."* God is that third strand that makes a marriage strong. Each marriage partner needs God's help to unite in a strong bond with their spouse and God. This strong union can be unraveled when relational boundaries are out of line with God's design, and there are continuing battles at those points of contention.

The best way a person can maintain right relational boundaries with one's spouse is to live in right relationship with God first. If they know God as their provider, protector, and Father, they will not be desperate for their husband or wife to take care of their every need. If they trust God as being all-powerful and faithful to answer prayer, they are not going to feel driven to control their spouse's life by manipulation. If they believe that God loves them dearly and is willing to help them work through whatever makes them afraid of intimacy, they will venture to have a close relationship with their spouse. You see, having your life united to God is what allows you to rightly unite to your spouse and makes marriage work well. Therefore, the ideal model of healthy relational boundaries between husband and wife includes the added dimension of an open relationship with God, like this:

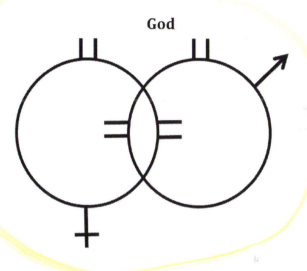

God knows where you are, where your spouse is and where all the lines are drawn. He can help you see where the boundary lines need to be redrawn and help you make the necessary changes to start living your life as He intended and to allow your spouse to do the same. If you are not in an open relationship with God, that is the place to start. Don't worry about your spouse's relationship with God. Just tend to your own. When you are close to God, living in the presence of God with your mind filled with biblical truth from His word—what Jesus called abiding in Him—you can ask God for whatever you want for your spouse and God will take care of it.

It looks so simple when I draw these little diagrams. I realize that the real changes these diagrams represent can be monumental.

When Patrick first told me about his infidelity, I was devastated but hopeful. He chose to share his secret with me because he wanted to save our marriage. He wanted to break free of the chains of sin in which his life was tangled. I went through the painful emotions, but deep down inside I knew that God could get us through this—if I would help him! (Ha!) I determined to do whatever it required to guard my marriage to make sure Pat was never unfaithful to me again. I went into overdrive, working to make sure I kept our marriage under control.

When we told the church and received their reaction, I was sent reeling. I never expected to lose my ministry. Patrick saw how badly I was hurt and he blamed himself. The church leaders blamed him too. Then a local newspaper reporter caught wind of the story. When he called to let me know he was going to run the story that put Pat over the edge. He became suicidal. I barely managed to get Pat into a Christian treatment program. His crisis superseded my own and I felt a strange sense of relief. With all my attention focused on his life-or-death struggle, I was distracted from my own pain. I flew down to southern California to join him at the hospital. Part of the treatment program includes family therapy. I went into the session feeling sorrowful but sure of my commitment to help my husband. I was going to do whatever it took to fix the situation, fix him, and fix our marriage (faulty boundary map #2).

The therapist, a woman named Denise, asked, *"Connie, why are you here?"*

"I'm here because I love my husband and I want to help him. I'll do anything I can to help."

"To help do what?" Denise asked, as though she were trying to get at something.

"To make sure he gets the help he needs, to make sure he gets over this, and ..."

"And what?"

"And to make sure he never does this to me again."

"So, you're here to figure out how you can control him?" Denise rephrased my statement.

"No! Well, I don't know. I'm here to help him," I insisted somewhat defensively

Later when Denise and I were in a private session, she went on. "Connie, what are you really doing here? You need to answer that for yourself. If you're here to learn how to control your husband's life, it won't work. You have to let him deal with his issues. If you really want to make the most of your time here, why don't we focus on helping you deal with your issues?" With that she invited me to check into the hospital to learn to live my own life, to allow my husband to live his, and let God be God. The prospect terrified me.

Through my conversations with Denise and other hospital staff, I realized that I was much more comfortable trying to direct the lives of others than to quietly reflect on my own. My boundaries were way out of line; my husband's crisis made that clear. I would gladly do anything to get his life in order but when the conversation turned to my life, I broke out in a cold sweat.

It was scary to let my husband choose whether or not to stay true to me—without trying to make sure that he did. It was just as scary to focus on my life, my relationship with God, and my responsibilities. The process of sorting out where his life ends and mine begins drove me to fix what was out of line in *my* life.

As our crisis deepened, I vacillated between all three faulty relational patterns. I had times I wanted to just stay in bed and cry, waiting for him to take care of me and make it all better. I became fearful that he would leave me and desperate to hold on to our relationship at any cost. Most times, I tried to control the situation and all the players. I tried to make everyone do what was right—the church, Pat, and anyone else who came into the picture. At other times I found myself disconnecting emotionally, obsessing over the possibility of divorce or the fear that Pat would kill himself. I spent hours rehearsing what I would do if my marriage ended. I planned his funeral. I entertained fantasies of finding a relationship with someone else. I tried to disconnect to distance myself from the pain.

If you're flitting all over the relational map, I understand. That's how we try to find a place of safety. Improperly set boundaries can help you feel safe temporarily, but they don't work out for the best in the long run. You can trust that God will be with you in this time of trouble. God is at work in the lives of all his children to get us to live in right relationship to Him and each other. God can use this crisis in your spouse's life, your life, and your marriage to help you get your relationships realigned properly.

I went through two weeks of inpatient care where I learned to sort out what belonged in my domain, what belonged in my husband's domain and what was rightfully shared. It took practice to make sure I wasn't trying to live his life or allowing him to take responsibility for that which was my responsibility. We both tended to gravitate to old familiar patterns. But as we agreed to what the boundaries were and began practicing living our own lives, we enjoyed the benefits of rightly aligned relationships. I want to share what we learned with you to help your marriage and family life. We had the help of counselors, but the truth is the truth. And it is the truth that sets us free. I trust that having a clear definition of where your spouse's life ends and yours begins will be useful, with or without the help of a counselor.

WHERE DO YOU DRAW THE LINES?

The following are boundary lines set out in God's word. Check to see where you draw the lines in your life. If your boundaries don't fall where God directs, I suggest you do the following:

> 1) Identify where you are out of line, specifically.
>
> 2) Confess to God what you recognize to be out of line.
>
> 3) Ask God to show you what step you can take right now to start correcting this error.
>
> 4) Ask God to help you make the needed changes and provide the guidance and support you will need to make permanent changes.
>
> 5) Do what you can to live within the healthy boundaries God shows you.
>
> 6) Devote yourself to continually repeat steps 1-5 until you learn and grow used to living within healthy, God-ordained relational boundaries.

This is a process. Don't get discouraged. You will need to reinforce the right boundaries over and over until they become more familiar than your previous unhealthy boundaries.

THE BOUNDARY LINE OF FREE WILL

Each person stands before God as an individual. God calls each of us to love Him with all of our heart, soul, mind, and strength. Each person is given free will to choose how to respond to God's desire for relationship. God calls each of us to love others—to treat others as we would like to be treated. He doesn't demand. He doesn't make us into puppets who will do what He knows is best. God allows each person to choose how he or she will live. He gives us clear moral standards of right and wrong. He warns us of the consequences if we disobey and the blessings if we obey. He explains that we will not be able to live in obedience by our own strength. He also offers to fill us with his Holy Spirit so we are empowered to fulfill his law. God makes all of this clear, but he never oversteps the boundary of our free will. Therefore, ==a wife oversteps== God-given boundaries whenever she tries to make her husband live the way she knows he should; and a husband oversteps his boundaries when he forces his wife to live the way he knows she should.

THE BOUNDARY LINE OF PERSONAL RESPONSIBILITY FOR SIN

Each person is a free moral agent who will reap what he or she sows in this life. Each person is held accountable before God. God does not hold anyone else responsible for the sin of another. Even in Old Testament times God made it clear that sin and punishment are not transferable to another person—except to Jesus Christ when we trust Him for salvation. God explains this using the proverb, *"[Shall] the fathers eat sour grapes, and the children's teeth [be] set on edge?" (Ezekiel 18:2).* Of course not; whoever eats sour grapes experiences the bitterness that comes with it. Likewise, whoever commits sin will experience the bitterness that is inherent in sinful behavior.

It is easy to identify sin in another person and feel noble by offering to help him or her get rid of their sin. That is especially tempting in marriage, where we are so close and think we see so clearly—as long as we are focused on our spouse's sins and shortcomings. Jesus had a strong response to this tendency in human nature to focus on the sins of others rather than our own. He said,

> *Why do you look at the speck of sawdust in your brother's eye and pay no attention to the plank in your own eye? How can you say to your brother, 'Let me take the speck out of your eye,' when all the time there is a plank in your own eye? You hypocrite, first take the plank out of your*

> *own eye, and then you will see clearly to remove the speck from your brother's eye. (Matthew 7:3-5)*

When it comes to cleaning up sin, we need to first look to our own lives. It is not our place to convict our spouses' of their sin. That's the Holy Spirit's job. If you feel inclined to look for sin, look first in the mirror. That's where God starts. That's your domain. If you see sin in your spouse's life – sin that is not against you – it is best to take your concerns to the Lord in prayer rather than to try to remove the sin directly.

When Pat sinned sexually, that crossed over into my territory. He made a commitment to keep himself solely for me. When he was unfaithful to our marriage vows, although I knew nothing of it, he sinned against me. This clear moral boundary helped us decide what he would share with me and what would only be shared with his counselor. We agreed that if he was struggling with sexual temptation in his mind that was between himself and God. But if he was on the verge of acting on those temptations or if he did act on those temptations, I had to know. It was not my place or responsibility to police his thought life. What a relief! For a while I was so fearful that I was constantly checking in, asking him what he was thinking. It annoyed him and did nothing positive for me. My time would have been better spent praying for him rather than trying to monitor his thoughts—as though I could!

The following is what I see to be in the domain of each individual:

- Personal relationship with God
- Moral choices and the consequences for those choices
- The soul: mind, will, and emotions
- Spiritual life and development
- Work (which, God has prepared for us in advance Eph.2:10)
- Negotiated family responsibilities
- Personal commitments
- Personal struggle with sin (including addictions)
- Recovery from ravages of sin

Once you recognize where your spouse's life ends and yours begins, it's time to start removing yourself from trespassing in your spouse's domain. It's time to start tending your own soul and spirit by nurturing your relationship with God. Then you can begin to focus on attending to your shared domain.

SHARED DOMAIN

Here are the areas of shared domain between husband and wife:

- Sexual intimacy
- Home
- Children
- Shared commitments (mortgage, finances, friendships, community involvement)

In times of crisis your spouse needs to see your continued commitment to the life you share. They may fear that their crisis — and the way they treat you because of what you two are going through — will cause you to want to leave the marriage. This will be especially true if you previously tended toward disconnecting. Ask God to help you pour yourself into these parts of your relationship, showing love and respect, without stepping over into your spouse's domain.

You will only be able to do this if your soul and spirit are secure in God. You may not *feel* love for your spouse. But godly love is more than a feeling; it's a commitment. Your commitment can be empowered by God's Spirit (who is Love) to see you through until you feel loving feelings for your spouse again. If you feel devoid of love for your spouse, disinterested in pouring yourself into sexual intimacy, children, home, or shared commitments, ask God to help you. Set your will in agreement with God's will—be willing. Use your connection to God as a conduit for God's love to flow through you to your spouse until your natural feelings of love revive.

SEXUAL INTIMACY

Do not neglect reaching out to your spouse sexually (unless there is risk of sexually transmitted disease). Use your privilege of sexual intimacy to shower your spouse with love and comfort. This is not an optional part of your marriage. First Corinthians 7:3-5 says,

> *The husband should fulfill his marital duty to his wife, and likewise the wife to her husband. The wife's body does not belong to her alone but also to her husband. In the same way, the husband's body does not belong to him alone but also to his wife. Do not deprive each other except by mutual consent and for a time, so that you may devote yourselves to prayer. Then come back together again so that Satan will not tempt you because of your lack of self-control.*

There is no rationalizing around that admonition. If you are not ministering love to your spouse sexually, there is something wrong. Granted, you may have issues that must be dealt with before you feel comfortable being sexually intimate again—for instance if there is the danger of contracting a sexually transmitted disease or there has been sexually abuse. If a problem of this nature exists, take action. Get professional help to resolve the problem. Your sexual union is essential.

Because our crisis involved sexual infidelity, it took quite a while to rebuild the bridges of trust to make that part of our relationship a source of joy again. However, we chose to maintain an intimate relationship even though that was not without heart-wrenching emotions at first. If you, too, have had to overcome sexual infidelity, I hope it helps to know that it is completely normal to have difficulty restoring those broken bonds of love and trust. However, it can be done. It takes time and devoted effort, but God can heal the brokenness to the degree that you can love each other freely and satisfy each other sexually.

HOME

Your home is your shared domain. It is a tangible place where you can demonstrate the solidarity of your marriage commitment in times of crisis. After Pat told me of his infidelity, I began to realize the importance of our home as never before. Each day we stayed together, took care of our children together and continued to make our home together was a living statement of our intent to stay in our marriage. When he first confessed to me, we were living in an apartment which didn't allow us the privacy we needed. Our counselor encouraged us to create a monument our determination to make our marriage work. He suggested that we buy a home. During this time, the Lord brought a passage of Scripture to my attention. It is found in Isaiah 54:2-3:

> *Enlarge the place of your tent, stretch your tent curtains wide, do not hold back; lengthen your cords, strengthen your stakes. For you will spread out to the right and to the left; your descendants will dispossess nations and settle in their desolate cities.*

I saw this as a confirmation of what my heart longed for anyway— that we could buy a home. Pat and I agreed that we wouldn't be tentative about our future together. We saw buying a home as our way to *"strengthen our stakes"* and *"enlarge the place of our dwelling."* This was before we told our boss and both lost our jobs. At the time, we assumed I would keep my position regardless of what happened with Pat's job.

My sister was a real estate agent; she found us a little house that we could afford and we moved in. While there was little joy in our lives, working on the house together brought respite from the pain and sorrow. We painted and wall-papered and stenciled our daughter's bedroom. Pat refinished a chest of drawers that had been mine when I was a baby for the baby I was carrying. That reassured me of the continuity of family. Somehow, our shared dedication to create a home for us and our children was balm for our broken hearts.

When we told the church about Pat's sin, just a month after we moved in, our home took on greater importance. After we were removed from ministry, I was home grieving my losses and waiting for our baby to be born. I didn't think I could find a job, being five months pregnant, so I turned my attention to processing the pain, trying to rebuild my relationship with Pat, caring for our daughter, and maintaining our home. Things were unstable; neither Pat nor I was very far into our grieving process. Pat took a job as a waiter in a dinner house, which was the only job he could find. Word of his fall had gotten out in our small town. There wasn't much demand for a fallen minister. So Pat became a server—a minister of another kind. His job brought in enough to scrape by financially, but it also subjected him to deliberate stares and outspoken ridicule. Our home became his place of refuge. When it was all we could do to manage our own pain and commit ourselves to each other, sharing the tasks of working on our home together was a source of comfort. In time it became a source of joy.

CHILDREN

Children are a shared responsibility. When your marriage is going through difficulty, it will have an impact on your children. You need to remain aware of how they are doing. It's easy to get caught up in dealing with your spouse's needs. Make sure you stay alert to signs that your kids may be hurting too. If your spouse is not functioning well as a parent, you will need to compensate in the lives of your children. Make sure you protect them and get them the help they need to process what is going on. If your spouse's problems are not debilitating, try to create time for the family to be together in a positive setting. Don't use the kids to try to make your spouse happy, but remember that one's children can be a source of joy and a reminder that there is something important for which to live.

SHARED COMMITMENTS

Husband and wife share mutual commitments: a mortgage, handling family finances, household duties, and involvement within the community. If your spouse's problems impact your life in tangible ways, you will need to adjust your daily roles and responsibilities. These shared commitments should be negotiated together. Wives should listen to their husband as the head of the family, but be sure to voice any hesitation about anything that impacts shared commitments. Consider all that needs to be done and how much you can carry without collapsing. Then come up with a plan together that will allow your family to weather the crisis while being faithful to shared commitments.

BUT I WANT MORE!

You may be thinking, *Is that really all there is to marriage? I just draw the lines between his life and mine in the right places and stay out of his life?* I understand that you want more than that. You want to know your spouse intimately—having not just a "one flesh" union but a love that reaches to soul and spirit. I want that too and I believe that is God's ultimate intent. But you cannot force your way into another person's soul or spirit. Even God Himself does not do that.

In the model of healthy relational boundaries, the line between the shared domain and each spouse's personal domain has a door. This is the door to the soul and spirit. This door will only open by means of love and respect. These are more than two more items on a list of what it takes for a good marriage. Love and respect can't be compartmentalized. Love and respect should color all your interactions with your spouse, love and respect should flow from God to you, and fill the life you share.

Ephesians 5:31-33 likens the marriage relationship to the relationship between Christ and the church, saying,

> *'For this reason a man will leave his father and mother and be united to his wife, and the two will become one flesh.' This is a profound mystery—but I am talking about Christ and the church. However, each one of you also must love his wife as he loves himself, and the wife must respect her husband.*

Even though the church is the bride of Christ, you don't see Him barging into the lives of those He loves. God respects the sanctity of each person He creates. However, Jesus gives us a model of how to enter into that deeper love relationship. In Revelation 3:20 we see a beautiful picture of Jesus knocking at the door of a human heart. We often hear this verse quoted when inviting people to open their lives to Christ for the first time. If you look carefully you will see that this is a picture of Jesus approaching a church. He is knocking at the door of His own bride. He loves, and knocks, and waits to be invited in. Likewise, you must not force your way into your spouse's heart, soul, and spirit any more than Christ forces Himself into yours.

The counselors helped me draw these guidelines for where Patrick's life ended and mine began, but they couldn't live them for me. I had to choose to let go of all the areas of his life I sought to control and focus my attention on living my life in a way that was pleasing to God. Once I focused my attention on aligning my life with God and taking care of what was rightly in the bounds of my life, I turned my attention to tending the areas of life Pat and I shared. He did the same and it changed the dynamics of our relationship in beautiful ways. Although we were still living with intense stress and ongoing troubles, we found moments and places of solace in the life and love we shared.

I know your situation is different from ours, but God is the same. His principles that helped us and many others like us can help you too. If you find that you can't sort this out alone, reach out to counselors trained in God's word and psychology who can help you. Establishing healthy relational boundaries will give you sure footing and definitive guidelines that will help you know how to get through this time of difficulty within your family. Therefore, I urge you, take action. Align your relational boundaries with God's design.

CHAPTER FIVE: God's Purpose in Pain and the Sanctifying Power of Suffering

God, Why Are You Allowing This to Happen?

At some point while your marriage is going through difficulties you will wrestle with the *"Why?"* questions. This is an important juncture in your spiritual development because you can get stuck here, demanding answers from the Almighty or reacting against God because of a misunderstanding at a time when you need Him most. Therefore, I will address the subject of why God would allow whatever is happening to your spouse or within your marriage with the specific focus of helping you deal with it.

Whole books have been written on the subject of the purpose of pain and why a loving God allows suffering. We cannot plumb the depths of this subject here; there are many excellent books you can read to explore the whole of this topic further. However, the goal of this chapter is specifically to help you have a practical and biblical framework in which you can view whatever you and your spouse are going through so that you develop three things:

1) The right attitude

2) Biblical understanding

3) A proper response to your particular trials or suffering

Your attitude toward trials and suffering in general is not dependent on what those trials might be but on God's command that his children can *"count it all joy"* when they encounter **various** trials.

Understanding the reasons why God allows suffering (as explained in Scripture) can help you wisely decide what approach to take in responding to whatever you and your spouse are going through. Understanding the purpose behind your spouse's pain will influence how you relate to him, and how you relate to God. If you misunderstand the purpose you may draw away from God or actually interfere with His purpose in your spouse's life.

Your response to the trials, your spouse, and God in the midst of the trials will be determined by your attitude and understanding of why God may be allowing what is happening. With the right attitude to begin with and a scriptural understanding of possible reasons why, your response becomes a matter of being obedient to God, applying the wisdom He gives you, and having faith that God does have some good purpose which He is working out.

About eight years after we had lost our ministry and gone through the worst of our situation, I was upstairs working at my computer when I heard Patrick singing downstairs. Patrick sings all the time, but this was different. He was singing worship songs using old performance tapes from when he was in ministry. I hadn't heard him do that in a long time. He graduated from Pepperdine with a music degree. When we first married, he aspired to a career in musical theater. When we were on staff at the church, he performed regularly as part of the worship team, doing special music and in the large-scale musical theater productions our church produced for the community. Singing is his gift and his joy. When he was fired from his position at the church there were many years when I didn't hear him singing at all.

Over the years Patrick occasionally sang at our new church, but not like he had previous to the crisis. And his dreams of using his gift for the Lord had been all but snuffed out. We hadn't talked about this much because it would fill him with remorse and make me very sad. I first fell in love with him when I heard him singing, and—most of all—I love to hear him singing about the Lord. So, when I heard him downstairs singing to his old performance tapes, it touched me deeply. I sat upstairs for a while and listened, not wanting to interrupt whatever was happening with him. Then I asked if he would mind if I came down to listen.

I sat across the room as he sang a few of the old, familiar songs that brought back bittersweet memories. The sweetness came from the way things had been before his fall, and the bitter edge came from realizing all the suffering that he (and we) had been through in the interim.

I asked him what prompted him to sing like this and what was going on inside of him. He grew quiet and then he said, *"I was just remembering, and wondering what I might be doing with my singing if I hadn't ruined everything. I was thinking back over every turning point in my life when I made the wrong turn. I was trying to imagine what life would be like if I had made right decisions at those points. I was trying to imagine what our lives might be like if all the dark threads of my sinful choices were removed. But every time I removed a dark thread I found that God had tied it into so many good things He did in us and our lives that all the good we now enjoy would unravel, even if I just removed the worst of the dark threads. So finally, I just gave up and gave thanks to the Lord. He has so redeemed all the sin and suffering that I could not find one thread of it that I would remove—now—even if I could."*

Somehow, God has used every wrong move, every sin, every mistake, and every bit of suffering we had endured to weave a beautiful tapestry of redemption. Our God is a redeemer. Whatever troubles you and your spouse are facing, whatever suffering comes your way, from whatever source, God can weave it around into something good. Don't ask me how because I can't figure it out even in retrospect. I only know that He does. I know this from the testimony of lives in the Bible, and I know it from what God has done in our lives and in the lives of the others I interviewed. Knowing and believing this up front makes going through the suffering and enduring the trials a far better experience.

ATTITUDE

Your attitude toward all trials and suffering must rest in your knowledge of God as a loving, almighty, and faithful Father. If you do not believe Him to be a loving God, you will doubt His good intentions toward you. If you do not believe Him to be almighty, you will doubt His ability to keep His good intentions toward you. If you do not believe God to be faithful, you may believe He has the love and the power but not the integrity to keep His word.

These are basic tenets of the Christian faith that are easy enough to mouth when recounting our creed. However, when tragedy strikes, when the unthinkable happens to someone you love, when adversity comes close to home, these beliefs are tested. They are tested in the secret recesses of your own heart, where you wonder, *How could a loving God allow such a thing? If God has the power to stop this, why doesn't He? God has promised us His protection, why is He letting us down?*

One of the purposes God achieves through all suffering and trials that touch your life is the testing of your faith. In practice that means that suffering and tragedy actually cause you to ask these questions and persevere in your faith until you have settled them for yourself. The Bible says, *"And without faith it is impossible to please God, because anyone who comes to him must believe that he exists and that he rewards those who earnestly seek him"* (Hebrews 11:6). Suffering and trials give you the chance to reaffirm your belief that God exists and that He will reward you if you earnestly seek Him throughout whatever you and your spouse are going through. This must be your basic predisposition, your spiritual attitude within which you address all your questions about *"Why?"*

Let's go on to consider three basic scriptural beliefs that form the framework for considering why God would allow whatever you are going through in your marriage (or any suffering). These beliefs carried me through all that we endured and were proved absolutely true. I will go on to illustrate the inter-relation of these beliefs with a story, but first, let me state them plainly:

1. God causes all things to work together for good to those who love him, who are called according to his purpose.

While your individual purpose in life may not be clear to you yet, God's purpose in this regard is clearly spelled out. Romans 8:28 says, *"And we know that in all things God works for the good of those who love him, who have been called according to his purpose."* Romans 8:29 tells what that purpose is: *"For those God foreknew he also **predestined to be conformed to the likeness of his Son,** that he might be the firstborn among many brothers"* (emphasis mine). God's purpose in the life of every believer is to have him or her be conformed to the likeness of Jesus: that is, to become like him in whatever trials life brings. So whatever you and your spouse are facing, you can know that God's purpose for you is that you become more like Christ through it.

This may raise the question of how these principles apply if your spouse is not a Christian and does not love God. While a non-Christian cannot assume the promises made to those in God's family, God's promises still apply to you in relation to the trials in your marriage, even if your spouse is an unbeliever. Beyond this, God's great love extends to all. He is not willing that any should perish but that all should come to repentance. If your spouse is not a Christian, God wants him to enter His family so that he can receive the benefits of redemption — including the redemption of all his suffering. Whatever other purposes God is working to accomplish through these trials, you can be sure that God will use the pressures of life to cause you and your spouse to see your need for help. Your prayers and proper attitude in the midst of suffering can be used of God to bring your spouse to faith. Then he can receive the benefits of God's promise to those who love Him, that God will work everything together for good.

2. God does not delight in the suffering of his children, any more than any loving parent does.

God only allows His children to suffer if necessary to accomplish some greater good that they may not understand. God is the greatest of fathers; how could He be callused to the pain His children suffer? No! God cares whenever you hurt. He only allows you to suffer when it is necessary to serve a greater purpose that you cannot understand at the time. If you are a parent, look at how your children react when you have to take them to get their vaccination shots. They cannot understand why you would allow the nurse to hold them down, much less why you would help her hold them down and hurt them. You could stop her! Why don't you? You can't explain it to the child at the time; but when they get older they will understand that you only allowed that pain to spare them the threat of a deadly disease. Were you untouched by their pain? No! Your heart broke because of the pain they suffered—not just the physical pain but also the pain they felt at what they considered to be your betrayal when they needed you to protect them from the pain. That is the heart of God toward you when you suffer, not just the pain of the circumstance but the deeper pain and confusion of wondering how God could allow such a thing if He really loved you.

3. Nothing is allowed into the lives of God's children without his permission.

The source of the suffering or trial may be evil, but if God allows it, He has a plan to make that which is meant for evil be used for your good in the long run.

God is not the source of all the pain and suffering that comes into your lives. Pain and suffering can come from living in a fallen world where things are not as God originally intended; they can come from the sin of other people; they can come as a natural consequence of sin within your heart or your spouse's heart; they can even come from spiritual forces of wickedness under the control of Satan (whom the Bible also calls the god of this world). Whatever the source, Peter tells us, *"In this you greatly rejoice, even though now for a little while,* **if necessary***, you have been distressed by various trials"* (1 Peter 1:6 NASB, emphasis mine).

Whatever the source, nothing can touch the child of God unless God allows it through his protective covering that surrounds all His children. The Bible tells us that Satan wanted to attack Job, but he had to get permission from God before he could do so. Even then, God put limits on what Satan could do. He was not allowed to take Job's life. This cuts two ways. You may be relieved to know that God has protective limits set around your life. But it may also make you hold God partially responsible for whatever is happening. While God may not be the source of the suffering, He did allow it. Yes, and you must keep in mind that He only allowed it if it can serve a good purpose that will offset the pain you and your spouse are going through or will go through. To better understand this, consider not only the outcome of Job's life but what he learned about God in the aftermath of his suffering.

THE INTERPLAY OF THESE PRINCIPLES
Now let me tell you a story that shows the interplay of these three basic principles:

1) **God causes all things to work together for good to those who love Him, who are called according to His purpose**

2) **God does not delight in the suffering of His children**

3) **Nothing is allowed into the lives of God's children without His permission and will ultimately achieve His purpose.**

The Chronicles of Narnia comprises seven books written for children by C.S. Lewis. These fictional stories magically take several British children into the land of Narnia, which is populated with talking beasts, mythical figures, sons of Adam, and daughters of Eve (human beings). All Narnia is ruled by the great lion, Aslan—who is a figure of Christ—sent by the Emperor beyond the sea—who is a figure of God the Father. These classic children's stories are brilliantly crafted to embody biblical truth in ways that allows us to see things that are true in story form that might have been missed when laid out directly in Scripture. Thus it was for me with the following story.

I will only describe this story from one of the Narnia books in barest detail. If you have not read the series, I heartily encourage you to do so now, and repeatedly—whether or not you have children! This story comes from the book **The Horse and His Boy**. The overall story is about how a talking horse and a boy prince saved Narnia from invasion. The central character is a young boy called Shasta, who is actually a prince but does not know that yet because he was kidnapped as an infant. He escapes a dreadful situation with the help of a talking horse. He is accompanied by a princess named Avaris and her horse—who is not a talking beast. In their journeys they meet with many dangers and trials. One of the most frightful is when they are chased by two lions, one of which scratches Avaris. They barely escape by arriving at a castle of refuge just before the drawbridge is raised for the night. They find themselves in one trial after another, until they come to safety where Shasta discovers that he is really Prince Cor of

Archenland. Without knowing it, all the trials he had been through on his journey caused him to fulfill the prophecy of his life, that he would deliver his homeland from *"the deadliest danger in which ever she lay."*

What strikes me about this story that illustrates our three points is the role of the lions. Near the end of the journey, Shasta finds himself accompanied by an invisible presence—a BIG invisible presence. He begs it to go away then says, *"What harm have I ever done to you? Oh, I am the unluckiest person in the whole world."*

The presence asks Shasta to share his sorrows. When Shasta relates his sad story, he especially focuses on how he and Avaris were chased by lions and how Avaris was wounded by one of the lions. Shasta is shocked when the Voice reveals that there was only one lion. Incredulous, Shasta asks, *"How do you know?"*

"I was the lion," the Voice answers.

Soon the Voice becomes visible as Aslan, the Great Lion, the Christ figure in the story. Aslan tells Shasta that he was the one who chased them because they needed to move faster to reach their destination. Aslan reveals to Avaris that he was even the lion who wounded her as recompense for the pain her actions had inflicted on another. Aslan explains to each of them that he had allowed them to be frightened, even hurt, along their journey, but assures them that he was watching over them for their own good and to bring them along to their intended destination. Though Shasta and Avaris ask Aslan about what will happen to others, Aslan explains that he tells no one any story but their own.

God knows your story, and he knows your spouse's story, and right now the two of you are on the journey together. There is much that you will not know in the midst of your trials that you will know later. There are some things you may never know because they may be parts of someone else's story. However, what you can know is that God, like the Great Lion, is with you at every point to bring about His good purpose in your life. There may be times you are scared and confused when you think He has surely left you to be prey to beasts. There may be times when it seems that God Himself has torn you to pieces, and indeed occasions when that may be true. However, you can know with absolute certainty that God loves you, God is almighty in power, and God is faithful. If you know that, you can get through anything—even when you don't understand why you and yours are suffering.

UNDERSTANDING

Now let's look at the possible sources of the trials or suffering and possible reasons that God allows suffering. This understanding will help you respond wisely to your spouse's situation if that is a source of suffering and to God as you and your spouse go through trials and suffering.

We will consider six reasons for and possible sources of trials and suffering that are clearly seen in Scripture. These do not operate independently of each other; usually more than one is involved in any trial. That's why you need to trust that God knows how to weave them all together for your good. However, in some particular instances, understanding the source of the trial will suggest how you get through it or hold up under it. These six reasons are given below in no particular order:

1. The trials may fit into a larger scheme of things that you are not able to see fully.

When Joseph, the son of Jacob, was sold into slavery by his brothers (in the book of Genesis), *they* meant it for evil. They were just trying to be rid of him because he had visions that God would raise him up to rule over them. Then he was sent to the house of Potiphar in Egypt, where he was falsely accused of trying to rape Potiphar's wife. This led to him being unjustly imprisoned in Pharaoh's dungeon. There he stayed for thirteen years. While imprisoned he interpreted dreams for two servants of Pharaoh. One promised to remember him to Pharaoh upon his release but forgot—for two years—until Pharaoh needed someone to interpret two strange dreams he had. Then the ex-prisoner recalled Joseph, who was still sitting in the dungeon. When Joseph was brought before Pharaoh, God gave him the interpretation of both dreams. These predicted seven years of abundance, followed by seven years of severe drought. The Pharaoh recognized the Spirit of God at work in Joseph and elevated him to be second in command over all Egypt and to oversee storage and distribution of all grain.

This brought Joseph into the position God had prophesied concerning him as a boy—the very same prophecy that prompted his brothers to despise him. This brought Joseph to the position where his brothers bowed before him several years later when they ran out of food. This in turn forced Joseph's father Jacob (aka: Israel), to move to Egypt with his entire family, which in turn fulfilled a prophecy God had given Abram (who became Abraham, Joseph's great-great-grandfather), which is recorded in Genesis 15:12-14:

> *As the sun was setting, Abram fell into a deep sleep, and a thick and dreadful darkness came over him. Then the LORD said to him, 'Know for certain that your descendants will be strangers in a country not their own, and they will be enslaved and mistreated four hundred years. But I will punish the nation they serve as slaves, and afterward they will come out with great possessions.'*

So all of this goes to show us that Joseph's trials and suffering were part of a much larger scheme of things that he had no way of fully comprehending. But he knew enough so that he did not despair in the midst of his sufferings. Instead, he was able to trust God and live his life fully, to the best of his ability, in whatever situation or enduring whatever suffering came his way in the midst of those trials. Even though much of his suffering came at the hands of those who intended it for evil, it had to pass through the hand of God, who turned what they intended for evil to accomplish what God intended for good.

2. Some suffering and trials come our way because we live in a fallen world.

That means that life often is not fair and things don't work out the way we know they should in a perfect world. King Solomon addressed this in the book of Ecclesiastes:

> *I have seen something else under the sun: The race is not to the swift or the battle to the strong, nor does food come to the wise or wealth to the brilliant or favor to the learned; but time and chance happen to them all (Ecclesiastes 9:11).*

Yes, accidents happen — even to Christians — and sometimes injustice wins out temporarily even in the lives of those who love God.

This is important because of the way our human nature reacts when bad things happen to God's people. It would be simpler to understand if we could assume that if God let something tragic happen to someone, they must have deserved it. This was the error Job's friends were chastised for by God, an error Jesus sought to correct in his disciples' thinking. This is recorded in Luke chapter 13:

> *Now there were some present at that time who told Jesus about the Galileans whose blood Pilate had mixed with their sacrifices. Jesus answered, 'Do you think that these Galileans were worse sinners than all the other Galileans because they suffered this way? I tell you, no! But unless you repent, you too will all perish. Or those eighteen who*

> *died when the tower in Siloam fell on them—do you think they were more guilty than all the others living in Jerusalem? I tell you, no! But unless you repent, you too will all perish. (Luke 13:1-5)*

Sometimes accidents and injustice happen; but that is not to be taken as evidence that God loves those involved less than others who happened to escape. Don't make the mistake of thinking that whatever has happened to you and your spouse means that God does not love you both or is punishing you for some unknown sin. Instead, trust that even if you or your spouse have been victims of accident or injustice in this fallen world, God can redeem the situation and—in the case of injustice— promises that he will bring justice to all who seek it from Him. It may appear that justice will come after death, but God will eventually bring justice.

3. The Bible tells us that Satan is real and that he comes to kill, steal, and destroy (see John 10:10).

It tells us that our enemy the devil *"prowls around like a roaring lion looking for someone to devour" (1 Peter 5:8)*. These are not descriptions of pleasant experiences when they are translated into real life.

There will be times when every true child of God, especially those who are accomplishing things for the kingdom of God, will undergo suffering that comes as a result of satanically inspired events. The apostle John writes,

> *We know that anyone born of God does not continue to sin; the one who was born of God keeps him safe, and the evil one cannot harm him. We know that we are children of God, and that the whole world is under the control of the evil one (1 John 5:18-19).*

Herein we see that the evil one cannot do us any harm unless God allows him to but also that the whole world system in which we live is under the control of the evil one. Within this context, there can be people and other spheres of influence that are directed against you by Satan.

We will address this issue more fully in the chapter about confronting hell head-on. However, the point for you to understand here is that trials and suffering can come from your spiritual enemy when you are doing God's work. Those are to be met as Scripture instructs us: *"Take up the shield of faith, with which you can extinguish all the flaming arrows of the evil one"* (*Ephesians 6:16*).

4. Trials and suffering may be allowed by God to purify your faith, to purge out that which is within you that is not holy as God would have it.

Scripture uses the analogy of purifying precious metals, where extremely hot fires melt the metal so that the impurities rise to the surface. Then as the metal cools, the impurities are removed from the surface. This denotes the process of repeated melting, surfacing impurities, removing them, and then melting the metal again to make it more pure. It also denotes the value and preciousness of that which is purified. This is what Peter referred to when he wrote to the persecuted early church, saying,

> *In this you greatly rejoice, though now for a little while you may have had to suffer grief in all kinds of trials. These have come so that your faith—of greater worth than gold, which perishes even though refined by fire—may be proved genuine and may result in praise, glory and honor when Jesus Christ is revealed. (1 Peter 1:6-7)*

When you go through suffering or prolonged uncertainty that tries your faith, that which is beneath the surface of your character becomes apparent. These may be bad attitudes, insecurities, issues from your childhood that still trouble you, bitterness, inclination toward a particular sin, resentments, unresolved anger, unforgiveness, lack of trust in God's goodness . . . the list goes on and on. God knows what is left within you that is not in keeping with the person He is making you to be, and He knows exactly what can turn up the heat to bring those things to the surface.

When the heat is on, and you notice things surfacing that are not pretty, don't avoid them or try to push them back down! No! God allowed the heat to bring them to the surface. At that point, you are to acknowledge them, confess any sinfulness you may become aware of in your heart or life, and ask God to take all the dross away. God is the refiner. He wants to take it away, and intended to do so all along. That's why He allowed the trials. Don't waste the pain! Give all the impurities it brings up to the Lord.

5. Some suffering and trials come because they are the consequences of what we have done.

As surely as the natural realm operates under the natural law stated as "every action has an equal and opposite reaction," the spiritual realm operates by the spiritual law that says what we give out will come back to us in kind. Even though God redeems, we also see that God holds us accountable. The apostle Paul stated it bluntly, *"Do not be deceived: God cannot be mocked. A man reaps what he sows" (Galatians 6:7).* Jesus stated it this way: *"For in the same way you judge others, you will be judged, and with the measure you use, it will be measured to you" (Matthew 7:2).*

It does no good to argue with the law of gravity; rather, it is wise to learn to work with it, not against it. So, too, is the way it works with the law of sowing and reaping. If this trial or suffering is something you or your spouse has sown and must reap, it does no good for you to pray that you or your spouse will not have to reap it. Rather, you should pray that as you or your spouse reap whatever must be reaped, your hearts would learn from the sorrow brought on by what was sown.

Also, you must not worry that God cannot sort out your life from your spouse's or that you will suffer unjustly at God's hand because you are married to someone who has brought these troubles to your door. This issue will be explored more fully in the chapter on tending a jointly held spiritual garden. But for now, you must rely on the verse that follows Paul's statement *"A man reaps what he sows."* That verse says, *"Let us not become weary in doing good, for at the proper time we will reap a harvest if we do not give up" (Galatians 6:9).* Even if your spouse has brought troubles and suffering into your marriage, you are to continue doing good. The same law that may have originated the suffering in your lives now can work to bring the good harvest in your lives in future seasons if you don't give up.

6. The last reason for some trials and suffering is that God may be disciplining you or your spouse.

Another way to put this is to say that there are times God punishes us for our sins and corrects us like a father corrects a disobedient child.

People tend to have strong prejudices concerning this idea. Some people gravitate to this as the explanation for all suffering. Anything bad happens and they immediately think God is punishing them and that they must have done something sinful to deserve such pain. Others take offense at the thought that a loving God would dare to punish His children. In this matter, your view of discipline or punishment will likely be influenced by the way you were disciplined or punished as a child by your parents. If you were abused, you may immediately associate God's discipline with that which God never intended to happen to any child. However, do not let your personal prejudices or childhood experience warp your understanding that there are times God will discipline his children. And when he does, it hurts, and the one being disciplined won't like it! But look at God's purpose in allowing painful discipline to come into our lives. Consider the passage below that explains God's discipline:

> *And you have forgotten that word of encouragement that addresses you as sons: 'My son, do not make light of the Lord's discipline, and do not lose heart when he rebukes you, because the Lord disciplines those he loves, and he punishes everyone he accepts as a son.' Endure hardship as discipline; God is treating you as sons. For what son is not disciplined by his father? If you are not disciplined (and everyone undergoes discipline), then you are illegitimate children and not true sons. Moreover, we have all had human fathers who disciplined us and we respected them for it. How much more should we submit to the Father of our spirits and live! Our fathers disciplined us for a little while as they thought best; but God disciplines us for our good, that we may share in his holiness. No discipline seems pleasant at the time, but painful. Later on, however, it produces a harvest of righteousness and peace for those who have been trained by it.*
>
> *Therefore, strengthen your feeble arms and weak knees. Make level paths for your feet, so that the lame may not be disabled, but rather **healed.**' (Hebrews 12:5-12)*

God's purpose is not to punish you with pain so that you will know how bad you are! God's purpose is holiness and healing! This is confirmed again by the prophet Hosea, who wrote,

> *Come, let us return to the LORD. He has torn us to pieces but he will heal us; he has injured us but he will bind up our wounds. After two days he will revive us; on the third*

day he will restore us that we may live in his presence. (Hosea 6:1-2)

RESPONSE

This leads us to our final section: how we are to respond to the trials and suffering God allows into our lives—including the ones associated with whatever is going on in your marriage.

James 1:2-4 instructs us,

> *Consider it pure joy, my brothers, whenever you face trials of many kinds, because you know that the testing of your faith develops perseverance. Perseverance must finish its work so that you may be mature and complete, not lacking anything.*

> Another version phrases this last verse, *'And let endurance have its perfect result, that you may be perfect and complete, lacking nothing"* (NASB).

Somehow, we are to come to the point where we can not only welcome trials into our lives but *"consider it pure joy"* whenever we face trials of many kinds. The reason given is not that these trials will work out but rather that God will use these trials to work something into our character. Furthermore, we are told that we are to let endurance of such trials have its perfect result, that we may be mature and complete, not lacking anything. This implies that our attitude toward the trial and our response in the trial will determine whether God's intention for the trial is completed. This tells us that God's intention is that we would be mature and complete, not lacking anything. That sounds good, but how can we understand it to be so good that we could *actually* consider it pure joy when we encounter various trials?

That's what I'm going to try to show you here. This is a hard concept to understand and apply because we don't easily associate pain with pure joy. We don't easily associate our weakness during pain with God's strength to accomplish His good purpose for our lives. I hope this illustration will help.

When I was pregnant with my first child someone gave me a book called **Childbirth without Fear**. It explained what would happen in labor, how my body would naturally constrict using rhythmic contractions to deliver the baby. It explained that, as labor progressed, each contraction would grow stronger and the timing of the contractions would come closer together. It then explained that the best way to go through labor was to cooperate with the natural birth process taking place. It explained that when a woman became afraid of the pain and resisted the contractions, her muscle tension actually worked against the natural process of her body. This meant that her body would have to work harder, producing stronger and more painful contractions to accomplish the goal of delivering the baby. The author then appealed to common sense by saying that if I would simply relax completely, go limp, and let my body do the good work it was about with the contractions, the birth would come sooner and with less pain.

The author also suggested that the woman who was in labor think of the joy she would have when she held her baby in her arms. He suggested that she think of each contraction as a wave of the sea that was meant to carry her ever closer to the joy of having her baby in her arms—and to labor being over! If she struggled against each contraction, the author said, that would not allow each contraction to take her as far as it could. Therefore, she was to think of becoming as cooperative as possible — meaning not resisting the contraction or tensing up in any way even though it was painful. When each contraction came she was advised to relax every part of her body, breathe slowly and deeply, focus on the joy awaiting her when she would hold her baby in her arms, and not resist the contraction in any way.

That sounded great, and it actually reduced my fear of giving birth the first time. However, while everything the author said was true, when the experience of labor began in earnest, living out those simple instructions became one of the greatest challenges of my life. But I did remember what he had helped me understand about the strength of the contractions being God's way of bringing forth my baby. Therefore, when the contractions became strong, I didn't resist them. I felt as weak as I ever have before or since, but in my weakness, I relaxed and trusted that the strength of the contraction would hurt less if I just went with it. I knew the purpose of the contraction, so I chose to relax and let it do its perfect work — bringing forth my baby. While I did have to endure pain, that pain came moment by moment so that it was never more than I could bear. And all the pain had a purpose: to bring me the joy of holding my baby in my arms.

When my twenty-seven hours of intense labor were completed—including having to endure abuse from a nurse I was sure came to torment me as an agent of Satan himself!—I held my beautiful daughter in my arms. Oh, the joy of that moment! Patrick looked at me and said, *"Honey, you don't ever have to go through that again. We can adopt if you want."* And my response to him was, *"It wasn't that bad. I could go through that again anytime if I knew I could count on this joy,"* referring to my baby nursing contentedly in my arms. That's what I think James meant by *"count it all joy."*

You can count on there being joy to come whenever God allows you to go through trials and suffering. And if you count on it while you are going through the trials, you can also count on the benefits you will receive at the outcome of the trials. You are encouraged to relax in the midst of the trials because even the pain of spiritual contractions is part of God's plan to bring about His good intentions for your life.

So now let's count some of the benefits of trials mentioned in the Bible. Then I will explain some practical ways you can respond as you go through your trials.

THE BENEFITS OF TRIALS AND SUFFERING

1. The first benefit is that we may be mature, complete and not lack anything that is good.

2. We learn obedience through the things that we suffer.

If life didn't give us opportunities to be anxious, how could we learn to be obedient to God's command *"Be anxious for nothing"* *(see Philippians 4:6)*. Even when we are not suffering because of disobedience, we can learn to be obedient to God in the midst of the pain we are going through.

3. Adversity can bring humility.

Psalm 107:39 tells us that oppression, calamity, and sorrow can humble us. When we are humble, we are in the best position for God to lift us up. This can be as preparation for ministry, as it was in my case where our suffering brought about humility and compassion that I did not have before. I later realized that these qualities were necessary for me to be the kind of person God could use.

4. Suffering produces that which God wants to develop in us.

God's word says,

> And we rejoice in the hope of the glory of God. Not only so, but we also rejoice in our sufferings, because we know that suffering produces perseverance; perseverance, character; and character, hope. And hope does not disappoint us, because God has poured out his love into our hearts by the Holy Spirit, whom he has given us *(Romans 5:2b-5)*.

The character and hope God wants to produce in us can be produced through suffering. So we rejoice in the blessings of God, and we rejoice in the sufferings God allows because we know He is doing a good work in us and through us.

5. The proof of our faith will be found to result in praise and glory and honor to God.

When we are in the trials, people are watching. When we truly believe God and take him at his word, He rewards our faith with substance. He answers our prayers and proves Himself faithful in our lives. This reveals Jesus Christ to the world in a way they may not be able to understand but cannot deny. Peter explained why our fiery trials are worth it:

> Now for a little while you may have had to suffer grief in all kinds of trials. These have come so that your faith—of greater worth than gold, which perishes even though refined by fire—may be proved genuine and may result in praise, glory and honor when Jesus Christ is revealed. Though you have not seen him, you love him; and even though you do not see him now, you believe in him and are filled with an inexpressible and glorious joy, for you are receiving the goal of your faith, the salvation of your souls (1 Peter l:6b-9).

There is something we must always bear in mind with regard to trials and suffering—whether our own or those our spouse endures. God is not nearly as concerned with bringing us out of our trials as He is with what the trials bring out in us. God is more concerned with what the trial gets out of you than when you get out of the trial. Therefore, when you and your spouse have trials, don't immediately ask God to get either of you out of them. Remember, God let you or your spouse get in those difficult situations for a reason. Therefore, our immediate response to any trial should not be, "Lord, take this away!" Rather, it should be: "Lord, accomplish your purpose!" "Complete your inner work through this as quickly as possible so You can take it away." "Lord, *cause me to relax and trust You in this so that You can do your perfect work in me." "Lord, let my spouse respond to You, to learn whatever You have to teach through this trial so that You can remove it as soon as Your work is complete."*

Do not respond to trials with surprise and shock. Trials are to be expected. Jesus promised that in this world we would have troubles. Why the shock? The apostle Peter wrote,

> *Dear friends, do not be surprised at the painful trial you are suffering, as though something strange were happening to you. But rejoice that you participate in the sufferings of Christ, so that you may be overjoyed when his glory is revealed (1 Peter 4:12-13).*

We are told to *"endure hardship as discipline"* (Hebrews 12:7). This was a key that helped Jan Dravecky get through all the trials she and her husband, Dave endured. Once she decided to endure all hardship as discipline, she began to look for what she could learn every time something was hard. She had seen that there was pain involved in the kind of discipline required to make her husband a major league baseball player. You know—no pain, no gain. She turned that understanding around to work for her. If there was pain, there had to be something she could gain. You don't even have to know why a trial or suffering came to your lives to be able to learn something from the pain and the process of going through it.

Whenever it's hard to endure whatever you are going through, switch from asking *"Why?"* to start asking, *"Lord, what can I learn from this? How can I have an attitude like Jesus in the midst of his trials?"* One of the things you may learn is the cause of the trial. If you do, you can know how to pray more effectively. If you think it may be a spiritual attack inspired by satanic forces of evil, pray against such forces; affirm your faith in God's promise to protect you; use the spiritual armor God has given you. If you learn that what your spouse is suffering is a direct result of personal sin, stand aside and let him bear the consequences. Love him and encourage him, but don't intercept the pain that he must bear as a consequence of wrongdoing. Ask God to show you anything He is trying to surface in your inner life, whether that is unconfessed sin or wrong attitudes God wants to adjust. If God shows you a bad attitude — or your spouse points it out — confess that and ask God to change you. If your spouse's trials reveal something in him that makes you trust him less, trust Jesus more to make up the difference. If the circumstances force you to have to do something you were reluctant to do, like get a job or go back to school, don't fight it. Trust that God is in control and has a purpose He is working out. When you are in the midst of trials, pain, and suffering, cooperate with God in every possible way you can. You can do so with joy because you can be sure God is working out a good purpose for you.

I know these may come off as sounding simplistic, but that which is simple is often not easy. I realize that doing these simple things is about as easy as using the simple breathing techniques learned in childbirth class during real labor. Just because it's hard to do doesn't mean it has to be complicated. In natural child birth class, the instructor says, *"All you do is relax and breathe like this."* And you think, *Hey this is easy!* This is all there is to having a baby? Piece of cake. Then when you're in the midst of labor and you have to relax and simply breathe through a contraction, you realize that simply breathing in the midst of intense pressure and pain is not easy.

Getting through the trials and suffering that may come because of whatever your spouse is going through or problems in your marriage will test your faith, test your endurance, test your patience, and test whatever else God knows needs to be tested. But that is good! You can get through it. God is with you all the way. If you remember and practice the simple things I've recounted for you in this chapter, they will prove true. But no, it probably will not be easy. God will bring you through it; and when He does you will be able to look back as my husband did and say, *"I wouldn't take out one dark thread. God has tied each one into all the good that he has brought about in our lives."* And when God does that, the people looking at the outer side of the tapestry of your life will see God's unmistakable handiwork.

CHAPTER SIX: TENDING A JOINTLY OWNED SPIRITUAL GARDEN

LORD, HOW CAN I DEAL WITH MY SPOUSE'S PROBLEMS & PAIN THAT INTERTWINE WITH MY LIFE?

I met Annette because she requested it of our Father in heaven. Annette was in a situation where she was crying out to God, *"Lord, how could you let this happen to me? I've devoted my life to serving you! I've loved my husband, served him, served the church, and done my best to live the life you called me to live. Why am I left alone to suffer because of what he did wrong?—against me! Lord, are my dreams going to come to an end because of the wrong he did?"*

As she was asking these questions, a friend gave her my book Dancing the Arms of God. She got to the part where I had lost my ministry, lost my reputation, and had to clear out my office alone—because my husband was in the hospital after becoming suicidal—and we had to move out of our home as a residual effect of my husband's sin. Annette later told me, *"I had assumed that my dreams were defeated because of what my husband's sins brought on us. But when I saw how God worked in your life, even by letting you suffer the ill effects of his sin, and how God still fulfilled your dreams and your calling, I felt hope for the first time in a long time. That's when I told the Father, I have to meet this woman.'"*

Annette called her friend Jo Ann and asked her to pray that she would be able to meet me. They prayed together. The following week I received an early-morning call from a friend inviting me to attend a women's conference. Someone had taken ill, she could not get a refund on the ticket, and she didn't want it to go to waste. I had wanted to attend but didn't think I could spare the money. So this seemed like it was from the Lord and I gladly accepted the invitation. When I arrived, I entered a large ballroom at the Red Lion Hotel where upwards of four hundred fifty women were seated at round banquet tables. I arrived late and couldn't find the woman who invited me. So, I took the only open seat I saw at a table with seven women I didn't know.

During the break we introduced ourselves. When I said my name, the two women to my left just stared at me—as if in disbelief. Then one of them — Jo Ann — asked if I had written a book. When I said yes, they got tears in their eyes and told me Annette's story. You see, this Jo Ann was the same woman with whom Annette had prayed that she would have the opportunity to meet me just days before. Jo Ann and her friend told me that Annette was the wife of their former pastor. That very day, Annette could not come to the conference because she was home alone packing to move. Then they told me what had brought Annette to that point. Annette and her husband met in Bible college. They fell in love, got married, and set out in life to serve God together. He became a pastor and she the overactive pastor's wife. Together they had planted several new churches, each time building a thriving ministry from nothing. They grew to be widely respected in their denomination. They raised a family and served God tirelessly— until Annette grew exhausted from overwork.

Her schedule did not leave any time for rest. Every night of the week she and her family were doing something to serve God and their congregation. Sunday, the day of rest for most people, was the most demanding day of the week. Saturday was spent in all-day evangelism training seminars. Leading Bible study and groups for young Christians and children took up other weeknights. Friday nights they spent picketing the local pornographic bookstores and sleaze clubs. This kind of schedule, after decades of ministry along with raising their teen-age children, proved exhausting. Annette asked her husband if she could pull back, but he had a hard time with that. She was the pastor's wife and people had expectations. She eventually collapsed with one physical illness after another. Some were caused by exhaustion and depression; others were caused by medical mishaps, accidents, or taking conflicting prescribed medication. Annette's life was in danger. She was hospitalized several times, twice for clinical depression and other times for medical conditions seemingly unrelated to her exhaustion.

She knew that she was burnt out and could see the same thing happening to her husband. She pleaded with him to slow down. Their relationship was suffering. She saw warning signs that something had to give, but she didn't know what that was. She insisted that they see a counselor, together. Her husband agreed, but the counselor couldn't get anywhere with him. Annette was doing everything she could to get well medically, spiritually, and relationally with her husband. Her husband didn't think the congregation would understand her stepping down from her various duties, so he agreed to let the counselor explain her condition to the congregation. A special meeting was called where the counselor told the congregation that Annette had exhausted herself from years and years of faithful service and needed to be allowed to rest and recover. She needed the understanding and support of their congregation. And for the most part she got it.

Her husband, however, refused to slow down. He kept up the pace. Rumors began to spread. A young girl had brought accusations against him. Annette and another woman on their church staff who was a trusted friend went to him. They demanded to know if there was any truth to these allegations. He assured them, *"No! Maybe there had been some ill-advised times scheduled when I was counseling her in private, but nothing happened."* Then word came that these allegations had been lodged against him at a district level in their denomination. Annette and the other woman confronted him again. They had been staunchly defending him; they had to know the truth. That's when he broke.

The story came out in bits and snatches. He would confess a bit, and then alternate that with self-defense and rationalization. Eventually, the ugly story emerged. Yes, he had been sexually involved with this teen-age girl. Her family members were part of their congregation. She was under age. Their sexual involvement had gone on for several months. Annette was stunned, outraged, and wounded by betrayal, devastated that she hadn't suspected, horrified that she had defended him blindly. And that was before the full impact of the situation hit her.

Within days her husband was arrested for child sexual abuse. He was shown every night on the local news shuffling into court in handcuffs and leg-irons wearing bright orange prison garb. The media had a hey-day juxtaposing pictures of him preaching in the pulpit next to footage of little four- and five-year-old girls parading in fluffy ruffled dresses (never mind the fact that he had been involved with a teen-ager and had never shown any propensity toward molesting preadolescent girls). The news media tore their family apart. Annette and her children were made subject to public humiliation the likes of which they had never imagined and did not deserve.

During the trial, Annette was subjected to harassment from several sources. She sat through the trial to see her husband convicted as a sex offender and taken off to jail. Of course, he had lost his job. The girl's family brought a lawsuit against their denomination and all church leaders were told not to communicate with Annette. She was cut off from the church family and all the relationships she had spent more than twenty-five years developing. Some members of her congregation rallied to her side—including the two women I "happened" to sit next to at this conference.

Annette also discovered that her husband was hiding more than his sexual sins. He had secretly gotten several credit cards that he used to buy all sorts of tools and toys that she knew nothing about—although she did have great fun selling them at a remarkable discount while he was in jail! She had done nothing to bring this on her family; but she was left to deal with it all alone while her husband was incarcerated.

She got a job in a Christian setting through a church friend, but even there she was subjected to innuendo and derision—as though no one could believe God would let her suffer so if she were not partially responsible for what her husband had done. Some dared to suggest—behind her back, of course—that if she had not been sick for so long he wouldn't have "needed" to look elsewhere for sexual gratification. Others suggested that when he got out of jail she should order sleepwear from Victoria's Secret. She was rightfully offended by such degrading suggestions, all of which implied the same thing—that this was partially her fault. Those who didn't remove themselves from her life completely found themselves limited in what they could do to help with the overwhelming fallout of real problems that came down on Annette because of her husband's wrongdoing.

She tried her best to make it financially; but within the year she had to declare bankruptcy. Their home went into foreclosure. She had to move into a tiny apartment. She sold off most of their possessions. She had to sell their boat—which broke her heart because that was the only place where she and her husband felt free from all the pressures they had borne. She had to do all the work of taking care of the stressful details. The creditors didn't call her husband in jail! He wasn't available to pack up all their belongings or to sort through a lifetime of family photographs and mementos to decide which ones could fit in the apartment and which would have to be put in storage. No! All of that fell to Annette.

Which raises the question that is the focus of this chapter: How could a just God allow someone who is not rightfully to blame share in the bitter fruit that grows from the bad seed of their spouse's sins, wrongdoing, or mistakes? It's the age-old spiritual and moral question of why God allows the righteous to suffer with the guilty. This chapter not only raises this question but will show you God's answers to the question and how God's word says you are to respond by the power of the Holy Spirit.

We're not talking here about general strategies for supporting each other while facing life's difficulties together. In this chapter, we're addressing the biblical principles of loving and supporting each other when the "hell" your marriage is going through can be traced to something your spouse did and the bad consequences intertwine with your life so that you suffer some of the ill effects even though you didn't do anything wrong. These same principles can apply if they are suffering for the wrong you've done. Here we focus on the situation where you are suffering for doing right, when your spouse has done something wrong. I trust you can apply the principles whichever way around applies in your situation. You can also apply these principles when someone's wrongdoing outside your marriage hurts you both.

WOULD GOD ALLOW THE BLAMELESS TO SUFFER WITH THE GUILTY?

One reason people often mistreat someone in a situation like Annette's is that they have a faulty understanding of God's justice as meted out in this life. If one holds a simplistic view that bad things happen as a result of deserving bad things or that good things always happen to good people, the inference would be that anyone who suffers does so because they have done something wrong to deserve it. I faced this in my own situation when my husband fell into sin and I was removed from my position of ministry. Part of my "restoration" agreement with our church was that I would meet weekly with an associate pastor on our staff for "counseling." Our first meeting was our last. This man's opening remark to me was, *"Connie, I know that we have not been able to find any sin on your part. However, God would not let you suffer all that you are going through if you did not deserve it. So why don't you go ahead and confess your hidden sin, then we can get on with helping you repent. Then maybe God will remove this judgment that is on your life."*

This attitude shows a common mistake in theology that leads to those who are suffering for doing right being mistreated by the church. God's word makes it clear that there will be times we suffer, not only for doing wrong, but for doing right. Didn't the apostle Peter write the following?

> *But even if you should suffer for what is right, you are blessed. Do not fear what they fear; do not be frightened. But in your hearts set apart Christ as Lord. Always be prepared to give an answer to everyone who asks you to give the reason for the hope that you have. But do this with gentleness and respect, keeping a clear conscience, so that those who speak maliciously against your good behavior in Christ may be ashamed of their slander. It is better, if it is God's will, to **suffer for doing good** than for doing evil. (1 Peter 3:14-17, NIV, emphasis mine)*

If your spouse has done something wrong or made a mistake and you choose to stay, then stay to do your spouse good. And you may suffer for it—even from the words and actions of other Christians (misguided though they may be). But remember, God can even use that experience to strengthen you. ==Your part is to not give in to fear; to set Christ as Lord in your heart and continue to obey Him.== We are told to be prepared to give an answer but only when someone asks. Don't waste your time trying to make others believe that you don't deserve the suffering you are going through. Just keep your conscience clear. In time, God will show those who say malicious things about you that they should be ashamed of their behavior. It says more about them than it says about you!

WHY WOULD GOD ALLOW THE BLAMELESS TO SUFFER WITH THE GUILTY?

Throughout the Bible we see God dealing with people within the context of families and nations. We see God deal with the nation of Israel and the tribes of Judah as a group. The prophet Habakkuk stood before God to address this same question. He saw the righteous suffering with the wicked, and the wicked even seemed to prosper. He saw the innocent falling prey to the violence of those who had thrown off godly restraint. He demanded to know what God was going to do about such injustice.

God didn't answer Habakkuk directly as to why he would allow what seemed like injustice to go unchecked. In fact, he told the prophet something Habakkuk found even more perplexing. God told him that He planned to raise up the Babylonians ("bad guys") to invade Judah (God's people). God himself called the Babylonians *"that ruthless and impetuous people"* and said they *"come bent on violence."* God was about to bring His judgment on His own people in the nation of Judah because the nation had become apostate. He was going to unleash a godless and ferociously violent enemy against them to overrun the entire country and take the people into captivity.

Habakkuk was literally weak in the knees at such a revelation. He was dumbfounded that God could allow such a thing. But God assured him that He had it all under control; He was in the process of bringing about justice. At the same time God would separate those who were really His from those whose hearts were not truly devoted. He would let the judgment of Babylonian captivity fall on the whole nation – the good people along with the bad. But in the process God would call those who had ears to hear to turn their hearts back to Him completely. God would sort it out and protect those who took refuge in Him. Then — God assured Habakkuk — he would judge the nation of Babylon for every bit of evil they did against the nation of Judah.

What would make the difference in terms of the experience of those caught up in the wide-reaching judgment against wrongdoing? It would be their faith in God and in His ability to work out a just end even when good people get caught up in the judgment upon the nation. Habakkuk is the one who first penned the saying *"But the righteous will live by his faith"* (Habakkuk 2:4). Habakkuk teaches us that those who have faith in God are to trust in God's providence regardless of circumstances. He declares that even if God should send suffering and loss, we are to trust that He can also bring justice in the end if we wait for Him to work it all out.

This sounds good in theory, but what does it look like in a person's life? Well, Daniel (as in the prophet Daniel or Daniel in the lion's den) was one of the good people who was carried captive into Babylon. He is one of the few characters in all of Scripture about whom we have no record of wrongdoing. He was the young man who refused to eat the king's food because it violated Jewish dietary laws. He and his friends refused to participate in idolatry. He persisted in praying openly three times a day, even though it was forbidden by law and punishable by death in the lions' den. In Daniel we see an example of a holy life being blessed even though it is being lived within the context of God's punishment for the sins of the nation.

God was fully able to let Daniel "suffer" captivity for the wrong that was done by the majority of the people in the nation of Judah. However, He also continued protecting and blessing Daniel as he set his heart to live righteously in a situation that he had done nothing to bring on himself. This is the attitude God would have you take also. And when you do, you can be assured that God will be with you to protect you, strengthen you, use you, and bless you as He did all those who submitted to Him even while suffering something they did not bring on themselves by personal wrongdoing.

GOD KNOWS HOW TO SORT OUT THE GOOD FIGS FROM THE BAD

Clear teaching on this matter is found in the book of Jeremiah, the prophet who addressed the nation of Judah before they were taken into captivity. After the king of Judah and the officials, craftsmen, and artisans of Judah were carried into exile from Jerusalem to Babylon, the Lord showed Jeremiah a vision of two baskets of figs placed in front of the temple of the Lord. Jeremiah writes:

> *One basket had very good figs, like those that ripen early; the other basket had very poor figs, so bad they could not be eaten. Then the LORD asked me, 'What do you see, Jeremiah?' 'Figs'" I answered. "The good ones are very good, but the poor ones are so bad they cannot be eaten."*

> *Then the word of the LORD came to me: "This is what the LORD, the God of Israel, says: 'Like these good figs, **I regard as good** the exiles from Judah, **whom I sent away from this place to the land of the Babylonians.*** [Then look what God says he will do for them.] *My eyes will watch over them for their good, and I will bring them back to this land. I will build them up and not tear them down; I will plant them and not uproot them. I will give them a heart to know me, that I am the LORD. They will be my people, and I will be their God, for they will return to me with all their heart.' (Jeremiah 24:2-7, emphasis mine)*

The prophet goes on to say who God sees as the bad figs and the bad that will happen to them. But the point that concerns you here is that you realize that God let the ones he saw as good be carried off from their homeland into captivity. To them, this was the worst thing imaginable. They lost everything they held dear; and God was willing to let that happen even though He said they were in His good graces. But look at what God was going to accomplish in their lives in the process. He had only good intentions toward them. He knew that those whose hearts were still receptive to Him would turn to Him with a whole heart when they were in the seemingly unfair and unfortunate circumstances that had come on them as judgment for the sins of the bad figs!

Look at what God told them to do in this bad situation; this is what Annette did, and it can apply to you in principle.

> *This is what the LORD Almighty, the God of Israel, says to all those I carried into exile from Jerusalem to Babylon: 'Build houses and settle down; plant gardens and eat what they produce. Marry and have sons and daughters; find wives for your sons and give your daughters in marriage, so that they too may have sons and daughters. Increase in number there; do not decrease. Also, seek the peace and prosperity of the city to which I have carried you into exile. Pray to the LORD for it, because if it prospers, you too will prosper. (Jeremiah 29:4-7).*

They were to settle down, cultivate faithfulness, put down roots, and live their everyday lives to the best of their ability. They were not to hold back living life fully. They were to trust that God had put them in the circumstances in which they found themselves, trust that he could prosper them in that situation—as God demonstrates in the life of Daniel—and trust that when the time is right God can punish everyone who deserves it.

One of the most widely memorized promises of Scripture was written in a letter Jeremiah wrote to the exiles of Judah. Jeremiah wrote,

> *This is what the LORD says: 'When seventy years are completed for Babylon, I will come to you and fulfill my gracious promise to bring you back to this place. For I know the plans I have for you,' declares the LORD, 'plans to prosper you and not to harm you, plans to give you hope and a future. Then you will call upon me and come and pray to me, and I will listen to you. You will seek me and find me when you seek me with all your heart. I will be found by you,' declares the LORD, 'and will bring you back from captivity. I will gather you from all the nations and places where I have banished you' declares the LORD, 'and will bring you back to the place from which I carried you into exile.' (Jeremiah 29:10-14)*

This promise was not just a positive affirmation; it is a historical fact that God kept this promise. Consider the implications for yourself and the added comfort of knowing that this promise is particularly given to those God considered good who were suffering judgment that fell on the sinful nation.

Know this: God does still have a good plan for your life even if your marriage is going through hell! God can bring about good for all those who seek Him in times of trouble. God is committed to bring it about when the time is right. You can settle down and live your life, trusting that God will not let anyone else's sin keep Him from fulfilling the good plans He has for you.

Both Annette and I can tell you with modern-day certainty that these ancient prophecies and principles prove true in real life when you find yourself in such situations. And this is not just true when there has been infidelity. I have seen this also applied in the life of a woman whose husband kept their financial condition under wraps until she discovered they were on the verge of bankruptcy. This came as a shock to her since they were living an affluent life. She had to severely alter her lifestyle, go back to work, and help him figure out how to get back to financial stability. She also had to help their children, who were almost ready to start college, adjust their expectations. The whole family suffered the financial setback that the husband/father had tried to keep from them, but God provided for them in the lean times and brought them out as they worked together.

I was finally introduced to Annette through her two friends I met at that women's conference. She participated in my focus group for this book, and she and I conferred at length about this particular issue, as did the woman who went through bankruptcy with her husband. I want to share with you the God-inspired principles and practical helps we used as we stayed in a situation where we had to suffer the consequences of our spouse's wrongdoing. These real couples saw the ramifications continue on for years, affecting family relationships, finances, and all the practical details of daily life. These principles work just as surely if it is the husband being hurt by his wife's misbehavior as it does the other way around. Let's look at how to respond to God, your spouse, and others in such situations.

HOW TO RESPOND TO GOD IN SUCH SITUATIONS

Don't turn away from God in anger. Rather, your first response to God is to do what the captives of Judah were called to do: come to Him; pray to Him; seek Him with a whole heart. You will seek God and find Him when you search for Him with all of your heart. And He will be found by you. And when you find God—not just words about Him—you will have all that you need to miraculously get through anything. You will even find that one day you will be able to say that it was worth going through whatever you went through so that you could find God again or grow closer. The restoration of that intimate relationship with God — where you have to depend on Him moment by moment and you see Him move on your behalf — really does make whatever you have to go through worthwhile. And that's coming from one of those people who swore they'd never say that!

Don't hesitate to express your questions to God. Habakkuk asked his questions and received an answer — not the one he wanted, but God did respond. God is not intimidated by your questions. However, keep in mind that you may be taken aback at how He answers you.

Don't hesitate to express your feelings to God. Read through the books of Jeremiah and Habakkuk and take note of how emotion-packed their writings are. God knows that you feel deeply; you need to know that God cares. Pour out your heart to God. Let Him know your fears, your sadness, your grief over the loss and devastation that has come to your life. There is something very therapeutic about pouring out your emotions to the Lord. Sometimes I found it helpful to write out my feelings. Many times when my emotions threatened to drown me I just literally cried out to God, turning my groaning and sobbing into a prayer that God fully understood.

Trust God! If you are saying, *How could I ever trust God if He would let me go through something so unfair?* You need to re-think this. Read through Habakkuk and Jeremiah and Daniel. Ask God to give you faith that He will take care of you in this situation, that He will bring you out, and that He will fulfill the good plans He has for you. Then trust Him, but keep in mind that it can take years for God's plans to unfold.

RESPONDING TO OTHER PEOPLE IN SUCH SITUATIONS

As previously noted, people don't feel comfortable with the idea that sometimes people suffer but don't deserve what they are suffering. Those people will tend to vilify you or withdraw. Personally, I found little was accomplished by trying to change their minds or draw them back. There will be some friends and loved ones who naturally gravitate toward you and extend grace to you. Take refuge in their love and try not to worry about the others. In time, God promises to clear your good name if you have been misjudged. I have found that many of the people who misjudged me later came back to apologize for doing so. Time will tell. Trust God to take care of those people.

There will be those who blame you. Don't accept such blame; instead, gently correct them by stating the facts. In my case, one of the girls in our youth group came to me and said,

"I finally got to the point where I could forgive you and Pat for what you did."

I replied, "What do you mean, 'what we did'?"

There was an awkward silence, followed by her saying, *"Well, you know ..."* to which I said,

"Look, I didn't do anything wrong to cause this situation. He is solely responsible for what he did wrong. However, I chose to stay with him because I love him. I support him. And I believe God can turn this situation around for good. Just because I am staying with him doesn't mean I had any share in what he did wrong."

That not only felt good for me, it helped her clarify that which was true and good.

One of the strangest things I encountered while we were going through hell was that people would attack my husband through me. They felt free to "share" their verbal assaults against him with me and tell me things they would never say directly to him. It's as if they wanted to let off steam about what he did. They didn't dare say it to him, but they said it to me in hopes that he would feel the sting. I never understood this and I still don't; but I did become adept at dealing with it. First, I would never join them in tearing down my husband. I would not argue with them either. It did no good, but it upset me considerably. Instead, I would just excuse myself and leave.

RESPONDING TO YOUR SPOUSE IN SUCH SITUATIONS

When you stay with your spouse and endure the consequences, stay to love. Annette didn't have to stay with her husband. She had clear-cut scriptural grounds for divorce. But she chose to stay initially; and when she chose to stay, she stayed to love. That is not easy to do, but I've heard it said, *"People need love the most when they deserve it the least."* Eventually, after her husband was released from prison, he decided to leave the marriage and she let him go. He wasn't willing to do the repair work that was going to be necessary. But Annette did her part and God took care of her. I found that to be true in our case as well, although we were able to work through the repairs and ended up with a good marriage.

When I approached writing this book, I asked Patrick what helped him the most of what I had done when he was going through hell. He said that one of the most powerful things I did was to repeatedly affirm my love for him and my commitment to him. If you choose to stay, reaffirm your love every day. Reaffirm your commitment even when the feelings are waning.

Don't stay to punish your spouse and make them endure seeing how much they have made you suffer. There were times when having me stay with him was one of the hardest things Patrick had to bear. I'm not saying that I spared him seeing the consequences he had brought into our lives; I was hurting openly. While you can be open about how you are hurting, don't use that as a weapon to wound your spouse vindictively. Granted, you may need God's help to pull that off.

Regardless of what your spouse has done and how it is hurting your family, you are still commanded to forgive. If you do not forgive your spouse, your heavenly Father will not forgive you. The New Testament is filled with that basic truth. Forgiveness takes commitment. It's a choice that you make, over and over again. You choose not to hold their wrongs against them. You choose to stop throwing it up to your spouse again and again. Not only are you to forgive, but your spouse will need your reassurance of God's promised forgiveness. This is not something you *feel*. It is something you *believe* based on God's word and knowing that Jesus Christ himself paid for your spouse's sins.

There will be a great temptation to fall into seeing yourself as "the good one" and your spouse as "the bad one," especially when some will see you as a saint just for putting up with whatever your spouse is putting you through. Taking on the role as "the good one" may make you feel superior, but it a form of judging that is not true. It will undermine your spouse's sense of self-respect, which will already have taken a hit, and it will destroy any growing intimacy in your relationship. I recommend taking the attitude given in Paul's letter to the Galatians, where he writes, *"If someone is caught in a sin, you who are spiritual should restore him gently. But watch yourself, or you also may be tempted."* You are not above falling into sin, even though your spouse may have been the one who fell in this round. Be careful! However you judge is how you will be judged. In the course of a lifetime both spouses will have their times of failure as well as triumph.

No matter what happens, maintain honesty. Let truthfulness be your aide in your relationship with your spouse. Be honest about what is happening and about how you are feeling, and relay the truth of God's word to each other whenever you can. Don't hide the truth of what is happening as a result of your spouse's actions to spare their feelings. But whenever you have to speak the truth —especially when you know it will be hard to hear — speak the truth in love.

GARDENING TIPS FOR THOSE WHO SHARE LIFE'S GARDEN

When you get married, you become part of a new spiritual entity. It's as if you now tend a jointly held spiritual garden where your life is united with your spouse's life, and therefore, you will share all of life — good and bad. You cannot help but be impacted by the consequences of each other's choices. At some point you have to stop railing against this reality — and the seeming unfairness that comes with it — and start cultivating faithfulness in that garden of life that you share. What follows is a series of "gardening tips" both spiritual and practical.

1. Don't be surprised that your life is intertwined with your spouse's life in real ways.

The statement that two become one flesh can be a beautiful spiritual truth. It can also be a painful physical reality. In that "one flesh" union there are real dangers that one dare not spiritualize. I met one woman whose first inkling that her husband had been unfaithful to her was when her doctor diagnosed a medical condition caused by a sexually transmitted disease. She had to have an immediate hysterectomy; and he had a lot of explaining to do. I say this to underscore the importance that you deal with the reality that you and your spouse are in a unique position to hurt one another because your lives are intertwined. And you would do well to realize this and be prepared to deal with whatever happens — not only with a spiritual response but also with a practical response when necessary.

2. Let your spouse reap the consequences of their wrongdoing as much as possible.

The principle of sowing and reaping is established in nature and in life. Scripture clearly states,

> *Do not be deceived: God cannot be mocked. A man reaps what he sows. The one who sows to please his sinful nature, from that nature will reap destruction; the one who sows to please the Spirit, from the Spirit will reap eternal life. (Galatians 6:7-8)*

It's part of God's plan that nobody should be deceived to believe that they can get away with anything. Therefore, if your spouse receives back the direct consequences of personal wrongdoing, you should not step in to take any of it.

God built natural consequences for wrongdoing into the overall scheme of things to teach us to do right and avoid wrong. The sooner any of us learn that disobeying God brings pain, the sooner we will see God's laws as a protection for us and be more eager to obey. If you keep taking the consequences that should be falling on your spouse, you will subvert the correction God meant to occur through bearing the rightful consequences of wrong choices and wrong actions.

Let your spouse bear the natural consequences of misbehavior as much as possible. Don't shield your spouse or take their consequences on yourself. If your spouse ran up the credit cards, let your spouse be the one to talk to the creditors when they call. There will be plenty of negative consequences that you will not be able to keep from falling on yourself and your children. Those are enough.

You are not doing your spouse a favor if you always come to the rescue. Instead, step back and let your spouse reap what he or she has sown. Proverbs 19:19 points out, *"A hot-tempered man must pay the penalty; if you rescue him, you will have to do it again."* Remember that when you let your spouse bear the consequences for their own conduct, you are cooperating with God's plan of correction and discipline.

3. Don't grow weary of doing what is right.

It is quite common to get discouraged when you are living with the negative consequences of someone else's wrongdoing. I kept thinking of all the years I spent doing what was right — all the good seed I had planted over the years — and I was deeply tempted to give up. When I felt angry about how hard life was, when I felt jealous of the supposed "fun" he had when he was doing wrong, when it seemed so unfair that I was suffering right along with him for something I didn't do wrong, I was severely tempted to sin. In my case, the temptation was to have an affair of my own. I was able to resist that temptation in large part because I do believe that just as surely as we reap for the bad we do, we also will reap for the good. The same passage that says whatever a man sows he will also reap follows with this positive note: *"Let us not become weary in doing good, for at the proper time we will reap a harvest if we do not give up"* (Galatians 6:9). God knows you will be tempted to give up while your marriage is going through hell. He knows it's easy to grow weary in well-doing. But don't give up. That which is sown takes time to grow. We saw God prove His word true over the course of time. The season of reaping the bitter harvest of sin passed; it was followed by reaping a good harvest of God's blessings for many years to follow. The seed for that harvest was planted when we were tempted to give up but didn't.

4. It is okay to sow in tears; you will reap in joy.

The psalmist wrote, *"Those who sow in tears will reap with songs of joy. He who goes out weeping, carrying seed to sow, will return with songs of joy, carrying sheaves with him"* (Psalm 126:5-6). Biblically, the seed that we sow can represent two things: God's word and our deeds. When we refuse to *"grow weary in well-doing,"* we may shed tears while we do what is right according to God's word. But God acknowledges our tears and assures us that our tearful beginnings will give way to joyful results. My good deeds were sown with lots of tears. Years passed when I continued doing the hard things that God said were right, while crying every day. But today, and for the past two decades we are reaping great rewards, and we are rejoicing! So are our children who have grown into well-adjusted adults in a stable home.

When Jeremiah prophesied about God's plans to bring back the exiles, he wrote, "*Their souls shall be as a watered garden, and they shall not sorrow any more at all*" *(Jeremiah 31:12)*. My soul was like a watered garden — watered with an abundance of tears! Those who have known this kind of deep sorrow can also be assured that God won't waste those tears. He will use them to water your soul, even to help grow a new life that is free from overwhelming sorrow. At one point, as we were going through the worst of it, my five-year-old daughter, Casey, asked me, *"Mommy, are you ever going to stop crying?"* I didn't have an answer and that made me cry even more. I was crying so much that no one wanted to be around me. And I didn't know when it would stop. If you are at that point, take hope! You will not cry forever. God has joy planned for you in the future. But also know that it's okay to cry.

5. Cultivate faithfulness.

This idea of cultivating faithfulness where you are currently comes from the admonition given to the exiles of Judah who were told to settle down in Babylon. We also see this in Psalm 37:3-6, which says:

> *Trust in the LORD, and do good.*
> *Dwell in the land and cultivate faithfulness.*
> *Delight yourself in the LORD;*
> *And He will give you the desires of your heart.*
> *Commit your way to the LORD,*
> *Trust also in Him, and He will do it.*
> *And He will bring forth your righteousness as the light,*
> *And your judgment as the noonday.*
> *(Psalm 37:3-6 NASB)*

If you read on in that psalm, you find encouragement to rest in the Lord, to wait patiently for him, and not to fret over evildoers who seem to prosper while you are suffering for doing what is right.

This idea of cultivating faithfulness is extremely practical. Life goes on, and there are responsibilities to be met. Some of those responsibilities will fall to you. You are to handle them faithfully, to the best of your ability, as unto the Lord. You will see the way the negative consequences of your spouse's life are impacting your household and your children. Don't just sit there. Use your practical and spiritual resources to counteract how the negative consequences impact your home and children as much as you can. Itemize your problems. Sort out those you can do nothing about from those you can do something about, and then do what you can. Look at the needs to be filled. If your spouse is unable to fill needs they used to fill, figure out another way to meet those needs if you can. Accept whatever you cannot do or change, but do whatever you can.

6. Keep weeding out the weeds.

There are lots of weeds that crop up in a jointly held garden. You've got to make sure to pull them out regularly. If you let any of these go unattended for any length of time, they will be harder to remove and will do more damage. These weeds include: anger, bitterness, and the deep roots that underlie whatever your spouse did wrong.

The Bible does not say that anger is always a sin. There are plenty of times God is angry; we even see times Jesus got angry. So there are times anger is warranted. However, we are also cautioned that anger can cause us to sin and must be dealt with daily. The Bible warns, *"In your anger do not sin: Do not let the sun go down while you are still angry, and do not give the devil a foothold"* *(Ephesians 4:26-27).*

Anger will sprout up every day. If it doesn't in such a situation, I suggest you see a counselor to help you get in touch with your real feelings. There will be many things that will happen that will make you rightfully angry. You need to get these feelings of anger out. Sometimes that means expressing these to your spouse. One of the most helpful things a counselor told Patrick and I when he first confessed his infidelity was that I needed to vent my rage and Patrick needed to hear it. He needed to hear what was happening within me as a direct result of his betrayal. He needed to acknowledge my right to be angry over what he had done to me and my life. Granted, it helped to keep me away from sharp objects when I was expressing my anger, and it helped even more to have a counselor to help us move past the anger; but I needed to get the anger out.

Patrick was willing to help by listening to my anger and respecting my right to feel it. Every time he did so, that weed of anger was removed. Certainly the weeds of anger did crop up again, even over the same root cause; but in a fairly short time, the anger was removed. However, my experience of dealing with anger with the church was the opposite. They would not listen to me when I wanted to talk about how I felt they had wronged me because I was angry. They wanted to push it down, stifle it, pretend it wasn't there. The result was that those weeds of anger grew and grew. They turned into the next kind of weed, a root of bitterness.

Bitterness is what grows from unresolved anger. Hebrews 12:15 warns, *"See to it that no one comes short of the grace of God; that no root of bitterness springing up causes trouble, and by it many be defiled."* Some would think it would be much harder to forgive my husband than to forgive the church, but that was not the case. I think this was true because while Patrick helped me weed out the anger as it arose, I was not allowed to honestly deal with my anger toward the church. I was convinced to try to stuff it down. When I did, its roots went deeper and spread within my heart. I tried not to sound bitter, but the bitterness that was spreading in my heart, caused trouble for me. There was no way to keep it from "springing up." Eventually, I had to deal with a much more pervasive feeling of bitterness; not only did I feel bitter toward the individuals in church leadership who hurt me, but I became suspicious of all churches and all church leaders. The roots had spread and defiled many. It took many years to root out all the damage that had been done.

Any time you see the ugly seeds of bitterness or you see bitterness springing up in your life, deal with it quickly. Confess it as sin. Ask God to help you go to the people toward whom the original anger was felt and follow the process Jesus lays out in Mt. 18. Do whatever you can on your part to remove that bitterness. Ask your friends to alert you to any bitterness they see in you or hear in your tone of voice. This one takes work to uproot, and it takes time – so be patient with yourself – but be relentless in rooting out bitterness. God will help you.

The last kind of "weeds" are the ones that may be under the surface. Sometimes it's not enough to deal with the wrong behavior. There may be roots beneath the wrong behavior that cause it to sprout up. Even after my husband confessed his sin, we did not understand what could have led him that far into sin. It became clear to us when we heard someone talk about the need to get to the root of sinful (and sometimes addictive) behavior, whether that involved inappropriate use of drugs, alcohol, sex, spending, food, or anything else used to inappropriately seek relief from the pain of life. There are roots that cause sins to grow. If you are to truly help your spouse deal with some kind of sin or wrongdoing that has devastated your lives, you must get to the roots.

These roots may go back through generations. They may go back to something traumatic that happened in your spouse's childhood or family history. Seek out knowledge to help you understand as much as you can about what was growing in your spouse's garden before your lives became joined together. Learn all about their family history and the roots of family problems that may go back for generations. The more you understand, the easier it will be for you to have compassion, to extend grace, and to help your spouse make wise decisions about how to deal with the roots of family sin that may have sprung up in their life.

If you don't understand why or how your spouse could do what they did, don't stop until you find a good counselor who can help you both identify the roots beneath the problem and deal with them. Otherwise, you may be able to stop one bad behavior but may find another kind springing up in its place. And don't just look for issues in your spouse's life; look for your own also.

7. Look for God to restore that which is lost.

Throughout the Bible locusts were seen as a judgment from God. In any land where the people depended on their crops to sustain them, a swarm of locusts that could sweep over the land and destroy all their crops was to be dreaded. Locusts came to symbolize the judgment of God. The book of Joel warns of God's coming judgment for sin, described as a plague of locusts. He calls for repentance, then promises that once they repent, God will restore all that the locusts have eaten. Joel prophesies,

> *I will repay you for the years the locusts have eaten—the great locust and the young locust, the other locusts and the locust swarm—my great army that I sent among you. You will have plenty to eat, until you are full, and you will praise the name of the LORD your God, who has worked wonders for you; never again will my people be shamed. (Joel 2:25-26)*

Here we see that while God will bring judgment for sin, He can also give back to you all that was lost as a result of sin. If devastation has come to your family because of some wrongdoing or sin, God may use the loss and the negative consequences to call for repentance and renewed devotion to Him. The devastation may bring shame, but it is not God's intention to leave you devastated or ashamed. Not only will God forgive sin, He will restore all that is lost as a result of sin. Just as people may see a warning against sin by seeing the negative consequences it brings, God can use your lives to show His redemption, His power to restore all that was lost and to take away your shame.

8. Even when it looks like everything is gone, trust God.

One of the things that impressed me about Annette when I finally met her was her unshakable faith in God. She stayed strong through an enormous amount of pressure of every kind while her husband was in jail. She got a new job. She was a source of strength for her children. She was able to graciously handle inappropriate remarks with good humor. She was able to smile at the future. While she was weak before the crisis hit, going through the crisis strengthened her remarkably.

When her husband got out of jail, she was ready to start working on their relationship. She was toughing it out, and it wasn't easy. He took a menial job. They had a mountain of regrets to sort through together. Their kids were still working through the difficult process of forgiving their dad. It was a mess; but she was determined to make it work. Some of the women in the focus group asked her, "Why?" She said, "*I have a sense that God is not finished with us yet. I believe in what God called us to and what God promised us more than I believe what I can see in our devastated lives.*" Then she quoted a verse from memory, declaring the truth that explained her extraordinary transformation. She said,

> *Though the fig tree does not bud and there are no grapes on the vines, though the olive crop fails and the fields produce no food, though there are no sheep in the pen and no cattle in the stalls, yet I will rejoice in the LORD, I*

> *will be joyful in God my Savior. The Sovereign LORD is my strength; he makes my feet like the feet of a deer, he enables me to go on the heights. (Habakkuk 3:17-19)*

Annette was living by faith, and while her faith had yet to be rewarded with restoration of all she lost she was living proof that God's word in this verse is true. The *Lord* is her strength. How did He give her the strength she needed to survive and rise above circumstances that would crush almost anyone? He changed her. The deer referred to is the mountain hind with remarkable feet designed by God to be able to scale jagged heights and sharp cliffs. These animals can go higher in rugged crags because they can climb over obstacles which would stop other animals. Not only can they climb what looks like insurmountable terrain, they leap from one jagged rock formation to the next and make it look fun. That's what God did for Annette. As her circumstances got more difficult, God changed her. He transformed her make-up so that she could handle whatever came with sure-footed confidence. She could do this because she knew *the Lord* to be her strength – not her circumstances, not her husband. She didn't succumb to depression. Sure, there were times she had to fight off bouts of depression; but she discovered that her sense of humor was a great gift of God. This woman was fun to be with; she was amazing. Later when her husband decided to leave her, she was able to trust God to give her a better future knowing she had done all she could to make the marriage work.

Annette is living proof that God can take a person through something that is unfair, provide for them in that situation, comfort them, and strengthen them to the point that that person becomes an inspiration to all who see their renewed strength. Take heart! If God has let you suffer unjustly, turn to Him with a whole heart. He will take care of you in the situation. He will bring you out. He will restore what you have lost. In the process, God will transform you so that you are stronger and able to go higher than ever before.

CHAPTER SEVEN: DO YOUR SPOUSE GOOD AND NOT EVIL ALL THE DAYS OF YOUR LIFE

LORD, HOW CAN I BE A BLESSING TO MY SPOUSE WHILE HE OR SHE IS SO TROUBLED?

When I looked for an example of a woman who had done her husband good throughout most of her life, the best example I found was my friend Sue. She has demonstrated the kind of miraculous love that God calls us and empowers us to demonstrate. As you read Sue's story, if you find yourself thinking, *I could never do what this woman did*, remember, she didn't do it in her own strength. She would be the first to tell you that the good she did to her husband was far more than she ever thought possible. And it was done by God working in and through her as described in the early chapters of this book. I will let Sue share her story with you in her own words, then I will follow up with specific principles and ideas to help you do your spouse good when it matters most—when they're going through a crisis or troubled times in your marriage. Here is Sue's story in her own words:

RUSTY & SUE LUGLI'S STORY
I was awakened from a sound sleep by being thrown across our motor home, hitting the wall with a thud. Dishes crashed all around me. Did we hit gravel? The sounds were deafening. Immediately a wall of flames separated me from my husband, Rusty, who was driving, and our twenty-seven-year-old daughter, Nikki, who was in the passenger seat. I cried out and screamed for my family. 'Jesus, help us! Help us all!' I was desperate to reach

Rusty and Nikki, but I could not stand. The wall of flames that had flared up between us blocked my way. 'God,' I screamed, 'take us all or none of us. Please!' Intense heat chased me away from them. I spotted a gash in the aluminum wall of the motor home and kicked my way through. I could see my skin melting even though I was not on fire. Blood ran down my forehead and into my eyes, blurring my vision. Constant stabbing pain shot through my back as I raced to escape.

The grass in the gully where I landed was on fire. As I crawled away from the motor home, the hellish flames pursued me. I crawled to a wire fence and tried to climb it but fell back because my feet were burnt and raw. I was only wearing shorts and a T-shirt. A man appeared across the fence. I screamed, 'Please, help me,' as I dug under the fence with my bare hands. The man and his friend picked me up like a sack of potatoes and raced away from the menacing flames. 'Save my family! Save my family!' I screamed. The thunderous crackling sounds struck terror in my heart. Billowing, black smoke blinded me as our motor home incinerated. I collapsed, sobbing, sure that Rusty and Nikki had burned alive. The seats where they sat just moments before were consumed in the inferno. The pain from my back and burns made it impossible to lay still. Finally, a policeman leaned over me to say, 'Your family is up on the road. They're alive.'

We had been headed up north to Washington from our home in Sacramento. The accident occurred August 28, 1993. Rusty needed to pull off the road for some reason. When Rusty pulled off, the motor home careened into a gully covered by tall grass, landing at a tilt. The gas tank ignited the dry grass and in less than three minutes, our motor home was a flaming hulk.

The pain was indescribable as I lay there, but I was able to praise God for sparing us. Then fear gripped me. I couldn't bear the thought of losing Rusty, whom I'd loved since I was fifteen, or my daughter. I'd felt this kind of fear before. When I was eight, I was napping with my mother when she had a heart attack and died. After my mother died, I lost seven other immediate family members by the time I was twenty-six. Now, I was terrified I might be left alone again.

I heard the paramedic say, 'Take the man first,' which told me Rusty was in the most danger. We were all taken by ambulance to Chico Hospital to be stabilized. From there, Rusty was taken away by helicopter to UC Davis Medical Center in Sacramento while Nikki and I stayed in the Chico Hospital emergency room.

My hands and body were swelling to twice their normal size. The emergency room nurse had to cut off my wedding ring to keep it from being embedded in my burned flesh. She had no way of knowing the depth of my sorrow as she cut away that symbol of our devotion. She had no way of knowing all Rusty and I had overcome to keep that ring on my hand. She was just doing her job. As she snipped the band of gold and carefully removed it from my left hand, all I could do was cry.

Our first twenty-five years of marriage were spent chasing our dreams. Rusty spent his time chasing his dreams of success in business and occasionally chasing other women. He was an excellent provider— financially. But that came at a high price. Rusty was a successful businessman—narcissistic, driven, focused, and determined— a man who had his priorities set. Unfortunately for me, I was lucky if I ended up fifth on his list.

I spent my life chasing my dream of being the best wife and mother I could be. I pretty much raised our two kids, Nikki and Todd, and ran our twenty-five acre ranch on my own. I was a Christian and Rusty was not, but I tried to create the kind of family that would make us all happy. I knew about his other women but dared not make an issue of it when I was younger and more insecure. One time Rusty decided to leave me. He didn't think he wanted to be married anymore. He came back out of guilt, and I *let him without any repercussions. I acted as if nothing ever happened. Dumb idea! But that was before I had the self-respect I have now. Knowing he was unfaithful only drove me to redouble my efforts to become more of what he needed me to be.*

My first twenty-five years of marriage were lonely. Without a mate to share my life with, I let the Lord fill my emotional needs. He was the husband I longed for when Rusty wasn't. During those years I held down a full-time job of self-improvement. I learned to depend on Jesus, which helped me shed many of the insecurities I carried from childhood.

Shortly after celebrating our twenty-fifth wedding anniversary in March of 1990, Rusty decided to leave me. Once again, there was another woman. But this time I wasn't going to play the game his way. The Lord had strengthened me since our previous separation.

I knew Rusty had a problem. I had done the best I could to make him happy, always sacrificing my own needs and desires for his. I had been praying for him to come to the Lord for over twenty years. This time I let him go, trusting this was the time for God to work in his life without me getting in the way. It was scary to be on my own. After much prayer, tears, and counseling, I gave Rusty up to the Lord and started to work on my own life for the first time. I devoted myself to being a godly single person. By July, I was sure our marriage was over. Rusty filed for divorce. I felt sad but relieved, confident that God still had a good life ahead for me. It was a difficult time, but it was also exciting—a time of growth and hope for the future. By August, Rusty was having second thoughts and talking about coming back. I didn't want that anymore. The tables had turned; now I was the one uncertain about continuing our marriage.

Rusty went through a time of searching that brought him to his knees. He finally surrendered his life to Jesus. Then he started sharing his heart with me for the first time. By October, I reluctantly agreed to work on our relationship. This time I understood that love included respect for me and accountability. I set the conditions: He couldn't move back until he was sure this was a permanent change and we had to stay in weekly counseling, both individually and together. It took time for me to change gears. At first I worked on our marriage only out of obedience to the Lord.

As I saw Rusty's commitment and change of heart, my heart softened toward him. By February, I was truly excited about our new life together with both of us in Christ. That new life made me hope that we could have a new marriage too. On our twenty-sixth wedding anniversary, we had a full wedding ceremony to renew our vows before family and friends. Rusty put the wedding ring on my finger, looked into my eyes, and said, 'Wear this ring as a token of my love.'

God's faithfulness gave us a new chance at life together. Life was so good after that. Our marriage was the marriage I had always longed for. We were friends and lovers, sharing all of life and enjoying the fruits of our labors together, until. . . Two years and five months after he placed that ring on my finger the emergency room nurse was cutting it off. Those years and days had been the happiest of my life. I couldn't bear the thought of all that hard work and devotion being lost. I wondered, Is this how our marriage will end?

I didn't have much time to ponder the possibilities. Once I had been stabilized, the helicopter that took Rusty to the burn unit returned to take me. Nikki wasn't burned but severely injured with a broken back, broken arm, and dislocated knee. The doctors kept her at Chico. As they were taking me away, I could hear Nikki screaming and crying for me. Everything inside me wanted to go to her, to hold her and comfort her. The burns covering my body and threatening my life made that impossible. But my mother's instincts were as keen as ever. Leaving her was unspeakably terrible.

News of our accident spread fast. When I arrived at UC Davis a few close friends and relatives were already there. They were allowed to see me. They told me that other friends and family were gathering in the waiting room, holding a prayer vigil on our behalf. I had been a devoted Christian for over twenty-five years. God had always seen me through, and I trusted he wouldn't let me down now. Even though it didn't dispel the incredible pain and fear, their prayers made those days bearable and preserved our lives.

When I was settled in the burn unit and finally lucid enough, they told me I had a broken back, with burns over 48 percent of my arms and legs. My prognosis was poor, but Rusty's was worse. The doctors gave him only a 9 percent chance of survival. Rusty was semi-comatose, fighting for his life three rooms from my own. There were days I wanted to die because the pain seemed unbearable. I endured numerous skin grafts and excruciating bandage changes. For burn victims, healing occurs from the inside out, so the exterior layer of skin had to be removed with each bandage change. The pain never went away despite the strong drugs.

As I watched from my hospital bed, the seasons changed from summer to fall. Friends and relatives continued to visit, but they were all going on with their lives while we were stuck in uncertainty and relentless pain. I tried to be thankful that my family was alive, but I was in so much pain and getting more depressed with each passing day.

The banner hanging across the top of my wall in the hospital read, **MIRACLE IN PROGRESS**. Rusty had a matching banner. That was our statement of faith. But each of us needed our own kind of miracle, and some miracles take longer than others.

Cards and posters covered my wall, reminding me of all the people who loved us and were praying for us. Friends took turns rubbing my forehead because that was the only place on my body that could be touched without hurting me. They urged me to eat and kept me company. The tape recorder was my constant companion; I listened to worship songs and the Bible on tape. Listening to these helped me focus on something other than the painful procedures necessary for my healing. The nurses waited for me to pray before every bandage change; they even learned the songs I sang. I guess they don't see miracles in progress very often.

Thank God I believe in miracles, because Rusty certainly needed one. I continued to love him and pray for his recovery, but I simply could not bear to see him. I struggled with such conflicting emotions. I was terrified at the thought of losing him; but I had a sense of peace about Rusty going home to heaven. I didn't want him to die—I couldn't imagine life without him—but if he were going to die, I wanted to remember him as the love of my youth. I did not want to mar those precious memories with images of him burned, swollen, and hooked up to machines.

Rusty's doctors kept insisting that I see him soon, in case he died. I kept refusing. I was determined to wait until I knew he was going to live. As I learned more about the severity of his injuries and realized the pain he would face, I accepted the possibility of his death. The confidence I'd gained during our separation gave me peace that I could go on even if he died. Our doctors said we'd know—one way or the other—by mid-October.

Almost every morning, I recorded a message for him so he could hear my voice and know I was okay, even though he was still unconscious. I chatted about who came to visit, sang him little songs, and told him how much I loved him. The nurses would take it to his room, play the tape, and return it to me—often with tears in their eyes.

My rehabilitation was long and painful. Whenever I was in an upright position I had to wear a brace that encased my body. I didn't have the strength to hold up my head, and it was hard not to faint. Apart from the burns, my broken back required surgery to fuse it together. I later learned that 85 percent of people with similar injuries end up as paraplegics.

My Bible verse for rehab was "I can do all things through Christ who strengthens me" (Philippians 4:13). I said it over and over. 'All things" was precisely what I had to learn to do over again. I had to learn to feed myself, walk, wash I my face, brush my teeth, even go to the bathroom; each was a major accomplishment. I was released from the hospital on October 3, 1993— six weeks after the accident. I chose to leave without seeing Rusty, still fearful that he might die. Rusty didn't lack visitors. All our family members and a few select friends visited him faithfully and continued in prayer.

October 15 proved to be the turning point the doctors predicted. Rusty almost died that day. When he pulled through, the doctors assured me he would live. After that, I agreed to see him. Our twenty-five-year-old son, Todd, had come from his home in Dallas to be near us. He and his wife, Gena, stayed at our house and visited us regularly. Todd took pictures of Rusty so I would know what to expect. He didn't look as I remembered, yet he was still the same inside and still the husband I loved. I had mixed feelings; I wanted to be with him, but I was also scared to death.

Our friend Don wheeled me into Rusty's room in the burn unit, with its familiar smell and sounds. I went to his side and watched him as he slept. He was still semi-comatose. Although he made small gestures on occasion, he was still unable to move or respond. Sixty-eight percent of his body was burned, his left ear was burnt off, his left eye destroyed, his face badly fractured, and four fingers of his left hand were amputated (from where he tried to get the seat belt off). They still didn't know if he had brain damage. The whole time I was there he didn't move.

I felt peace surrounding him but longed to be able to hold him. He was so broken, swollen, and burnt. I longed for him to be able to live the active life he had before. Don anointed him with oil, and we prayed together. We didn't stay long. I was glad I finally found courage to go, but I struggled with the realization that Rusty was disfigured.

I always knew it was my decision to be either sad or glad about whatever situation I was in. There were a lot of sad times during this season of my life, but I continually chose a positive attitude, as much as possible. The doctors said it wouldn't be long before Rusty would be coming home too. I hoped that Rusty would be able, one day, to accept these realizations for himself. In the meantime, I continued my rehabilitation and tried to prepare myself mentally for Rusty's rehab that would follow. The thought of the kind of adjustment his homecoming would present was overwhelming to me.

When you are in the hospital you always think of coming home, but the reality of being back in the place you were before the accident—seeing pictures on the wall of the way it used to be and the way you used to look and knowing it will never be that way again—is hard. Rusty regained consciousness and we brought him home on December 22, 1993, just in time for Christmas.

A young man who was like a son to us, Frank, became Rusty's primary caretaker for the next five months. I was glad to have him home but missed what we had previous to the accident. After our marriage was restored, we had become very close in every way—spiritually, sexually, in our communication, and in shared activities. We did almost everything together and were best friends. I wondered if we'd ever have that kind of closeness again.

During the first year after the accident, we slept in separate bedrooms because we both had to get good sleep and it hurt too much to be touched. I was so lonely with him in one bedroom and me in another. There was another kind of loneliness brought on by our differing rates of healing. Rusty was hurt worse than I, and his head injury caused him to be in the hospital two months longer. His healing was much slower than mine, even with my broken back. It felt like I had gone on alone without him.

My rehab and learning to do everything over again took about all the patience I had. I didn't think I had the patience to help Rusty through the recovery process in which I had preceded him. Once Rusty came home, everything seemed to move in slow motion just when I was ready for life to speed up to normal. I found it difficult to wait for Rusty to learn to live over again, especially because he was unconscious when I went through the process. He woke up without realizing what I had gone through. Somehow, we adjusted.

I took over Rusty's care from Frank five months after he came home. By the grace of God, I found the patience to help Rusty make the transition from being a burn victim to becoming a burn survivor. When one is used to being an invalid—which is easy after a four-month hospital stay— and being legally blind – as Rusty was – it takes time and effort to get out of that mode of I thinking. Sometimes I felt like Rusty's mother, encouraging and motivating him when it took so much of my strength just to encourage myself. It was a sad and weary time in my life, but the moments came when I could see improvement. Rusty's progress and my own made the hard work of recovery worth the effort. Our struggles, emotionally, physically, and spiritually, drove us to prayer. And God faithfully answered our prayers, day by day, as he healed us. By the grace of God we beat the odds, and by his grace we will continue to do so.

As I write this (1996), it has been more than three years since the accident. Physically I can do almost everything I did before, even ride my bicycle. Rusty has undergone several operations to complete his program of plastic surgery. Nikki still struggles both physically and emotionally. But we are all still moving ahead. We are all still miracles in progress.

Rusty and I have learned many valuable lessons through these trials: Our love for each other has deepened. The devastation on the outside of our bodies allowed the beauty and strength on the inside to come out. I try not to look back too much but to look forward and appreciate the gift of life. We don't take anything for granted anymore. Our compassion has grown too, comforting others with the comfort we received. God brought us out of the fires—scarred but strong—to be a testimony of his faithfulness, with our love purified, our faith refined, our priorities in order, and our marriage renewed.

As Sue recovered, she went on to encourage others that they could get through any of life's fiery trials and that they could help their spouses do the same. To meet Sue, you probably wouldn't notice her scars; you would notice her kindness, vibrancy, and restored gift of hospitality. In fact, Sue hosted the focus group for this book in her home. Rusty, who is back running his business, stopped in to greet the women. As I listened to Sue tell her story, I saw how she did him good all the days of her life since she met him. She exemplified the words in the book of Proverbs that describe an excellent wife:

> *A wife of noble character who can find? She is worth far more than rubies. Her husband has full confidence in her and lacks nothing of value. She brings him good, not harm, all the days of her life.* (Proverbs 31:10-12)

Another Bible translation phrases that last line, "*She does him good and not evil all the days of her life*" (NASB). That's what God calls wives to do for their husbands and I would think how He would have husbands treat their wives. And God helps us do so.

God created you to help your spouse, and the times when your marriage is "going through hell" are the times they will need your help the most. God created woman unique from all creation to be able to help the man to whom she devotes herself in marriage. That means we have what it takes to be of help to our husbands in time of crisis as no one else can. It is no secret that wives have tremendous influence over their husbands. Look at Eve, Sarah, and Jezebel in the Bible. Women always have and always will influence their husbands. If you are a wife, determine to use your influence for your husband's good.

The admonition for how husbands should treat their wives shows a similar call to love your spouse beyond a normal capacity to do so. The Bible says, "Husbands, love your wives, just as Christ loved the church and gave himself up for her" (Ephesians 5:25) and *"In this same way, husbands ought to love their wives as their own bodies. He who loves his wife loves himself."* So, husbands and wives need to seek God's supernatural love to be able to do the other good and not evil every day of your lives.

How can we make sure our influence and what we do for our spouse is good? If you are going to do your spouse good and not evil all the days of your life, you can only do so by living according to God's word. You need to know what it says and how to apply it to your own life then access God's wisdom and the power of the Holy Spirit to give you the power to do the good that you want to do.

ALL THE DAYS OF OUR LIVES
Since we are called to do our spouse good all the days of our lives, it's obvious that doing so can't be based on reciprocal love. It can't be, *I'll do him good if he does me good* or the reverse of the same sentiment, *He'd better not tick me off or he'll be sorry!* (And a wife

knows better than anyone how to make her husband sorry; and vice versa.) If that were the case the best we could muster would be, "She does him good MOST of the days of her life."

So, how do we do our spouse good ALL the days of our lives? The trick is to do all that we do for *our spouse "as unto the Lord."* If you see doing good to your spouse as a demonstration of your love for Jesus (which is how we are told to demonstrate that love — see 1 John 3:16-18; 4:11-12, 19-21), you can do your spouse good every day.

Consider this example: Mother Teresa of Calcutta was able to love people who were repulsive to others; she loved people others saw as unlovable. She explained how she was able to abound in such love — day in and day out — regardless of how unlovely the person on whom she lavished her love. When she became a nun she became a bride, married to Jesus Christ. However, she demonstrated her love for Jesus by loving every person she met as if that person were Jesus. When she loved them she was living out her love for Him.

This understanding came from a story Jesus told about how God will judge our lives. In Jesus' story, the king rewarded those who cared for the unlovely, saying, *"I tell you the truth, whatever you did for one of the least of these brothers of mine, you did for me"* (Matthew 25:40). But to those who failed to care for "the least of these," the king said, *"I tell you the truth, whatever you did not do for one of the least of these, you did not do for me"* (Matthew 25:45).

Therefore, all the service Mother Teresa did to "the least of these" she did "as unto the Lord." She demonstrated her love for Jesus in caring for the practical, spiritual, and emotional needs of those who were within her reach. This is how a Christian husband or wife can do their spouse good and not evil all the days of their life. There are some days we may think our spouse truly is one of "the least of these." On those days — and every other day — our devotion to love our spouse and do them good is done "as to the Lord." That makes our choice to do our spouse good independent of how lovable he or she is on any particular day. This also means that a person married to a non-Christian or someone who isn't heartily following the Lord can still succeed at being a godly spouse even if their spouse is not godly. As you set about determining specific ways in which you can help your spouse through this difficult time, I trust that you will keep in mind the spiritual disposition established in the early chapters. These prepare you to do whatever you will be called upon to do by the power of the Holy Spirit. Here's a recap:

1) Set your will to agree with the will of the Father.

2) Remain completely dependent on Jesus Christ and let Him remain in you.

3) Let God's word remain in you (study, memorize, "keep it" until God fulfills it in your life).

4) Look to the Holy Spirit to guide you as to how to do your spouse good in your situation.

5) Know that it is God who works in you to will and to act according to His good purpose so you are free to do your spouse good however you choose.

6) Do it! Take action!

Don't just tell your spouse about your faith; show it! Do your spouse good. James wrote, *"Faith by itself, if it is not accompanied by action, is dead. But someone will say, 'You have faith; I have deeds.' Show me your faith without deeds, and I will show you my faith by what I do" (James 2:17-18).* Up to this point we have focused a lot on internal faith. If that faith is operative, it will come out by doing your spouse good. Here's how:

DOING YOUR SPOUSE GOOD
Doing Good as Your Spouse Goes through a Crisis

Sue didn't have guidelines to follow when she was helping her husband through his crisis. However, as I identified what worked for me when I was trying to help my husband and compared notes with Sue, we discovered that the same principles applied. These principles applied whether Sue was helping Rusty deal with recovery from a devastating accident, or I was helping Patrick get through the crisis caused by his besetting sin and the devastation that it brought to our lives, or Jan Dravecky was helping Dave get through cancer and losing his career. I don't know what your spouse is going through, but I hope these principles on how to deal with various phases of a crisis will help you help your spouse while your marriage is going through hell. These principles should also continue to help into the next season or phase of the crisis. There will come a day where you will look back in wonder at how God gave you the strength and super-natural love to keep going through all the phases of the crisis. Here's an overview of the process I and some of the contributors to this book went through in phases. Maybe it will help you anticipate and bear the various phases you will need to go through in your marriage.

PHASE ONE: AT THE ONSET OF THE CRISIS

When Sue saw her husband trapped in that motor home engulfed in flames, she tried to reach him but couldn't. She quickly took a turn to get out of the flames and call for help. You need to do the same. When you see your spouse or marriage in trouble, your first inclination may be to go to your spouse, to try to help them yourself. But you need to practice going to God first. Think of it like calling 911. In physical emergencies, you realize that you sometimes can't adequately help directly. Think of other kinds of crises in the same way. Step back and call on God for wisdom. Consider who could provide the resources your spouse needs. If someone knows how to deal with the kind of problem your spouse is facing, encourage your spouse to get help. If they are unwilling to get professional help, don't force it, but gather information that can help when your spouse is ready to receive it.

The onset of the crisis is often the most dangerous time. If your spouse is unable to make decisions, educate yourself to understand the condition or situation, and take decisive action in their best interests. When Patrick was devastated by the aftermath of confessing to the church, I realized he was suicidal. I didn't ask him, *"Do you think you should go to the hospital?"* I called the hospital. I made financial and travel arrangements to get him the help he needed immediately. If I had not acted decisively at that moment, I truly don't know if he would be here today. Later, when he was more stable, I no longer made decisions for him. When he could make decisions for himself, I respected that.

If you act quickly to get help at the onset of a crisis, you may minimize the severity of the problems. Say your spouse loses a job after many years. If he settles into a routine of avoiding re-entry to the job market, that can compound any sense of inadequacy. It can contribute to feelings of worthlessness that will be counter-productive. However, if your spouse came home despondent because he got a pink slip and you encouraged him to do something immediately to help prepare to re-enter the job market, it would have a more positive impact the first week of unemployment than after six months off the job.

Seek Professional Help When Necessary

Managing a crisis in the initial phase can be overwhelming. If professional help exists to deal with the kinds of issues impacting your family, seek out someone who understands the issues better than you do. Encourage your spouse to seek help if that's appropriate or if you have tried to overcome your difficulties on your own but have reached an impasse. If you think your spouse needs help but isn't willing to seek it, get help for yourself to learn how to deal with your spouse.

Phase Two: Helping Your Spouse through the Ongoing Crisis

There's a surge of adrenaline that gets you through the onset of a crisis. That's when you may still be in shock or denial so you aren't fully aware of all the ramifications of what has happened. You may be fighting so hard to survive that you are focused and energized. The toughest phase of helping your spouse comes after the onset of the crisis has passed and before you can see your way clear to resume a normal life. These are the months Sue described as the most difficult, the slow-motion time when it takes all your strength just to make it another day but you feel like you haven't made any progress. These are the days you have to heed the admonition not to *"grow weary in doing good,"* trusting that in due season you will reap good rewards if you don't give up.

When a major crisis hits, you, your spouse, and your family won't get over it quickly. When someone drops a rock in a pond, the ripples don't stop until they extend all the way out to the edge. The rock is the crisis, and the pond is the whole of your spouse's life, your life, your marriage, and your family life. There will be ripples that go on for a long time. And God will be with you all the way, until the crisis and its myriad effects are gone. But you must prepare yourself to help your spouse all the way through.

Phase Three: Helping Your Spouse during the Recovery Stage

When whatever caused the initial crisis is over, there will be people who are wounded, relationships that are broken, and much that needs recovery or redemption. The two of you will need help of some kind. Assess your situation together, and come up with a plan to work toward that end. Just as Sue consulted doctors to get a plan for Rusty's recovery, a plan will help you help your spouse and family recover from whatever happened. Patrick and I did the same thing. No one can walk the road of recovery for you, but there are others who have been down that road. It helps to know what the process looks like, what pitfalls you might encounter, and that there are those who have come through triumphant. Having a plan and the hope of others who've successfully gone before you will help you persevere for the long haul in the aftermath of a crisis. You are already doing this in part by reading this book.

Encourage Your Spouse to Seek Outside Support

Encourage your spouse to find a support group. It may be a support group designed to deal with particular issues or a group at your local church. Your spouse may feel more comfortable just going out with a few friends on a regular basis to work through the issues. Patrick didn't feel comfortable going to a public support group in our area. Instead, he invited men he trusted to become a support group for him. They didn't have any formal education about his problems, but they agreed to follow a good Christian book that dealt with those issues. They read the book and discussed it with him week by week, and then they prayed together. What started as a group to support Patrick ended up helping everyone who participated. The other men realized that many had similar struggles — perhaps in different areas — and God helped them as they helped each other.

PHASE FOUR: CELEBRATE THE MILESTONES AS YOU MAKE PROGRESS

Whenever you see signs of progress, celebrate. Take time and effort to recognize accomplishments and anniversaries of progress. Remind each other that there is a good future before you, however different it may be from the past. You can do your spouse good in this regard by commemorating any positive milestones you see. In this way you can give your spouse a new and brighter perspective.

When your spouse or marriage is going through a prolonged difficulty, you and your spouse may lose perspective. Goals may be all shot to pieces. Plans for the future may be irrevocably altered. Your spouse may not be able to look to the future with hope. Proverbs 31:25 says this of the excellent wife: *"Strength and dignity are her clothing, and she smiles at the future."* This ability to smile at the future is a gift you can give your spouse. Ask God to show you how to help your spouse look toward the future with hope.

Here's how I was able to do this: Patrick confessed his infidelity to me shortly after our ninth wedding anniversary. The year that followed was hellish, and we were living in emotional darkness. I prayed that God would give me an idea of how we could truly celebrate our upcoming tenth wedding anniversary. The idea I got was a tangible way of smiling at the future. I went through all of our photographs, from the time we were first dating, our wedding, the birth of each of our children, parties with friends, birthday parties, our trip to Israel, Christmas mornings and the like. Then I assembled key pictures in chronological order representing the course of our lives up to the point of the crisis, year by year. After the pictures from the most recent time, I left many blank pages, representing the uncertainty in which we were living. But on the last page of the photo album I put a photograph of a beautiful sunset. This was my photo history of our happy life together before the crisis, my assurance that we would have happy times ahead, and my vote of confidence that we would reach a happy ending.

I took this photo history with me as we went out to dinner to celebrate our tenth wedding anniversary. This was my surprise gift for him. When we arrived at the restaurant, I put a recording of the Kenny Rogers song **Through the Years** into the car stereo. As the lyrics spoke of love lasting through the years, I turned the pages that depicted our love through the years for Patrick to see. As it ended with, *"I'll stay with you, through the years,"* I turned the blank pages until I came to the sunset. That was my way of smiling at the future. And it did my husband's heart good!

Yes, life can get so hard that you forget there will ever be happy days again. But remember, even if you have to remember as an act of faith! For your spouse's sake and your children's sake and your own sake, remember that God will bring you through. Then help your spouse remember. And one day, you too will reach the point where you realize that you are talking about whatever is troubling you now, and you are using the past tense. That's when you can celebrate having made it through the crisis.

Recently, I was cleaning out the family sideboard with my 26-year-old daughter. She pulled out a dusty photo album and flipped through it, noticing the many blank pages toward the end. When she asked about it, I was able to share the story of our 10th anniversary. Together, she and I marveled at the wonderful years that came after that – 22 years now – in amazement at the blessed years in our marriage and family that fulfilled the hope I depicted in those blank pages.

GENERAL GUIDANCE FOR HOW TO DO YOUR SPOUSE GOOD

LET YOUR SPOUSE DO THAT WHICH IS HIS OR HERS TO DO

Doing your spouse good does not always mean doing things for them — especially things that are their responsibility to do. In fact, Sue says the best thing she did for Rusty — and the most difficult — was to stand back and insist that he do for himself that which was his to do. There is often confusion over how much husband and wife should cover for each other. We are taught that we are to *"carry each other's burdens"* and so fulfill the law of Christ (Galatians 6:2). That statement is often misunderstood to mean that we should come to the rescue whenever anyone is weighted down with troubles. Some spouses interpret that to mean that whenever their spouse is burdened, it's their responsibility to lift that burden off of them. That is not what the statement means. The verse that says we should bear each other's burdens is made in the context of the next verse that says, "...each one should carry his own load" (Galatians 6:5).

The *burden* that we should help carry refers to an overwhelming weight that one person could never lift. In Rusty's case that was when he was truly disabled and had to be cared for by others. **His own load** that each one is to carry describes a knapsack or backpack that contains personal belongings. This represents individual responsibilities. There are times when your spouse's life is so overwhelming that they will need your support to bear up under it. Certainly, in those instances, you are to join with the body of Christ to uplift your spouse and help relieve the overwhelming pressures keeping them down. But that never negates each person's responsibility to carry **his own load**. Your spouse's own load includes that which they can do (with God's help) and should do for themselves: their job, role in the family, personal commitments they agreed to fulfill, responsibility for their own choices and the consequences of those choices. If your spouse fails to carry **"his own load"**, you are not obligated to carry it. In fact, to do so is to do your spouse a disservice.

Those who misunderstand this portion of Scripture will end up weighted down with loads that God never intended them to carry. They will not only exhaust themselves, they will also contribute to negligence on the part of others. The husband who makes excuses to cover for his alcoholic wife and bears the consequences for her drinking is carrying her load. God never intended a spouse to do that. In time, the resentment and the exhaustion will take their toll. It is better to do as God says: Let each person carry his own responsibilities. The wife who takes on the job of carrying all the responsibility in the family — acting as both father and mother when the father is able but abdicates his role, covering for her husband's irresponsible behavior with regard to his job, stepping in to fulfill commitments he made but does not keep, or otherwise doing for him what he should rightfully do for himself—is carrying his load.

Deciding on what those specific responsibilities are, especially within the family, takes negotiation between husband and wife as to who will do what. I don't have a one-size-fits-all plan for what the roles of husband and wife are in your marriage and specific situation. There was a season of our marriage and family life when my husband was a full-time, stay-at-home dad (along with approximately two million other American fathers). During those years he took on responsibility for managing the business details of my book sales and speaking, while also carrying primary responsibility for managing our entire household. Now that he is in full-time ministry, I have taken up some of what he used to do, like paying the bills. The two of you can work out the particulars of who is responsible for what, but it is important that you both define what is in each one's backpack of personal responsibilities. Then, you carry yours and let your spouse carry theirs. God may have allowed this crisis to get you or your spouse to accept your rightful responsibilities. God may use this challenge to strengthen you and your spouse. If you rob your spouse of carrying their own load, you may be doing far more harm than good in the long run.

Demonstrate Love and Respect

There are a few essentials called for in Christian marriage. One is that the husband is called to love his wife, and the wife must respect her husband. Paul wrote the Ephesians, *"A husband also must love his wife. He must love her just as he loves himself. And a wife must respect her husband. "* (Ephesians 5:33). Whereas the emphasis for the husband is that he must love his wife, the emphasis for the wife is that she must show respect for her husband. Notice, these are not presented as a suggestion or helpful hint but the word MUST is used in both directives to husbands and wives. A wife can choose to demonstrate respect, even when her husband's respectability may be at a low ebb. A husband can choose to demonstrate love to his wife even when she is not being particularly loveable. There are plenty of places where the Bible talks about showing respect where respect is due and addresses being a person worthy of respect. These apply to both men and women. However, Scripture instructs us that those who are younger are to demonstrate respect to the elderly; children are to demonstrate respect to parents, wives to husbands, and subjects to governing officials. Whatever the nuances, wives are told to concentrate their efforts on showing respect to their husbands and husbands are to concentrate on demonstrating love and not being harsh toward their wives. This is another example of something you do as an act of faith and obedience to God. The kind of marital relationship God designed is meant to function with mutual love, mutual deference to each other, and mutual respect. However, there is a greater emphasis placed on husbands demonstrating love and wives demonstrating respect. Perhaps God knows what each of us needs the most, or what each of us is most likely to neglect if God didn't say we must demonstrate it.

Uphold Respect for Your Spouse

If others are disrespectful toward your spouse, do not listen or join in. When it's appropriate, you may defend your spouse; if others speak ill of them. Differentiate between what your spouse has done and the person you have vowed to love throughout life. They may have done wrong, but their life is more than their errors or frailty.

Take Care of Your Spouse's Sexual Needs

Do not neglect reaching out to your husband/wife sexually. In God's design, no one else is allowed to take care of their sexual needs. Therefore, this is not an optional part of your marriage. First Corinthians 7:3-5 plainly states:

> *The husband should fulfill his marital duty to his wife, and likewise the wife to her husband. The wife's body does not belong to her alone but also to her husband. In the same way, the husband's body does not belong to him alone but also to his wife. Do not deprive each other except by mutual consent and for a time, so that you may devote yourselves to prayer. Then come back together again so that Satan will not tempt you because of your lack of self-control.*

There is no rationalizing around that admonition. If you are not ministering love to your husband or wife sexually, or neglecting each other, something is wrong. Granted, you may have issues that must be dealt with before you feel comfortable being sexually intimate — for instance, if there is the danger of contracting a sexually transmitted disease or if you have been sexually abused in some way or there is a medical condition as when Sue and Rusty were burned so badly they could not bear to be touched. Also, sexual dysfunction is often a side-effect of depression. If there is a lack of interest in sex, educate yourself to understand what this lack of interest means. It could be related to many things: depression, marital issues that need to be resolved, physical problems, exhaustion, or distraction because of outside pressures. Address this issue sensitively with your spouse and perhaps with a therapist who understands the link between crisis, depression, and sexual relations. Whatever the cause, if a real problem of this nature exists, take action. Get professional help to resolve the problem. Your sexual union is vitally important.

Because our crisis involved sexual infidelity it took quite a while to rebuild the bridges of trust to make that part of our relationship a source of joy and unmixed pleasure again. However, we chose to maintain an intimate relationship even though that was not without heart-wrenching emotions at first. If you, too, have had to overcome sexual infidelity, I hope it helps to know that it is completely normal to have difficulty restoring those broken bonds of love and trust. Just know that it can be done. It takes time and devoted effort, but God can heal the brokenness to where you can love each other freely and satisfy each other sexually again.

Use your privilege of sexual intimacy to comfort your spouse as no one else can. In the Old Testament, when Isaac was grief stricken because of the death of his mother, Sarah, he was comforted by marrying Rebekah. The Bible specifically notes that he *"brought her into the tent."* In that culture, the tent was used as the honeymoon suite. It says, *"So she became his wife, and he loved her; and Isaac was comforted after his mother's death"* (Genesis 24:67). Do not neglect comforting your spouse sexually when he or she needs it.

BE THERE TO LIFT YOUR SPOUSE UP WHEN THEY FALL
King Solomon wrote,

> *Two are better than one, because they have a good return for their work: If one falls down, his friend can help him up. But pity the man who falls and has no one to help him up! Also, if two lie down together, they will keep warm. But how can one keep warm alone? (Ecclesiastes 4:9-11).*

You know when your spouse is down. Whenever you see them fall — whatever that means in your situation — ask the Lord to show you how you can lift your spouse up. Then do it.

REAFFIRM YOUR LOVE FOR YOUR SPOUSE OFTEN
In preparation for writing this chapter, I asked Patrick how I helped him the most when our marriage was going through hell. He said, *"You reaffirmed your love for me. You always seemed to know when I needed to know, and you made it clear that you were committed to me. You let me know that you still loved me and weren't going to leave me. And I always needed to hear it."*

Times of crisis can shake a spouse's sense of security. If they think you only love them for what they do for you or provide for you, they may become insecure if the crisis threatens their ability to do what they think causes you to love them. Make sure your spouse knows you are firmly committed to love them — no matter what happens in their life (excluding ongoing sexual infidelity). Don't assume your spouse knows it. You can't reaffirm your love too often when you are in crisis mode.

OFFER GENUINE PRAISE, APPRECIATION, AND THANKS
As life drags on through a season of crisis or recovery, a little praise can go a long way. Be genuine. Let your spouse know what they mean to you. Tell your spouse specific things you respect and appreciate about them. Your praise, appreciation and sincere thanks will encourage your spouse, even if they have a hard time believing you.

In our family we joke about Pat's signature on greeting cards; it's usually just "Pat" while I tend to be wordier. The kids have taken to counting the number of characters he writes or suggesting that he at least add oxoxox (for hugs and kisses). Pat and I just celebrated our 32nd wedding anniversary. I was expecting the minimalist signature. Instead, he bought a blank card and wrote a note saying that in response to our joking he decided to think of all the words he could to describe what he loves about me. The bottom of the card was filled with positive descriptive words. That meant SO MUCH to me. I turned the card inside-out and put it on the mantle for all to see. I passed it around to my friends, and the kids all read it. See, a little thoughtful and specific praise goes a long way.

ENCOURAGE YOUR SPOUSE
Even the greatest men and women in the Bible needed to be encouraged: Moses. Joshua, David, Mary the mother of Jesus, Elijah, Mary of Bethany, Jeremiah, Sarah and many others. Your

spouse needs it too. Encourage your spouse by reminding him or her of past successes, by pointing out how much you love them, by letting them know you have faith in them and believe the best of them.

Remind Your Spouse of the Truth of God's Word

If your spouse is open to it, offer encouragement with the word of God as it applies to their situation. Remind them often that God forgives completely and redeems, that God loves him or her and will cause all things to work together for good to those who love Him. Remind your spouse that God has plans for your shared life — for good and not evil — to give you both a future and a hope.

Don't Nag—Especially Not with God's Word

Use God's word as an encouragement to your spouse, never a weapon against them. If your spouse is not open to God's word, don't badger with it or use it to nag. Your first impulse may be to *"reprove, rebuke, and exhort."* Resist it! While Scripture gives this instruction, it is given to a pastor with regard to his congregation, not to a husband or wife with regard to their spouse. Whether or not your spouse is a Christian, they probably don't want a sermon from you. I searched the Scripture to see if there was any such instruction to wives to *"reprove, rebuke, and exhort"* their husbands or husbands to wives. I didn't find any. What I did find is this bit of wisdom in Proverbs 21:19, *"Better to live in a desert than with a quarrelsome and ill-tempered wife."* And *"Husbands, love your wives and do not be harsh with them"* (Colossians 3:19).

You can help your spouse, but not by nagging, complaining, speaking ill of him or her, or telling them how to live their life. These are the kinds of direct approaches that tend to fail. There are accounts of women who nagged their husbands into action (like Sarai nagging Abram into conceiving Ishmael or Eve getting Adam to taste the fruit), but their nagging certainly didn't do their spouses or anyone any good.

Pray for Your Spouse

The best way you can help your spouse may seem like a circuitous route. It is to go directly to the Lord Himself to pray for your spouse. If you feel compelled to nag, nag at God in prayer. Jesus described a widow who had been treated unjustly. She wouldn't stop pestering the judge until he gave her what she wanted. Jesus said that it's good to pray like that, to persist in prayer until God answers. Nagging at God is fine; nagging at your husband or wife is not. If you turned every temptation to nag your spouse into a prayer for them, you would surely see better results. Seek the Lord to help your spouse; that will have a better effect than you trying to change him or her by nagging. The best way to reach your spouse's heart is by demonstrating your love and doing good.

Educate Yourself with Regard to Your Spouse's Problems

Learn all you can about your spouse's condition, kind of problem, or situation. Do this without overstepping healthy relational boundaries; if your spouse is having problems at work, don't call the boss to find out what's going on. But it might be helpful to educate yourself about the effects of stress on the job. Don't butt in to solve your spouse's problems, but try to learn how these problems will affect your spouse. This prepares you to help in practical ways without overstepping healthy relational boundaries.

For instance, if your spouse is overworked, irritable, and wakes up in the middle of the night thinking about work, it will probably do no good to say, *"Honey, you shouldn't work so hard. You need your sleep."* But if you read a book like **Adrenaline and Stress** by Dr. Archibald Hart, you would better understand the dynamics of what your spouse is going through. You would then be in a better position to help in practical ways or to help them understand the dynamics of how the job is taking its toll. If your wife is becoming unbearably irritable, moody, and it's at an age that indicates it might be menopause, you would be ahead of the game to educate yourself on the symptoms and remedies to manage the symptoms of this physical condition that can impact your marriage and home life.

EXTEND GRACE TO YOUR SPOUSE WHEN THEY ARE SUFFERING

Ask God to give you His view of your spouse when he or she is suffering. Dave and Jan Dravecky deal with families every day where someone is suffering and others are trying to help them through it. When I asked Jan for her advice for you, she said, *"Don't judge him for how he bears his suffering. God uses suffering to purify us; that means it's going to bring up the dross that is under the surface in anyone's character."*

Jan continued, *"When Dave was suffering I felt compassion because I knew the heart of the man as he wanted to be. But when the pain gets to be unbearable, a guy can't be the man he wants to be. Even the most spiritual man may be able to act spiritual short term when he is hurting, but long term pain brings out the worst in any man. God knows that; sometimes that is the purpose of allowing suffering into a man's life, to purify him of all the dross. Expect it; suffering causes the "uglies" to come out. When you see the ugly side of him, don't be surprised! Trials are meant to bring the impurities to the surface so that God can remove them. They may bring up issues that were never dealt with from his childhood. Seeing the darkness of his soul rising to the surface may be painful for him, but that is God's business. It's God's place to deal with him. It's your place to do him good."* When your spouse is suffering, God can give him or her the grace to bear it, but you can do your spouse good by extending grace and kindness.

COMFORT YOUR SPOUSE EMOTIONALLY

Scripture says that we are to *"weep with those who weep; rejoice with those who rejoice" (Romans 12:15 NASB)*. Share your spouse's joys and sorrows. Do not reprimand him for his sorrows. Allow your spouse to express their deepest feelings, doubts, and struggles without reproach.

Sometimes your spouse will need to vent their feelings. If they know that they can speak honestly to you without getting a major reaction, they will find in you a source of comfort. This was one lesson I learned from our experience. I used to try to pry Pat's feelings out of him (which tends to be a wife's inclination more than a husband's). I resented that I readily shared my feelings with him but he didn't share his with me. As we progressed through counseling, he finally explained why.

He said,

> *"Whenever I share what's really going on inside of me, you react. You don't just listen; you either get upset, defensive, or fearful or try to correct how I'm feeling. If I express doubts, you immediately try to banish them. When I'm feeling uncomfortable feelings, I don't need an adjustment from you. I just need to talk things out. If you want me to share deeply with you, you're going to have to let me know that I'm not going to get a major reaction, a sermon, or a lecture."*

After this explanation and a few times when he was able to point out this kind of reaction whenever he was trying to share his heart, I understood. It took practice, but I learned to listen and care—and not demonstrate a major reaction. This has caused him to feel safe to open up. As a direct result, our communication has deepened and he shares more freely. I do fall back into this pattern and have to be reminded but I allow myself to be corrected and it helps.

If you simply cannot bear to hear your spouse voice unsettled feelings, doubts, or fears, don't force yourself. Just make sure they have an outlet for honest reflection. As you grow more secure in the assurance that God will take care of you and your spouse, you won't be as shaken by the fact that they struggle with human emotions.

Don't Worry!

Most married people are inclined to worry when their marriage or spouses are in deep trouble. And although men don't tend to show their worry as openly as women, when a wife is in deep waters her husband bears that burden too. You can worry, but that won't do you or your spouse any good. Besides, it is direct disobedience to the Word of God and Jesus' commands. Jesus recognized our tendency to worry and counteracted it. He taught,

> *So do not worry, saying, 'What shall we eat?' or 'What shall we drink?' or 'What shall we wear?' For the pagans run after all these things, and your heavenly Father knows that you need them. But seek first his kingdom and his righteousness, and all these things will be given to you as well. Therefore, do not worry about tomorrow, for tomorrow will worry about itself. Each day has enough trouble of its own. (Matthew 6:31-34)*

You don't have to let worry consume your life. If your spouse is already burdened by their problems, you can help him or her tremendously by refraining from worry. The Bible treats worry as a choice, not something you cannot help. If you constantly worry, even if it is related to your personality type, it is also part of your daily practice that God can help you change.

Here's how the Bible says to do this,

> *Do not be anxious about anything, but in everything, by prayer and petition, with thanksgiving, present your*

> requests to God. And the peace of God, which transcends all understanding, will guard your hearts and your minds in Christ Jesus (Philippians 4:6-7).

God's promise of peace is made to those who choose to turn every worry into a requisition then give that requisition to God. Your worries are already itemized in your mind. Just turn each worry into a request, speak it or write it out to God; then thank Him that He will take care of it. Repeat this process every time the worry comes to mind.

I do this with amazing results, not only seeing God's provision but also receiving the peace that passes all understanding which is promised. This worked when we needed food, when we needed school clothes for our little girl to start kindergarten, and generally for all our needs. If I had gone about worrying over these and giving voice to my worries, I would have brought more shame on my husband because these financial difficulties came as the result of his actions. Instead, I chose to believe God's promises of provision. He always sent what we needed when we needed it. We never missed a meal. Unsolicited packages arrived days before school started. They held the most beautiful school clothes! I never went around whining about how my husband couldn't provide for his family; I never would have dishonored him is such a way. But you better believe I told God every single thing we needed, everything I would have worried about if I hadn't been speaking it out in prayer. This simple practice can do your spouse good directly when prayers are answered and indirectly when your heart and mind are guarded by the peace of God.

PRAY SPECIFICALLY, CONSISTENTLY, AND SECRETLY FOR YOUR SPOUSE'S NEEDS

Your spouse needs you to believe God enough to pray for them.

> Jesus said, "When you pray, go into your room, close the door and pray to your Father, who is unseen. Then your

Father, who sees what is done in secret, will reward you" (Matthew 6:6).

You have the inside scoop about your spouse's struggles. Never use that information to dishonor him or her before others; but don't waste it either. Use the inside scoop you know about your spouse to shape specific prayers for their situation. I use blank journals to write my prayers to keep me focused. I recently reviewed these prayers from the times when Pat was going through his darkest times. I was amazed as I saw the specific requests I made secretly that have been answered for all to see. Pray for your spouse; pray persistently and pray in secret.

CONCLUSION

If you practice doing these things, you will do your spouse good all the days of your life. As you start out, this may be foreign to you. Don't give up. Each time you see yourself responding otherwise than God would have you, don't berate yourself. Simply confess where you fall short and trust that God will forgive you and *"cleanse you from all unrighteousness,"* as is promised in 1 John 1:9 (NASB). As you continue to practice doing your spouse good and not evil, God will give you the grace and power to do so all the days of your life — one day at a time.

CHAPTER EIGHT: COMBATING HELL HEAD-ON

HOW CAN I BRING THE POWER OF HEAVEN AGAINST THE FORCES OF HELL ON BEHALF OF MY SPOUSE?

Karen was fed up! She was ready to take the kids, move out, and leave her husband to his misery. It took a lot to bring her to this point. She and her husband, Jim, used to be the life of the party — the Christian party, that is. They were happy together. Their home was always the center of activity, always activity that advanced the kingdom of God and honored Jesus Christ. They had home Bible studies, fellowship groups, and church get-togethers; sounds of worship could regularly be heard coming from inside their beautiful home located in an affluent neighborhood.

God had blessed them in every way. They appeared financially sound. Their kids were healthy and happy, loved God, and loved their parents. Jim had a great job that provided a solid base income. He operated a side business in real estate development that allowed them to live in comfort. Jim was known as a Christian at home, at church, and at his place of business. His strong work ethic and moral integrity brought him favor with his boss, who promised him a promotion if he would supplement his education. So Jim went back to college for an advanced degree, expecting the promised promotion.

By the time he finished his schooling, his boss fell ill and had to be replaced. The new management team did not take the same view of business or of Jim. They disregarded all previous promises of advancement and began to put into effect many unfair business practices. They abused employees, were blatantly disrespectful, and showed total disregard for ethics. Anyone who opposed them was fired or demoted. Many cowered before this new management team. Some brought lawsuits. Jim stayed and tried to make a stand for what was right.

At first this seemed like the thing to do, but the effect was that Jim became obsessed with the need to right the wrongs he saw being done, not only to him, but also to his co-workers, who were not in any financial position to jeopardize their jobs. He became the point man for righteousness in the face of clear wrongdoing on the part of those who could get away with it because they held the power.

For more than two years, Jim fought what he saw as evil practices. But this took a terrible toll on his disposition. He grew depressed, more and more obsessed, and spiritually beaten down. He could not understand why God would not overthrow such injustice. The battles he was fighting at work became the whole focus of his life. Every conversation he had at home related to his troubles at work. When Karen suggested that he quit and find a new job, he refused. He wouldn't quit without having a new position, and yet he was in no shape to interview for and win a new position. Every prayer Karen and the children were asked to pray was to resolve the problems at work. It got to the point that, not only was Jim miserable, he was making Karen and the children miserable right along with him.

Karen and Jim began fighting over what they should do. She was upset that he would continue in a situation that brought such unhappiness to their family. The more depressed he became and the more things at work became out of control, the more he wanted to control things at home-But he couldn't even control himself. He abdicated all responsibility at home, where he had once been a very active partner in running the household and helping with the kids. His problems at work seemed to have sucked him dry. He couldn't even help with the kids' homework.

When Karen tried to get him to see how this was hurting his family, he would add her apparent lack of caring to his list of woes. He'd cry out to God, *"Now, I have a wife who doesn't understand me. She keeps getting on my case, pushing me to quit my job."* He was consumed with self-pity, thinking, *"Oh, poor me! There is no one who understands and takes my side!"* This only aggravated the conflict between him and Karen. She had done everything in her power to help him, to show him compassion, and to be understanding, and this was the thanks she got?

This didn't go on for weeks or months; it went on for more than two years — day in and day out. No matter how Karen tried to get him to see what this was doing to his family and their home life, he was blind to see it. He would cry all the way to work and cry on his way home. But he seemed trapped. He would not stop the battle until he saw justice win out. He felt it was his Christian duty. But he did not seem able to focus on how that was keeping him from fulfilling his Christian duty at home. She felt compassion for him but found herself wondering if the whole family was supposed to go down with him. Karen thought that maybe if she moved out he would wake up and realize what was happening.

So, Karen stopped praying for God to change things at Jim's work and started praying for wisdom, particularly whether or not she should move out. As she prayed, she was impressed with the verse that says, *"For our struggle is not against flesh and blood, but against the rulers, against the authorities, against the powers of this dark world and against the spiritual forces of evil in the heavenly realms"* (Ephesians 6:12). A light went on in her mind. She had been focusing all her energy trying to help Jim fight the battles with the people at work, and even trying to defend herself as she fought with Jim. Could this be the Lord showing her that she was fighting the wrong battle? She thought so.

Her new strategy was to do battle against the forces of evil on her husband's behalf. Without telling him, she actively began spiritual warfare on his behalf. She committed herself to pray three times a day, just as she had seen modeled by Daniel in the Old Testament. She got on her knees on his side of the bed and prayed in Jesus' name to bind the work of Satan against him. She took authority over all the forces of wickedness that were in any way assaulting him and cast them away from him in Jesus' name. Then she laid her hands on his pillow where he laid his head. She prayed that the enemy would lose control of his thoughts. She prayed that if Jim's mind had been blinded in any way he would be given clear thoughts. She put her hands where his eyes would have been and prayed that God would open his eyes and heal any spiritual blindness the enemy had caused. She put her hands where his ears had been on his pillow and prayed that if Satan had closed his ears to the truth God would give him ears to hear what the Holy Spirit said to him. She moved her hands down to where his heart would have been and prayed that God would heal the hurts that had been inflicted by the abuse at work. She prayed against any work of the enemy that had broken his heart and left him in depression. She put her hands on the bed where his hands had lain. There she prayed that God would release the bonds that kept him spiritually bound in this situation. She continued praying over his space, as the Holy Spirit led her, three times a day. Each time, she took authority over the work of the devil in his life in the name of Jesus. And she said nothing to anyone about this.

On the morning of the fourth day, Jim was on his way to work. He was so distraught and crying so much that he couldn't drive. So he pulled the car to the side of the road to pray He prayed, *"Oh, Lord, I need a word from you. Please, show me something."* He opened his Bible and looked on these words:

> *Be on your guard, that your hearts may not be weighted down with dissipation and drunkenness and the cares and worries of this life catch you unaware and choke out the word"(Luke 21:34).*

He thought, *"I'm not drunk. And I don't dissipate (carouse and party)."* Then the next line hit him like a two-by-four in the head:

> *...and the cares and worries of this life catch you unaware and choke out the word.*

It was as if God were right there speaking the words to him directly. And suddenly, Jim could see it. He could understand it. He could recognize how he had fallen into a trap of letting the cares of this world choke out God's word from his life.

When Jim came home from work, he said, *"Karen, I've had a breakthrough!"* Then he told her how God had opened his eyes, cleared his mind, and revealed what needed to change. What Karen had been trying to tell him for years, what might have taken months in counseling, God showed him in an instant. Karen knew this breakthrough was related to her prayers and spiritual warfare on his behalf, but she felt impressed that she should continue to pray for him in secret. She didn't want to act like she was taking credit or making herself out to be more spiritual than him. Besides, she knew that although this was a breakthrough the battles were not over yet.

That night they had a wonderful time of celebration Jim gathered their family together and recounted the story and confessed that he had let the cares of this life choke out God's word in his life. Together, they praised God for what he was doing and asked him to continue his awesome work.

The next day, one of Karen's friends called her crying. She had been having problems with her husband and wanted to know if Karen had any advice. Things had come to an impasse, and she was at her wit's end, tired of fighting but not sure what to do to turn things around. Karen was careful not to act like she had the answer, but she asked her friend if she would like to hear about something that had an amazing effect on Jim. Her friend was eager to hear. So Karen told her the whole story I've told you up to this point.

Her friend said, *"Let's do this together for our husbands."* They set the time and agreed to continue praying in this way three times a day, combating the forces of hell with the power of heaven on their husbands' behalf. After four days of praying for both husbands, Karen's friend's husband came home and said, *"I've blown it. Spiritually, I've gotten off track."* He said he felt led of the Lord to begin meeting with Jim for Bible study, prayer, and fellowship. They agreed, *"If nobody else comes, if we are the only two men in the world who are focused on the Lord, we are going to stand together to worship God, pray for each other, and read the Word. We need it, and we committed ourselves to do this every week."*

The men still didn't know about their wives' secret prayer pact. Karen and her friend were so happy. They said, *"Praise God! Thank you, Lord!"* Every Saturday morning their husbands continued to meet together. One day, Karen's friend came over and said, *"I found this brochure at the Christian bookstore. It sounds like something the guys would be interested in, this thing called Promise Keepers* [this was before anyone in California had heard of Promise Keepers]. *It's a men's conference, but they would have to go all the way to Boulder, Colorado. What do you think?"*

Karen said, *"That takes money, and we don't have any. And it's all the way in Colorado. I don't think there's any way. Jim would never go."*

But her friend countered, *"Well, I'm just going to lay it by the phone, and I'm going to pray about it."*

Karen's friend figured her husband would be even less likely to want to go than Jim. But a few weeks later, the friend's husband called Jim and said, *"Hey, I just picked up this brochure, and we've got to go."* Jim agreed.

They needed miracles to happen to make it work, but miracles happened. The whole time they were at the conference they saw little miracles one after another. And their wives kept praying the whole time they were at the conference. When the two guys returned from Promise Keepers, their faces shone. When Karen felt a release, she shared what she had been doing. She told Jim how God had led her to pray and do spiritual battle on his behalf, beginning three days before his breakthrough. Jim said, *"That day in the car, when the Lord showed me that I was weighted down with the cares of the world, I purposed in my heart to let them all go. I chose to give them up. I chose not to be entangled like that anymore. Even getting caught up in good causes can be a trap. I knew I had to seek the kingdom of God, to seek the Lord, because that is where life, and peace, and joy, and everything worthwhile can be found."* What a miraculous change this was from the man who had been crying and obsessing every day for more than two years. And this transformation took place in a few months.

After the conference, Jim was so uplifted that he would bring the family together, with the Promise Keepers worship tape on full blast, to worship the Lord together. The kids saw the deliverance of God for their dad. They saw God's word proved true. They saw the Holy Spirit move the way the Bible says He does. And the whole family was filled with joy over what God had done.

Karen notes that Jim's situation at work did not change one bit. And the temptation of the enemy would still entice him to be drawn back into the struggle that had entrapped him before. His anger would still flare up at the injustice he witnessed. He would still want to retaliate when he was humiliated and provoked by his bosses, but the power that situation had over him was broken. He was never entangled in the depression and obsession again.

Whenever he started to feel himself being sucked back into the old pattern, he and Karen would pray that God would give them the right focus. Then they would turn the situation over to the care of God, detach emotionally, and be able to leave what he could not change in the capable hands of God. Two years had passed since the initial breakthrough when I interviewed Karen and Jim for this book. While God had not seen fit to move Jim out of the situation, God gave him power over the spiritual forces that used to hold him in bondage because of the situation. He came home from work every night free of depression. Their family prayed together. And he continually got better and better. The fights with Karen stopped; they again united in their love for the Lord and for each other. Joy returned to their home. And all this was set in motion when Karen stopped fighting her husband and started fighting the spiritual forces of evil on his behalf.

This brings us to the point of this chapter: the authority God has given you to wage spiritual warfare. As a spouse, this is something you can do on your spouse's behalf. And, as seen in Karen's story, there are some times when this seems to be what is necessary. So, if you find yourself caught up in fighting against your husband or wife and getting nowhere, stop fighting against your spouse and try fighting against the enemy on their behalf.

Spiritual warfare cannot be left to those you consider super-spiritual. The Bible tells us that we are in a spiritual battleground, whether we acknowledge it or not. When you become a Christian, you put on the uniform of God's soldier. It's not a matter of whether you're in the battle but whether you're wearing protective gear and wielding your spiritual weapons to advance the kingdom of God and beat back the forces of darkness.

As Christians we must begin with a basic understanding of the two conflicting spheres of power that operate in our world: God and Satan (also referred to in the Bible as the evil one, deceiver, father of lies, thief, the devil, and the serpent). We must also never lose sight of the fact that God's purposes for us are always benevolent and Satan's purposes for us are always malevolent.

When I use the phrase "your marriage goes through hell," that is sometimes an apt description of the spiritual source of the pain you and your spouse are suffering. Satan delights in causing pain, suffering, confusion, and discouragement in the lives of human beings made in the image of his arch rival. Jesus said of him, *"The thief comes only to steal and kill and destroy; I have come that they may have life, and have it to the full" (John 10:10).*

Some of the pain and suffering you're going through may come directly from Satan and the spiritual forces of wickedness that are under his authority. The Bible says that Satan is the *"god of this world" (2 Corinthians 4:4).* Therefore, many things that happen in this world that result in pain and suffering have their source in the forces of wickedness, ruled by Satan.

Jesus also pointed out the intent of the "thief": *"he comes only to steal and kill, and destroy."* The thief opposes Jesus, who comes *"that we may have life and that more abundantly."*

Each life, and each marriage, is lived out in the midst of this basic spiritual conflict. If we understand the purpose of our lives, marriage, and even the purpose of difficulties in life, we will recognize the efforts of the thief who has set himself against God with the intent to thwart God's purpose for your life and marriage.

Scripture says we are not to be ignorant of his schemes, so that we do not fall into his traps. At one point, Paul wrote,

> *I have forgiven in the sight of Christ for your sake, in order that Satan might not outwit us. For we are not unaware of his schemes* (2 Corinthians 2:10b, 11).

Again he wrote, in a general letter to the whole church in Ephesus,

> *Put on the whole armor of God, that you may be able to stand against the schemes of the devil"*(Ephesians 6:11 NASB).

This is not advanced Christianity, but a basic awareness and stance of life in which every Christian should prepare to participate. This understanding is also very powerful in being able to help your spouse at times when the "hell" your marriage is going through is influenced by those for whom hell was created, the devil and his fallen angels.

BASICS OF SPIRITUAL WARFARE

Let's look at the basics of spiritual warfare that will help you even if this is entirely new to you. This is not something you approach lightly, as if it's some magic trick you can learn to play to amaze your friends. In the Book of Acts we see Paul and the other disciples driving out demonic forces in the name of Jesus. It looked easy enough, so others decided to try it. We find this account in Acts chapter 19:

> *Some Jews who went around driving out evil spirits tried to invoke the name of the Lord Jesus over those who were demon-possessed. They would say, 'In the name of Jesus, whom Paul preaches, I command you to come out.' Seven sons of Sceva, a Jewish chief priest, were doing this. One day the evil spirit answered them, 'Jesus I know, and I know about Paul, but who are you?' Then the man who had the evil spirit jumped on them and overpowered*

> them all. He gave them such a beating that they ran out of the house naked and bleeding. (Acts 19:13-16)

SOME RULES OF ENGAGEMENT FOR SPIRITUAL WARFARE

You and I have no power to do battle with the enemy of our souls apart from Jesus Christ. As members of the body of Christ on earth, Jesus has given us authority to conduct spiritual warfare in his name. Think of this as if God has given you a court order that allows you to take back in prayer whatever the devil has stolen. God has deputized you with authority to arrest the evil work of the devil in the lives of others and in your own life. To do this you pray in the name of Jesus, commanding the devil to stop his assault. You pray the promises of God, affirming that God's word is true and trusting God to apply His word to those for whom you pray. When you see that the devil has come in as a thief to steal, you can pray that God will restore what the thief has stolen. You don't have personal power to do this; you have been given authority by the power that is in Jesus. He was given all authority in heaven and earth when he defeated Satan by dying on the cross and proved his victory with His resurrection.

PROTECTIVE COVERINGS AND SPIRITUAL WEAPONS

Ephesians 6:12-18 lays out how the Christian is equipped by God for spiritual warfare. The verses are in bold. Here are the basics taken from that passage of Scripture:

1. **Recognize that our battles take place within an ongoing spiritual battle. "For our struggle is not against flesh and blood, but against the rulers, against the authorities, against the powers of this dark world and against the spiritual forces of evil in the heavenly realms."** We approach this issue by recognizing — as Karen did — that we already are in a battle and that essential battle is not against our spouses!

2. **God issues protective gear. It's our responsibility to put it on and use it. "Therefore put on the full armor of God, so that when

the day of evil comes, you may be able to stand your ground ..." God provides spiritual armor that will protect us. It is our responsibility to put it on and to stand our ground. This isn't done automatically.

3. There will be times you will have to stand your ground against the forces of darkness "... and after you have done everything, to stand. Stand firm then . . ." If your spouse is besieged in a spiritual battle, there may be times you will need to stand firm spiritually with him in the midst of those battles. I came to believe that part of my husband's struggle against sexual sin was influenced by spiritual forces of wickedness. Even after he had confessed, repented, and was in counseling, I sensed that I had to wage a spiritual battle together with him to break the power of spiritual forces of wickedness that worked overtime to tempt him, accuse him, tell him that God could not forgive him, and torment him. These came in the form of persistent thoughts that went against what we believed and what God affirmed in the Bible. So, in addition to getting the counseling we needed, we decided to stand our ground against any unwholesome or untrue influence of the enemy.

This took persistence, but it paid off after we stood together and prayed together with a determination that we would not give up until these false and sinful beliefs lost their power over him. It was as if our determination to stand firm against the forces of evil was necessary. As Paul tells us in 2 Corinthians 10:5, **"pulling down strongholds" in spiritual warfare includes "bringing every thought into captivity to the obedience of Christ."**

Let me suggest an analogy to underscore the importance of standing firm together against the powers of sin and darkness. It comes from the 1995 movie **Jumanji**. Granted, I know that this is not a Christian movie, but it paints a positive picture of a truth of how to deal with forces of darkness.

In the movie, two kids are caught up in an occult "game" that unleashes demonic forces against them. The game sucks the boy into a dangerous jungle, where he is held captive until someone rolls a certain number. The rules say that the only way to make the bad effects go away is to keep playing and finish the game. But the girl gets so frightened when the boy disappears into the game board that she runs away. She does not stand firm against the forces of evil. Twenty-six years later, another boy and girl are drawn into playing the game. They free the first boy (who has since grown into a man), and they find the first girl (now a woman) to complete the game. The forces of evil unleashed by the game can only be stopped if they finish that original game. In the process of being forced to combat demonic assaults together, the man and woman have to stand firm. They have to resolve the unforgiveness they hold toward each other. They also have the opportunity to lay down their lives for each other. He wrestles a crocodile to protect her, and she jumps in front of a bullet that was meant for him. They keep playing the game until it is over, even though they are terrified. They complete the game, and all the demonic forces disappear, just as the rules stated. All the evil that had been unleashed through the game is sucked back into the game. Somehow, it all works together so that the bad that would have happened if they had given up never had a chance to happen. They find themselves back in time before it all started, yet with the knowledge of what had happened. The original boy and girl who played the game grow up, get married, and share an intimacy, trust, joy, and appreciation for life that they never would have known if they had not battled the demonic forces together, stood firm, and won.

Here is the application that applies to all Christian husbands and wives: Demonic forces and spiritual forces of wickedness are operative in our world. They can and will, at times, assail your life and your spouse's life. The only way out is to face the forces of darkness with the light of God, to meet their lies and deception with the truth of God's word, and to persevere — standing firm against them — until the purposes of God are accomplished. In the midst of the conflict with demonic forces, you and your spouse will find opportunities to love and be loved and to express your love by laying down your life for each other. God could stop the assault at any time if He exerted His power over the forces of evil. Therefore, if He allows it to continue even though you are asking Him to remove it, and waging spiritual warfare according to His instruction; that implies that He is developing your endurance. You must determine to stand firm, to continue to resist evil until the demonic assault has run its course. You press on, being strong in the Lord and the strength of His might. When the Lord brings you through, you will see that He is able to *"work all things together for good"* (see Romans 8:28) because you love Him and are called according to His purpose. When you have been through this kind of conflict together with your spouse, or successfully on behalf of your husband or wife, your love and devotion for each other will be solidified and deepened. Your trust in the Lord will be strengthened too.

4. **Truth holds all the other protective armor in place. "…with the belt of truth buckled around your waist…"** The armor familiar to the people who read this letter originally is the armor of the Roman soldier. The centerpiece of his armor was the belt, to which all the other pieces attached. So, too, truth must be the centerpiece of your spiritual covering. You must know the truth of God's word. You must trust Jesus Christ, who called himself the Truth. You must judge all by whether it is true. Anything that is deceptive, that shades the truth or diminishes the truth in any way, is not how God will protect you. Take refuge in the truth. Test everything by whether it agrees with the truth revealed in the Bible.

5. **Make sure you have the righteousness of Jesus firmly in place: "…with the breastplate of righteousness in place…"** The breastplate covers the heart, a soldier's most vulnerable area. So,

too, your heart must be protected with the strong assurance of your righteousness — not how righteous you are by doing good but the unassailable righteousness of Jesus that is yours by faith in Him.

Whenever you begin to pray against the forces of the devil, he will go for your heart. He will remind you of things you have done wrong or your weaknesses or jealousies in an effort to get you to believe you are disqualified from praying in the full authority of Jesus Christ to defeat evil. This reminds me of a scene in the final episode of the Harry Potter books and movies *Deathly Hallows Part Two*. Ron Weasley is attracted to Hermione but his insecurities make him think she is more attracted to his best friend, Harry, while she thinks of Harry as a brother. When they are trying to destroy a locket that contains part of the evil Voldemort's soul, it fights back. The locket emits a false image of Harry and Hermione and tells Ron everything he fears about himself and every distorted thought that would make him back down. Harry has to shout the truth to Ron to jar him into not listening to the enemy's lies that would cause him to give up his fight against evil. Finally, Ron courageously stops listening to the lies that cut him to the heart and destroys the locket, along with the voice of the evil deceiver. We too have to resist the evil one and guard our hearts against his hurtful lies that may whisper in our own inner voice echoing our deepest insecurities and most foul emotions. We must remind ourselves that it is the sinless Christ who died for us and gave us His righteousness as our breastplate to guard our hearts. The apostle Paul, who wrote the letter to the Ephesians instructing them about spiritual armor, also wrote,

> ...that I may gain Christ and be found in him, not having a righteousness of my own that comes from the law, but that which is through faith in Christ—the righteousness that comes from God and is by faith. (Philippians 3:8b-9)

Your breastplate of righteousness is nothing less than the unassailable righteousness of Jesus Christ himself. That is what protects you as you do battle. Remind yourself of this any time you feel beaten down so as to be tempted to give up the battle against evil for yourself, your spouse, or your marriage.

6. **Be ready to move out with the protection and support of the gospel. "...with your feet fitted with the readiness that comes from the gospel of peace."**

7. **Hold up your assurance that God will keep His word. "In addition to all this, take up the shield of faith, with which you can extinguish all the flaming arrows of the evil one."** Roman soldiers of ancient times didn't just want to wound one person with each arrow. They shot flaming arrows so that the arrow would not only wound but spread fire to destroy all around it if the flames found anything that could catch fire. Your faith can be like a Roman shield, made of leather, which could be dipped in water so that when the arrows hit there was no way the destruction could kill the initial target or spread. The shield would extinguish any flaming arrows. Satan is not satisfied to wound one victim at a time. The arrows that are aimed at your life or your spouse's life, your family or your marriage are afire with flames of hell that are meant not only to wound one but to destroy as much as possible in your life, in your family and finances, and in the lives of your children. Therefore, you must know how to use your faith in the truth of God's word to stop those fiery missiles whenever they come near you, whether they are aimed at your spouse or at you. Whenever the attacks come, and in whatever form they take, you must meet them with absolute faith in God's promises and the truth from the Bible. If you have to choose whether to believe a fear that you will run out of money or God's assurance that He will provide, you should affirm that God has promised to take care of you. If you feel condemned for some sin that is already confessed and forgiven, don't let that wound your heart. Instead, thank God that you have already been forgiven as promised in His

word. If you are induced to hold a grudge or refuse to forgive your spouse for some sin committed but since confessed and repented of, don't go along with the unforgiveness that is clearly wrong. Instead, thank God that your spouse is forgiven, and affirm your choice to forgive even if the feelings aren't there yet. Act on God's word. Hold it up in prayer by stating that you believe it. This will help protect your heart with the shield of faith.

8. **Let your assurance of salvation protect your mind. "Take the helmet of salvation ..."** The helmet protects the head, and salvation protects your mind. The Bible says, *"Therefore he—Jesus—is able to save completely those who come to God through him, because he always lives to intercede for them"* (Hebrews 7:25). We must know, understand, and be sure in our mind that Jesus brings salvation. That salvation involves being saved for heaven, but it also means being saved from the power of sin and being saved from the rule of Satan in everyday life. If this is not your assurance, I encourage you to fill your mind with Scripture that addresses the full salvation God promises His children. When you see the salvation God promises, you will become aware of the areas where the enemy may be keeping you or your spouse from enjoying that full salvation. With the assurance of knowing what God intends, you can know and discern intelligently how to pray for your marriage and your spouse's specific needs.

9. **Your only offensive weapon is the Bible, the word of God: "...and the sword of the Spirit, which is the word of God."** Look at how Jesus did battle with Satan while being tempted. Three times the devil tried to tempt him, and three times Jesus replied, **"It is written . . ."**

Jesus did not argue with the devil. He simply used the word of God — which he knew by heart — to combat the deceptive suggestions of Satan.

The Bible says,

> *Do your best to present yourself to God as one approved, a workman who does not need to be ashamed and who correctly handles the word of truth (2 Timothy 2:15).*

Since the word of God is our only offensive weapon in this passage, we need to know how to handle it. When I was a youth pastor, a kid named Kevin came to youth group with a real, sharp, two-edged Samurai sword. He had no idea how to handle it, and he therefore posed a great danger to everyone nearby. It's the same way with us and the Bible. God's word is living and active and likened to a two-edged sword; it's powerful. And if we don't take time to get to know how to handle it, we can be dangerous.

Learn the basics of the Bible. Learn how it applies to your lives. Never use Scripture to try to put your spouse in their place or bring them down a peg. Rather, use God's word as a weapon against your spiritual enemy in a way that benefits your spouse.

10. **Stay alert and keep on praying! "And pray in the Spirit on all occasions with all kinds of prayers and requests. With this in mind, be alert and always keep on praying for all the saints."** Notice the stress here is not on how you pray but that you keep on praying. It was as Karen kept on praying for her husband that she was directed by the Holy Spirit as to how she should do spiritual warfare on his behalf. You may want to pray for your spouse as Karen prayed for hers. I think any prayer for your spouse or any spiritual warfare on behalf of your marriage would be good. Just keep on praying and don't give up.

PRAYING THE LORD'S PRAYER

One of the things I have learned to practice in my daily prayers is to pray the Lord's Prayer for myself and my husband. Here's how I do it:

"Our Father in heaven, hallowed be your name. May your kingdom come…" That means allowing God to rule your life and being willing to submit to God's will for loving your spouse. Pray that God's kingdom comes to rule in your spouse's life too.

"Your will be done." Pray that you would agree to God's will rather than insist on your own. Pray that God's will be done in your spouse's life rather than praying that your will be done in his or her life. You may have a clearly envisioned will for your spouse. Have your prayers been more about YOUR will being done in your spouse's life than God's will being done in their life? If so, that could be why God is not answering those prayers.

"Lead us not into temptation." Realize that your sins and temptations may be quite different than your spouses, but they are just as reprehensible to God. Check to see if you are praying like the Pharisee, *"Oh, Lord, I thank you that I am not like him . . ."* That kind of spiritual snobbery will cause your prayers to go nowhere.

"Deliver us from the evil one." Praying this daily allows us to recognize that we live in the midst of a spiritual battle. As I pray this, I wait to see if God brings to mind any specific areas where my husband or I might need to be delivered from the evil one. If any come to mind, I pray for those specifics. **"For yours is the kingdom, and the power, and the glory, forever and ever. Amen!"**

KEEP A BALANCED VIEW

A word of warning may be in order here. God is a God of balance and peace. While He does not want us to be unaware of the devil – but rather wants us to be prepared to go to battle fully dressed and fully armed – there is another common trap of which you must beware. That is to become so focused on Satan and the forces of evil this supersedes focusing your attention on the Lord and his kingdom.

When someone discovers the power we have to do battle against the devil they may see every facet of their life struggles to be a trick of the devil. That is not the whole picture. While the forces of evil may influence and delight in every sinful and hurtful thought or deed that takes place on earth, they don't necessarily deserve direct credit. The Bible tells us that human beings are influenced by the world (cultural influences), the flesh (our own sin-inclined nature), *and* the devil. There's plenty that can go wrong by yielding to the influence of the world and our own nature, without forces of evil being credited.

Don't give the devil more attention than he is due. Be aware of the possibility of satanic influences. Learn to pray against them, to take authority over them, and to deal with them the way God says we should. But don't look for a demon behind every bush. If you believe that your spouse's issues are somehow tied up with occult forces or that he or she is in some kind of bondage to spiritual forces of wickedness, seek out prayer support from those in your church community who are better equipped to deal with this kind of thing. You may also want to better educate yourself on the subject by reading good books on the topic recommended by spiritual leaders you trust.

Be on your alert for the devil, but don't get out of your secure position in Jesus or get sidetracked to chase him down. Let me show you a picture of what I mean, using something that happened to me when my children were young. I was driving my car in a hot and dry rural area near my mother's home where my children were playing outside. As I drove up the dirt road approaching the house, I happened to run over a rattlesnake. It kept slithering along in the direction of my children. Once I saw that the snake was still moving and that it was indeed potentially deadly, I backed my car over it. Then I tried to hit it again going forward. It slithered off into the grass, wounded but alive. Now, I did all of this within the safety of my car. I didn't dare jump out of the car because I was not equipped to safely handle that venomous rattlesnake on my own. I just made sure I took my children away from the danger and did my best from my protected position in my car.

That's a pretty good picture of how I approach our spiritual enemy. I know he's in the grass. I know he'd strike and try to kill me in an instant if I stepped out of my covering in Christ and came after him apart from my position in Christ. The danger would be the same whether my intention was to engage him to protect someone I love or I was just wandering off the "highway of holiness" (Isaiah 35:9-10) that God has established for me. So I don't go looking to pick a fight with the devil. I trust that as long as I stay abiding in Christ, just like I stayed in my car, I can remain protected and can also strike a blow against the forces of evil whenever I see them at work or posing a threat to someone I love. If I happen to encounter satanic opposition, if the forces of darkness get in the way of where the Lord is taking me, I use all the power of Jesus at my disposal to do as much damage to the forces of evil as I can. I use the power and privileges of prayer that God has given me to stop any forces of evil from getting near my loved ones. If I see danger or spiritually malevolent forces moving that way, I use the power of God to fight against them.

I don't focus my attention on looking for demons under every rock. I focus my attention on seeking first God's kingdom and His righteousness and the work God has given me to do each day. But I am not ignorant of the devil's schemes, and when necessary to confront evil, I do so from my protected position in Christ. If I approach evil in my own strength, I am overwhelmed with fear and at great risk. If I approach the forces of wickedness from my secure position in Christ, I may still feel afraid, but I am protected and can deal with evil directly if it comes across my path.

CHAPTER NINE: STAYING TRUE TO GOD WHEN YOUR SPOUSE GETS OFF TRACK

LORD, WHAT SHOULD I DO IF MY SPOUSE IS DRUNK, DISOBEDIENT, OR PUTTING ME IN DANGER?

I was tempted not to write this chapter. By doing so, I take a risk of stirring up controversy and generating criticism from those who have taken strong positions on issues related to what I must discuss here. However, I dare to take on these issues because I know that some husbands and wives reading this book need to understand how to apply the principles I will share here. Whenever I speak to groups, I bring up real issues that are not usually mentioned in a Christian context, particularly those associated with being married to someone who may be way off track spiritually. Whenever I speak publicly, there are some who need to speak with me privately. I have been brought in to help churches deal with delicate and difficult issues.

The same kinds of questions are raised repeatedly. These questions are at the heart of some of the most difficult marital and family situations that occur – and, sadly, they occur even in Christian homes. In such situations there are no easy answers. Since I'm writing this book to help husbands and wives hold on to heaven in real life situations and deal with real problems that arise while their marriage is going through hell, I chose not to shy away.

Let me give you an example of some of the real situations I have been asked to address from a scriptural perspective. I know that these may not describe your situation. You may even think that these are so rare as to make this section irrelevant to you. Please read this chapter anyway. While the situations that prompted me to write this chapter may be far removed from your own, the principles can be applied in any Christian life and can equip you to help others who may confide in you when their lives get into deep trouble.

Here are some of the questions and situations I've been asked to address:

"I'm pretty sure my husband is sleeping around. I beg him to get tested for sexually transmitted diseases, but he won't. Should I be sleeping with him knowing that it could put my life at risk when we have four small children?"

"My wife has a substance abuse problem but she won't admit it. I work full time and she is home alone with our children. We can't afford outside daycare but I don't really trust that she's in control of herself."

"My husband has knocked me around some, but he's a good man. He only does it when he's drunk, and I am a Christian. He's not. Shouldn't I just stay with him and love him to the Lord?"

"My husband wants me to watch hard-core pornography with him. He's a Christian and says I have to submit to him. He says this is part of my wifely duty and that if I don't meet his needs he'll be forced to look elsewhere for someone who will. But I know it's a sin, it's degrading to women, and I can't do so with a clear conscience. What should I do?"

"My wife and I are both Christians and have been married a long time. She keeps things secret, especially her out-of-control spending and gambling. We are on the verge of losing everything.

No matter how hard I work I have no hope of catching up and I am sick of her deception."

"My husband sometimes wants me to lie for him or do something else that I know is wrong. Is that something I have to do as part of submitting to him as my husband?"

"My husband is involved in some shady business dealings. I don't know much, but I wonder if I should turn him in to the authorities or try to force him to stop. What do you think?"

"I've caught my husband behaving inappropriately with one of my daughters. I'm not sure what was going on. He's her step-father. She is afraid of him now and won't tell me anything, but she's been acting out. I think he's molesting her; but I'm not sure. What should I do?"

See what I mean; no easy answers! And yet God doesn't desert us when we face problems where we need His wisdom most. I will not give direct answers to these questions because you might apply those answers to your situation, which has specific circumstances that I cannot factor in here. What I will do is show you how to apply biblical principles that will allow you to make good decisions in your particular situation. God has given principles in the Bible that can be applied—carefully, prayerfully, and advisedly—to such perplexing problems. I dare not make pronouncements about what you should do in your situation since there are so many variables that must be taken into consideration. However, I will do my best to explain the principles and how you can use them when dealing with these kinds of perplexing situations.

PRINCIPLES YOU CAN APPLY

PRINCIPLE #1
God's authority rules supreme over all other God-ordained authorities. Whenever you have to choose to obey God or a human authority — whether that authority is set up in the church, family, military, or country — you must always obey God rather than man.

All human authority is set up under God's ultimate authority and subject to him. Everyone fits into various places in various authority structures at any given time. Right now you are subject to the rule of God's law to which all are held accountable and you are under the governing authority of your country, state, and local laws. In your workplace, you may be the CEO who exerts authority over the men and women operating under your leadership. Or you may work under the authority of a supervisor, who in turn may be under the authority of a manager. If you are in the military, you are additionally under the authority of those whose rank is higher and subject to military law — which in some cases is more restrictive than civil law. In the family structure, God has given the husband a special position of leadership and parents have authority over the children.

While the Bible says that wives are to submit to their husbands, this does not mean that the husband becomes the supreme authority in his wife's life. Zondervan Study Bible Notes for 1 Peter 3:1 explain, *"The same Greek verb as is used in 2:13, 18 [is] a term that calls for submission to a recognized authority. Inferiority is not implied by this passage. The submission is one of role or function necessary for the orderly operation of the home."* Within the home, the husband/father has the higher rank and the greater responsibility and therefore stricter accountability before God.

In all situations, regardless of the authority structure that applies, no one is called to obey someone in authority over him or her if they call for disobedience to God. The Bible repeatedly tells us to obey God. Deuteronomy 13:4 says, *"It is the LORD your God you must follow, and him you must revere. Keep his commands and obey him; serve him and hold fast to him."* The entire chapter of Deuteronomy 28 lists one blessing after another that will come to those who obey the Lord, including blessings for their children.

The Bible cites an example of a wife protesting her husband's decree while also demonstrating a civil protest. This comes in the book of Esther when the evil Haman called for a holocaust of the Jews because they refused to disobey God by bowing to him. The Bible says,

> *Then Haman said to King Xerxes, 'There is a certain people dispersed and scattered among the peoples in all the provinces of your kingdom whose customs are different from those of all other people and who do not obey the king's laws; it is not in the king's best interest to tolerate them. If it pleases the king, let a decree be issued to destroy them . . . ' (Esther 3:8-9)*

The Jews did not bow to civil authorities but remained true to God and resisted the attempt to destroy their race. They also fasted, prayed, and appealed to God for protection. Esther was not reprimanded for refusing to obey her husband's edict because that edict violated God's higher law. Rather, she and the Jews were commended for remaining true to God rather than submitting to a lower authority. For Esther that authority was her husband who also happened to be the king; for the rest of the Jews it was the king and his government. However, Esther and the Jews took their petitions to the highest authority of all, God Himself. God worked out everything so that Haman was hanged on the gallows he built for Esther's uncle and *"the tables were turned and the Jews got the upper hand over those who hated them"* (Esther 9:1b).

Jesus' Take on Submission to Authority

Jesus respected the position of authority held by the Pharisees (Jewish religious leaders who opposed him). Matthew 23:1-4 says,

> Then Jesus said to the crowds and to his disciples: 'The teachers of the law and the Pharisees sit in Moses' seat. So you must obey them and do everything they tell you. But do not do what they do, for they do not practice what they preach. They tie up heavy loads and put them on men's shoulders, but they themselves are not willing to lift a finger to move them.' (Matthew 23:1-4)

The Apostle's Take on Conflicting Authorities

Look what Peter and John did when commanded not to speak or teach in the name of Jesus, after Jesus had told them to do just that. Acts 4:18-20 says,

> Then they [the religious authorities] called them in again and commanded them not to speak or teach at all in the name of Jesus. But Peter and John replied, 'Judge for yourselves whether it is right in God's sight to obey you rather than God. For we cannot help speaking about what we have seen and heard.' (Acts 4:18-20)

God gave His approval of their decision by continuing to work through them miraculously, which got them in trouble again. Acts 5:27-29 reports,

> "Having brought the apostles, they made them appear before the Sanhedrin to be questioned by the high priest.' We gave you strict orders not to teach in this name,' he said.' Yet you have filled Jerusalem with your teaching and are determined to make us guilty of this man's blood.' Peter and the other apostles replied: 'We must obey God rather than men!'" (Acts 5:27-29)

PRINCIPLE # 2

You are to look to the Lord as your ultimate provider. If your spouse gets off track, you can still trust God to protect you and provide for all your needs.

I have had women come to me who are in dangerous situations or are putting up with sexual infidelity but dare not challenge their husbands because they are afraid they will be cut off financially. The woman who puts her trust in God cannot be subject to such blackmail. Whatever decisions you have to make because of what your spouse is doing need to be made with the understanding that God can be a husband to you if your earthly husband abdicates that responsibility. Isaiah 54:5 declares, *"For your Maker is your husband—the LORD Almighty is his name—the Holy One of Israel is your Redeemer; he is called the God of all the earth."*

Psalm 146:3-10 says:

> *Do not put your trust in princes, in mortal men, who cannot save. When their spirit departs, they return to the ground; on that very day their plans come to nothing. Blessed is he whose help is the God of Jacob, whose hope is in the LORD his God, the Maker of heaven and earth, the sea, and everything in them—the LORD, who remains faithful forever. He upholds the cause of the oppressed and gives food to the hungry. The LORD sets prisoners free, the LORD gives sight to the blind, the LORD lifts up those who are bowed down; the LORD loves the righteous. The LORD watches over the alien and sustains the fatherless and the widow, but he frustrates the ways of the wicked. The LORD reigns forever; your God, O Zion, for all generations.*

There were times when I had to weigh out whether or not I would stay married to my husband; times when he was not sure he was going to stay true to our marriage vows and true to the Lord. At that time, since I had scriptural grounds for divorce, my counselors had me consider that possibility. I decided that I wanted to do all I could to keep our marriage together; but I was not willing to stay in a marriage where my husband would not honor his vow of fidelity. I did not know how I would make a living, but that was not what determined my choice to stay in my marriage. I knew that God would provide for all my needs, especially if I remained true to Him regardless of what Patrick chose to do. That helped overall because Patrick knew I stayed with him out of love, not out of perceived desperation. My strong stand called for a marital commitment from him — which he decided to renew — and was not weakened because I looked like I had to stay with him out of financial need.

PRINCIPLE # 3

You have authority in your family and areas of responsibility that are yours to oversee to the best of your ability, using all your intelligence, strength, and resources. The husband's authority extends over his wife and family. The wife's authority extends over minor children and household. Therefore, even in cases where the husband is demanding submission and demanding the wife to stay. The wife is obligated to protect herself and their children — even from her husband if he is the one who is endangering them. Similarly, if the wife is endangering the children, the husband has the responsibility to protect dependent children.

I base this on two things. The first is the Bible's commands that children are to obey their parents (not just their father) thus giving the mother governing authority over her children. The second is the example of Abigail, whose story you can read in 1 Samuel chapter 25. I feel comfortable drawing from her example because Paul wrote, *"For everything that was written in the past was written to teach us, so that through endurance and the encouragement of the Scriptures we might have hope" (Romans 15:4).*

Abigail lived at a time when David had been anointed king of Israel by God's prophet but was on the run from King Saul. She was married to a man whose name suited him completely. His name was Nabal, which means fool, and so he was! It was customary for David's band of men to provide protection for the field workers and shepherds in whatever area they were staying. In return, the owners of the fields that received protection were expected to reciprocate by giving David's men food and provisions. When David's men provided this protection for Nabal's shepherds and asked for the customary provisions,

> *Nabal answered David's servants, 'Who is this David? Who is this son of Jesse? Many servants are breaking away from their masters these days. Why should I take my bread and water, and the meat I have slaughtered for my shearers, and give it to men coming from who knows where?' (1 Samuel 25:10-11).*

This was very foolish! But the Bible describes Abigail as very intelligent. The servants understood what this could mean and who they should turn to in such a dangerous situation. While David's men were reporting this to David and were strapping on their swords, Nabal's servant ran to Abigail. I'll let the Bible tell the rest of this story here:

One of the servants told Nabal's wife Abigail: 'David sent messengers from the desert to give our master his greetings, but he hurled insults at them. Yet these men were very good to us. They did not mistreat us, and the whole time we were out in the fields near them nothing was missing. Night and day they were a wall around us all the time we were herding our sheep near them. Now think it over and see what you can do, because disaster is hanging over our master and his whole household. He is such a wicked man that no one can talk to him.'

Abigail lost no time. She took two hundred loaves of bread, two skins of wine, five dressed sheep, five seahs of roasted grain, a hundred cakes of raisins and two hundred cakes of pressed figs, and loaded them on donkeys. Then she told her servants, 'Go on ahead; I'll follow you.' But she did not tell her husband Nabal.

As she came riding her donkey into a mountain ravine, there were David and his men descending toward her, and she met them. David had just said, 'It's been useless—all my watching over this fellow's property in the desert so that nothing of his was missing. He has paid me back evil for good. May God deal with David, be it ever so severely, if by morning I leave alive one male of all who belong to him!'

When Abigail saw David, she quickly got off her donkey and bowed down before David with her face to the ground. She fell at his feet and said: 'My lord, let the blame be on me alone. Please let your servant speak to you; hear what your servant has to say. May my lord pay no attention to that wicked man Nabal. He is just like his name—his name is Fool, and folly goes with him. But as for me, your servant, I did not see the men my master sent.

'Now since the LORD has kept you, my master, from bloodshed and from avenging yourself with your own hands, as surely as the LORD lives and as you live, may your enemies and all who intend to harm my master be like Nabal. And let this gift, which your servant has brought to my master, be given to the men who follow you. Please forgive your servant's offense, for the LORD will certainly make a lasting dynasty for my master, because he fights the LORD'S battles. Let no wrongdoing be found in you as long as you live. Even though someone is pursuing you to take your life, the life of my master will be bound securely in the bundle of the living by the LORD your God. But the lives of your enemies he will hurl away as from the pocket of a sling. When the LORD has done for my master every good thing he promised concerning him and has appointed him leader over Israel, my master will not have on his conscience the staggering burden of needless bloodshed or of having avenged himself. And when the LORD has brought my master success, remember your servant.'

David said to Abigail, 'Praise be to the LORD, the God of Israel, who has sent you today to meet me. May you be blessed for your good judgment and for keeping me from bloodshed this day and from avenging myself with my own hands. Otherwise, as surely as the LORD, the God of Israel, lives, who has kept me from harming you, if you had not come quickly to meet me, not one male belonging to Nabal would have been left alive by daybreak.'

Then David accepted from her hand what she had brought him and said, 'Go home in peace. I have heard your words and granted your request.'

When Abigail went to Nabal, he was in the house holding a banquet like that of a king. He was in high spirits and very drunk. So she told him nothing until daybreak. Then in the morning, when Nabal was sober, his wife told him all these things, and his heart failed him and he became like a stone. About ten days later, the LORD struck Nabal and he died.

When David heard that Nabal was dead, he said, 'Praise be to the LORD, who has upheld my cause against Nabal for treating me with contempt. He has kept his servant from doing wrong and has brought Nabal's wrongdoing down on his own head.'

Then David sent word to Abigail, asking her to become his wife. His servants went to Carmel and said to Abigail, 'David has sent us to you to take you to become his wife.' (1 Samuel 25:14-40)

The significance of this story for our purposes is that Abigail did not run to ask her husband's permission to do what she knew to be best for her household. In fact, she didn't even inform him as to what she had done to protect their household from his foolishness until he sobered up the next morning. Even though that culture was far more patriarchal than our own, Abigail understood that she had been delegated authority to protect her household. She used this authority along with their shared resources and her keen intelligence to protect herself and those under their authority. In this case it was their employees.

Notice also that Abigail appealed to David according to God's law, to which he was still subject even though he would one day be king. Abigail did not usurp her husband's authority; rather, she fully used her own to the benefit of all. Also note that Abigail did not leave her husband, even though he was a sorry excuse of a man — one whom God himself called a drunken fool. Instead, she did what she could within her marriage. It was God who arranged to get her out of that commitment when he struck Nabal dead and blessed David with a godly and intelligent wife.

The principle I draw from this for us is that you have plenty of room to make wise decisions on behalf of your family. If your husband is drunk or just acting like a fool, you don't have to ask him every little thing about what to do to look out for the well-being of yourself and your minor children. Use your intelligence, your understanding of what God says is right, and your responsibility to protect your family to make good decisions when your spouse — whether husband or wife — is in no condition to do so.

PRINCIPLE # 4

There are times marital separation is allowed under conditions specified by God.

The Bible is clear that God wants marriages to stay together, but it also allows for separation — while not encouraging it — under certain conditions. Paul wrote the church at Corinth,

> *To the married I give this command (not I, but the Lord): A wife must not separate from her husband. But if she does, she must remain unmarried or else be reconciled to her husband. And a husband must not divorce his wife (1 Corinthians 7:10-11).*

The Zondervan Study Bible Notes on this verse say, *"Paul argues that in the light of Christ's command she (or he) is not to marry again. Rather, the separated or divorced couple are to be reconciled. Clearly the idea is that marriage should not be permanently disrupted."*

I believe separation should be considered any time your spouse poses a danger to you or your children, when you or your children are being physically or sexually abused, or when you or your children are otherwise having your lives put in danger perhaps by addiction or dangerous associations. This separation is to be for a season, to get help for the problems, to actively seek to remedy the behavior that causes danger, to pray, and — if your spouse is a Christian — to invoke church discipline in accordance with the instructions given by Jesus in Matthew Chapter 18.

DEALING WITH DOMESTIC ABUSE

I have heard erroneous and highly dangerous teaching given that says biblical submission gives a husband the right to beat his wife. This is wrong! I knew of a pastor's wife who appealed to her husband's senior pastor to call for him to stop physically abusing her or to give up his position in the church. Instead of reprimanding the abusive husband in this situation, the pastor to whom the woman appealed for help told her to *"submit to his beatings as Christ submitted to the lash of those who crucified him."* This is a grave misapplication of Scripture, and such teaching has caused untold damage!

I know of another woman who is taking the right approach. Her husband abused her for a number of years. A few years back she came to understand that God has not commanded her to live in such danger or to subject her children to it. She is a God-fearing woman who decided to separate from her husband. She made it clear to him that she does not want to divorce him. As she said to me, *"I still respect my husband — but I do so from a safe distance."* She has no intention to date anyone else. She is using this time of separation to get counseling for herself and her children, to encourage her husband to get counseling, to pray, and to rebuild their relationship. They reconciled a few months later. But he was not able to control his temper, so she separated again. They went through more counseling and have since reconciled a second time. He understands that she remains committed to him, continues to pray for him, and continues to love him; but she will not subject herself or her children to his abuse.

PRINCIPLE # 5

When it is appropriate to submit to another's leadership you do so by trusting God — whether that is the leadership of a pastor in your church, your husband, a general in the military or governing authorities in your country. You are not necessarily trusting or endorsing the rightness of the decisions being made.

King Solomon wrote,

> *Obey the king's command, I say, because you took an oath before God. Do not be in a hurry to leave the king's presence. Do not stand up for a bad cause, for he will do whatever he pleases. Since a king's word is supreme, who can say to him, 'What are you doing?' Whoever obeys his command will come to no harm, and the wise heart will know the proper time and procedure (Ecclesiastes 8:2-5).*

We are also instructed in the Bible to...

> *...obey your leaders and submit to their authority. They keep watch over you as men who must give an account. Obey them so that their work will be a joy, not a burden, for that would be of no advantage to you (Hebrews 13:17).*

There will be situations where you are not in danger but don't think the person who has the authority to make the decision is making the right one. If God has given them a position of authority, God will protect you from their mistakes or misuses of that authority. In such cases, including when a husband "pulls rank" in a family decision over the wife, she can trust God even if it's not the decision she would have made. I have seen God protect me and guide me when I submitted to those in authority even when I disagreed in whole or in part with what they were doing. When I did submit to their authority, I did so out of obedience to God not necessarily as an endorsement of their decision.

The first case was when the pastor and leaders of our church chose to remove me from my position on the church staff. I made it clear that I thought they had no legal or scriptural grounds for doing so. I thought it was the wrong decision, but I recognized that it was their decision to make. So I followed the proper time and procedure. I did not rebel against the pastor and church leaders. We stayed in the congregation and fully submitted to their leadership. I did pray that God would vindicate me, prove to them that they were wrong, and reinstitute my ministry apart from them. In time, God proved me right, those leaders later apologized, and God reinstated my ministry outside that church. As I submitted to the governing authority in that situation, I demonstrated faith in God, even while being quite sure their decision was not right. It was still their decision to make, and they were not asking me to participate in wrongdoing.

On the occasion when Patrick wanted to move away from that town, I did not want to move. After we talked and prayed, I thought God was leading us to move, but I still didn't want to move. So, I chose to simply follow Patrick's leadership, trusting God would take care of us even if this was not the best decision. As it turned out, it was the best decision, and by following Patrick's leadership I took a short-cut to having my dreams come true and my prayers answered.

PRINCIPLE # 6
Marital submission does not equal obedience. You must draw the line when your husband or wife, or anyone else calls you to participate in sin or conspire with them to go against God's will.

Throughout the Bible we are repeatedly told to obey God, to obey His commands, and to obey His precepts. There are verses telling us to obey the leaders of the church within the context of the church, telling slaves to obey their masters (as slavery was common in that culture; today one could apply this to mean obey your employer), and telling children to obey their parents. However, nowhere in the Bible does it say, wives should categorically obey their husbands.

Ephesians 5:22 says, *"Wives, **submit** to your husbands as to the Lord."* Taken out of the context, some would try to make this say that women must blindly obey their husbands as they would obey the Lord. The Zondervan Study Bible Notes explain the distinction between submission and obedience with regard to Ephesians 5:22, saying, *"Wives, submit"* is *'An aspect of the mutual submission taught in v. 21. To submit meant to yield one's own rights. If the relationship called for it, as in the military, the term could connote obedience, but that meaning is not called for here. In fact, the word 'obey' does not appear in Scripture with respect to wives, though it does with respect to children (6:1) and slaves (6:5). [The phrase] 'as to the Lord' does not put a woman's husband in the place of the Lord, but shows rather that a woman* *ought to submit to her husband as an act of submission to the Lord."*

Let's consider an example that shows that submission does not equal blind obedience, even when the one giving you a command may have authority over you. Let's use a military example to avoid stirring up the strong emotions that may be evoked by dealing directly with husband-wife submission.

There have been many stories in the news of senior military officers making improper sexual advances toward those of lower rank. An officer's rightful authority to pull rank in military situations does not give him any authority to command someone under his authority to disobey military law to which all military personnel are subject. Obedience in such situations would be wrong. In fact, when such is demanded it is the lower ranking person's obligation to resist such an abuse of authority, get out of the situation, and appeal to higher authorities for protection on the basis of the law.

The same idea of submission versus blind obedience applies for wives and husbands. Both the wife and husband are subject to the higher law of God. Any time a husband tries to use marital authority to get his wife to join him in sin or commit a sin, he is overstepping his God-ordained authority. That is where a wife should draw the line and refuse to cooperate with him. In such cases, the wife can appeal to other governing authorities and laws set up to protect her in her particular situation. That may be the leadership of the church or civil authorities. She should also appeal immediately and directly to God. Neither should a husband allow his wife to lure him into sinful or bad decisions (that didn't work out so well for Samson with Delilah, even though they were not married).

We see a New Testament example of a woman who went along with her husband when he set out to lie to God. Ananias and

Sapphira, a married couple, became Christians in the early church. At that time many sold property and gave it to the church. Ananias and Sapphira chose to sell their property, but they decided to keep back some of the money for themselves and lie about how much they received when they sold it. When they agreed together to try to lie to God, they were both struck dead. However, God gave each of them an individual chance to choose whether or not to lie. Each was held accountable before God individually for his or her moral choice. You, too, are held accountable before God for your moral choices. While it is understood that spouses can exert influence over each other, God doesn't excuse sin on the basis of saying, *"Well, my spouse told me to do it."*

PRINCIPLE # 7
Both non-Christian and Christian spouses can get off track; and God can take care of you regardless of your spouse's spiritual state.

Some people will liken what Sapphira did — lying — to what Sarah did in the Old Testament — saying she was her husband's sister when he told her to do so (see Genesis 12:13). This can cause confusion, because in Sapphira's case God struck her dead and in Sarah's case God holds her up as a good example for us. There is a good explanation for this, and it holds lessons that can help you when your spouse gets off track with the Lord — whether or not your spouse is a Christian.

First off, Sarah's story only makes sense if you keep in mind that Sarah married her half-brother (see Genesis 20:12). When her husband told her to tell someone that she was his sister, she was only telling half the truth; she was misleading, but she was not telling an outright lie. There were two times Sarai, or Sarah, was told by her husband Abram, or Abraham, to say that she was his sister. Once was early on when they were Sarai and Abram, before entering into a covenant relationship with the living God.

The second was after God changed their names and they had entered into a covenant relationship with Him (the time, the New Testament tells us, when Abraham's faith was accounted to him as righteousness). Therefore, Abram/Abraham is shown both before and after his conversion experience making the same error — commanding his wife to say she was his sister.

This can give us comfort because both times God protected Sarai/Sarah from Abram/Abraham's mistakes when he got off track. If you are unfamiliar with the story, you may wonder why it mattered whether she was his sister or his wife. It mattered because, at that time, women were treated as property. If a more powerful clan leader or ruler wanted to take a woman into his harem or as a concubine, he might kill the husband so that he could have her. If the other men thought she was his sister, they wouldn't kill him; rather, they would pay him a handsome price for her — say gold, slaves, and livestock! Talk about an indecent proposal! Sarai/Sarah was very beautiful, and twice we see that her husband told her to say she was his sister. Both times unsuspecting men took her into their harems, thinking she was available. And both times God protected her by intervening miraculously and revealing her husband's deception.

You have to consider this passage in its cultural context: Women did not have any option other than to depend on a man to provide for them. They could not hold jobs or earn money in any respectable way. Sarai/Sarah was entirely dependent on her husband to protect her. This situation was out of her control. She couldn't just leave; if she did, she would just be walking out into the desert to die. She surely didn't trust her husband's judgment; she put her hope in God (as we are told in 1 Peter 3:5).

Her husband got off track when he grew afraid of what men might do to him, even though on the latter occasion God had already proven himself numerous times to him. God had just finished telling him that within a year Sarah would give birth to a child of their own, the child through whom all the promises God had made would find their fulfillment.

Now, what was Abraham thinking to let Abimilech take his wife? No telling! But this seems a source of great encouragement in the times when we just shake our heads and wonder, *"What is my spouse thinking to do such a thing?!"* Whatever your spouse may do that puts one or both of you at risk is out of your control. But you can choose to put your hope in God and seek Him for protection. At such times, your responsibility is to do the best you can while still trusting and obeying God.

Sometimes we have to walk a fine line. A wife may know that her husband is getting off track with the Lord, say doing something at work that isn't exactly ethical. A husband may know or suspect that his wife or doing something illegal or unethical but not want her or their family to pay the penalty. So where do we draw the line?

Lessons from Sarah

I think Sarah's example gives us some guidelines. She did not usurp Abraham's authority. Not only was he her husband; he was the leader of their clan. In their culture it was the clan leader's place to interact with other clan leaders. She went along with him as far as she possibly could — telling the half-truth that she was his sister — but she never entered into sin.

Regarding Sarah, Peter tells us, *"You are her daughters if you do what is right and do not give way to fear"* (1 Peter 3:6). So, for our purposes here, I draw out the principle that spouses are not to necessarily interfere directly when their spouse is getting off track. There are times its better to let God deal with them and reveal the error of their ways. We go as far as we can to support them, but we refuse to cross the line into sin. If there is a decision to be made for your family that you cannot agree upon but that does not require sin on your part, the husband is the designated tie-breaker. But if he makes a mistake, God can still take care of your family, especially if you go along with it to honor the roles God established.

Keep in mind that God's purpose is not always to have everything go great for you and your spouse. There are times God can use a mistake on your spouse's part to teach them a lesson they need to learn.

My friend tells a story where she and her husband could not come to an agreement about making an investment. She was an accountant and was usually the one who handled their finances because that was her area of expertise. He received a substantial bonus and wanted to make a risky investment. She tried to tell him this was a bad investment and to persuade him away from it, but they came to an impasse. Finally, he said, *"We are not going to agree here. Whose way will it be, yours or mine? Are you going to insist that I submit to you here even though I am the head of our household?"*

She consulted several Christian advisors. One professional counselor told her,

> *"Don't get in the way of God developing your husband's maturity. Every time you step in to rescue him from himself, you get in God's way. Let him make his own decisions and, if need be, learn from his own mistakes."*

Her Bible study leader told her,

> *"Go ahead and submit to his will in the matter. Then pray for him. God cares more about dealing with him than he cares about having you both making money on an investment."*

When she saw that the goal was not for the situation to turn out the way she thought best but rather for God to deal with her husband, she could yield. She made it clear that she still did not think the investment was a wise financial move but she would stop resisting him on this decision. It was his call and his responsibility. So he made the investment, and it was a major financial disaster. But God used it to refine him without her having to say another word. He promptly gave the area of finances back to her since they agreed she was obviously the one in their family best equipped to handle financial matters.

APPLYING THESE PRINCIPLES

These are principles, not pronouncements. Therefore, I encourage you to think them over and apply them as follows:

- In situations where you are not sure if or how these principles apply, pray for wisdom and for God to provide wise counsel to help you make important decisions.
- Seek godly counsel from your pastor and Christian professionals who have expertise in dealing with the kinds of issues you're facing.
- Get some unbiased opinions by seeking out advice from reputable groups or organizations who do not know you like Family Life, Focus on the Family, http://www.hearts-at-home.org/, or HomeWord with regard to the issue, irrespective of who's involved.
- If you or your children are in danger, get to a place of safety first. Once they are safe, you can take time to sort out the issues with the help of wise counsel.
- If your spouse is in danger of hurting him or herself, get professional help immediately.
- When you have a perplexing decision to make, use all God has given you: intelligence, resources, support systems, and the power to make choices for the good of your household, especially your children. Don't hold back because you're not sure you have the right to make such decisions. There are times your decisive action is needed.

- Keep a clear conscience. There are some situations where what is right for one person might not be right for another. If you cannot do something in faith that it is right, don't do it. Keep seeking in God's word for clearance so that you can do it with a good conscience.
- Remember to ask God to guide you, and look for Him to do so. Practice applying all the guidelines given in the chapter on God's guidance.

In closing, please remember, I'm not a theologian. I've done my best to find biblical principles to help married couples in perplexing situations make tough decisions in keeping with God's word. My main point is you don't have to get off track if your spouse does. Stay true to God even if your spouse strays God will protect you and use you to protect your children and household. I hope these help. If any are confusing or out of sync with your beliefs, seek out further spiritual guidance within your church.

Also, bear in mind that God's goal is to get your spouse on track, to have your husband or wife following the Lord with a whole heart. You can help bring this about by living according to God's word and demonstrating love for your spouse as you do so. Instead of just looking down on your straying spouse, you can do these things:

- Speak the truth in love (as defined in 1 Corinthians)
  "Love is patient, love is kind and is not jealous; love does not brag and is not arrogant, does not act unbecomingly; it does not seek its own, is not provoked, does not take into account a wrong suffered, does not rejoice in unrighteousness, but rejoices with the truth; bears all things, believes all things, hopes all things, endures all things." (1 Corinthians 13:4-8 NASB)

- Demonstrate your love with actions
- Show respect
- Pray specifically and persistently

CHAPTER TEN: KEEP YOUR BALANCE

PRACTICAL ADVICE FROM THOSE WHO'VE BEEN THROUGH HELL AND SURVIVED

The foundational part of this book has dealt with spiritual truths and principles. But spiritual understanding is meant to be put into practice. Radio Host Rich Buhler says that if something isn't practical, it probably isn't spiritual; I agree. Therefore, this chapter is chock full of practical advice and tips that you can use if they fit your situation.

All the stories I've drawn from and shared with you came from real people. Each couple faced a different set of circumstances, but they all held on to heaven while their marriages were going through hell — of one sort or another. After interviewing these people, I invited them to come together to pray and discuss how we could encourage those of you who are in the midst of such a situation.

We had a great time together. Although we each had a story to tell that had brought with it loss, pain, discouragement, and some sadness, we also had gained much through that experience. We found, that as a group, we had encouragement, joy, and good advice we could share with you. What you find in this chapter is a collection of the good advice that we all agreed would help you get through whatever you are going through in your marriage.

As I set about to organize all the tidbits and tips that were shared on that day, a central theme emerged: KEEP YOUR BALANCE! You are probably already focused on taking care of others; you need to balance that with taking care of yourself: body, mind, emotions, and spirit. You are probably already focused on helping your spouse; you need to balance that with getting help (for yourself, your kids, and whatever practical help is needed). You've probably already become pretty good at finding strength for today; you need to balance that with maintaining hope for the future. The following is the shared advice of that assembly of those who know (to some degree) what you are going through. They send it with their sincere prayers — prayed that day — that you and your marriage will come through this season happier, healthier, and more blessed than before.

TAKE CARE OF YOURSELF

The most common mistake people make in such situations is to neglect themselves while expending themselves entirely to take care of their spouse, work, and whoever else needs care. This tends to be more of a problem for wives than husbands. If you start out trying to be superhuman without taking care of yourself or replenishing your inner reserves, you will eventually come crashing down. You can only give and give and give so long before you are depleted.

Taking Care of Yourself Allows You to Take Care of Your Spouse Too

Bottom line: You have to take care of yourself or you won't be able to take care of others. So it is not a selfish thing to do, it is a healthy thing to do. Taking care of yourself is one way you can make sure you are able to help take care of others for the long haul. Think in these terms: *I have to do whatever is going to strengthen me so that I can be there for my spouse and family. I have to take care of myself spiritually so I can go before the Lord on my spouse's behalf. I need to stay healthy so I can help my whole family get through this difficult season.* Remember, you want to do more than just survive. You want to have emotional, spiritual, and physical reserves so you can have something to give your spouse.

Recognize Your Limits

If you are going to be able to help your spouse for the long haul, you must recognize your limits. You can only do so much physically. You can only work so much. You can only bear so much grief. You can only uphold others so long without having someone uphold you. You need rest, nourishment, and some time for recreation.

If You Ignore Your Limitations, You Will Eventually Collapse

Be forewarned: If you try to do more than is humanly possible, you are setting yourself up to collapse in some way. You may collapse physically because the exhaustion takes its toll on your immune system and you will get sick. You may have a moral collapse. When you push yourself on and on, with very little room for joy or rest, you will grow hungry for a little pleasure in life. It just happens that way. If you are toiling beyond your limits, you will start to think; *Don't I deserve a rest once in a while? Don't I deserve a little fun?* The answer is yes! You do! But if you neglect your legitimate needs for a little respite and fun in life, you'll be prone to fill those needs in unhealthy – even sinful – and destructive ways. You may start drinking too much, depending on sleeping pills, developing a "friendship" with someone other than your spouse who gives you the attention you need. Beware! When those feelings of resentment begin to arise or you hear yourself thinking, *I know this isn't good, but I deserve this!* Take that as your cue. Find a legitimate way to make life pleasant, otherwise you may be tempted to find a quick fix that will create problems in the long run.

TAKE CARE OF YOURSELF PHYSICALLY
Do Not Neglect Your Physical Health

Now is not the time to let yourself go physically. Take extra care to be physically fit. Take vitamins, even if you don't usually. Get enough rest. Eat enough but not compulsively; and eat healthy foods. Get plenty of exercise. You know all of these things, and you know how easy it is to neglect them (or to stop eating or overeat to comfort yourself). But think of each good thing you do to take care of yourself as something you are doing for those you love as well as for yourself. If you tend to neglect yourself, get a friend to help you monitor taking care of yourself in these ways.

Listen to Your Body's Signals

If you are so focused on what is going on in your marriage, you may ignore your own emotions, your intuition, and your spirit when your inner being is trying to get a message to you. If you ignore your intellect, emotions, and spiritual sensibilities, your body will start to let you know that you need something. This can come in the form of physical exhaustion, panic attacks, nightmares, eating disorders, sleep disorders, physical pain, memory loss, and a host of other physical ailments that will interrupt your daily life.

When your body starts trying to tell you something, you'd better listen. Get to a doctor. Be sure to tell your physician not only your physical symptoms but also the stress you are carrying due to your marital situation.

TAKE CARE OF YOUR MENTAL ATTITUDE
Maintain a Positive Mental Attitude

Philippians 4:8-9 says,

> *Whatever is true, whatever is noble, whatever is right, whatever is pure, whatever is lovely, whatever is admirable—if anything is excellent or praiseworthy—think about such things. Whatever you have learned or*

received or heard from me, or seen in me—put it into practice. And the God of peace will be with you.

Do whatever helps to maintain a positive outlook. Listen to motivational recordings. Limit your exposure to upsetting material. Keep your focus on that which is good.

Understand What is Happening in Your Spouse's Life & Yours

Whatever your situation, you will be helped by knowing what you are dealing with and how best to respond to it. Educate yourself in any way you can to better understand your situation. Find out whatever you can to help you make good decisions and gain hope from others who have made it through something similar. (That's what you're doing right now.)

TAKE CARE OF YOURSELF EMOTIONALLY
Do Things that are Emotionally Uplifting

Remember, Ecclesiastes 4:9-10 says, *"Two are better than one, because they have a good return for their work: If one falls down, his friend can help him up. But pity the man who falls and has no one to help him up!"* You aren't both supposed to fall down at once. So do whatever you can to lift yourself up emotionally in healthy ways. This may mean doing a hobby you enjoy, spending times with a special friend, taking a walk in the park, taking a class, going out to lunch with encouraging people, attend a sporting event, or whatever you find emotionally uplifting. This is not neglecting your spouse; it's keeping yourself up so you can help lift your spouse up. You may also focus on doing emotionally uplifting things together.

Acknowledge Your Feelings and Process Them

Acknowledge the reality and validity of your needs, feelings, hurts, and losses. Grieve as necessary, even if your spouse thinks their suffering is more severe than yours. You cannot wipe away one person's suffering by comparing it to another's. Don't pretend that you are not hurting if your spouse happens to be hurting more.

You cannot divorce yourself from your feelings, or your feelings from those of your spouse. When your spouse is hurting or in danger, you will hurt too. You can't deny the pain without compounding the problems. When you're married, what happens to your spouse touches you, and what touches you will touch your emotions. Taking care of yourself includes being honest about how you are feeling, venting your emotions, talking out your feelings. It is common to minimize your losses and struggles especially if your spouse is going through something that makes him or her seem like the "identified patient" (like when Dave Dravecky was battling cancer and his wife, Jan was struggling emotionally). Your spouse's problems and the resulting losses in their life is one thing; your problems and the resulting losses in your life are another. Neither can be neglected without adding to your problems. You dare not ignore your feelings and your emotional pain because you don't think what you are going through is as bad as what your spouse may be going through. If you do, you will have to deal with these suppressed emotions later. The most common way these suppressed emotions surface is through what we know as burnout or depression.

Look for Signs of Depression, and Don't Hesitate to Get Treatment if Necessary

Depression is more than just feeling down in the dumps. Long term stress often causes biochemical imbalances in the brain that result in clinical depression. If this condition exists, it can take medical care to get well again. Certainly emotional and spiritual conditions play a role in depression, but there is a physical element that must be considered. Depression causes feelings of hopelessness and lethargy so that you would not be inclined to seek help if you are clinically depressed. If you have any of the symptoms of clinical depression, get the help you need. Most of the people in our support group benefited from a combination of medical, spiritual, and psychological help.

These are the symptoms of depression: sleep disturbances (either sleeping too much or not being able to sleep), low energy, loss of interest in things that used to be pleasurable, lowered sex drive, feelings of hopelessness and worthlessness, feeling sad and empty, uncontrollable crying (crying every day for more than two weeks), loss of interest in normal activities, appetite changes, physical aches and pains, difficulty concentrating, and thoughts of death or suicide. If you have these symptoms, consult a counselor or physician.

TAKE CARE OF YOUR SPIRITUAL HEALTH
Secure Your Personal Relationship with God Before Trying to Help Others

In cases of emergency on an airplane, oxygen masks will drop from above to make sure you keep breathing. If you are seated next to someone who needs help securing their oxygen mask, you are instructed to first secure your own mask. Then you will have enough breath to help those who need it. Think of your relationship with God as your oxygen mask. He is your life line. You need to secure your own relationship with God first, then you will be able to help your spouse or others.

Don't Let Your Spouse's Lack of Spiritual Interest Keep You from Spiritual Support

Let your spouse know that you intend to remain spiritually strong so that you can be an encouragement and help to him or her. If your spouse doesn't want to go to church or do things to build himself up spiritually, don't look down on him. Instead, maintain your commitment to do those things that build you up spiritually. When I strengthened my faith — even when Patrick wasn't sure about where he was with the Lord — I took the weight off him and put my hope in God. As I actively looked to God to restore and rebuild our lives, Patrick's load was lightened. In time, when he was ready to fully re-establish his spiritual disciplines, I was happy about that; but I never let his times of spiritual disillusionment cut me off from God. This helped us both.

Do the Things That Build You Up Spiritually

Go to church. Go to Bible study. Read inspirational books. Learn what God's word has to say about your particular situation. Memorize Bible verses. Claim God's promises. Pray without ceasing. Worship God. Thank God in everything. Find a prayer partner to uphold you in prayer (as long as they will keep your prayers confidential). You know what helps you grow spiritually and what nourishes you spiritually. Do those things.

BALANCE HELPING YOUR SPOUSE WITH GETTING WHATEVER HELP IS NEEDED

Taking on the role of helping your spouse when he or she really needs your help can be heady business. It's nice to be needed, but beware of a common pitfall: thinking that you are the answer to your spouse's every need. Seeing yourself as the answer to their every need is to play God's role in another's life. This is idolatrous. Therefore, don't wallow in your spouse's burdens as though you alone must uphold them. You play a special role, but God has provided sources of help on every hand. Make part of your role not only to help your spouse but to get whatever outside help is necessary for you and your family. The following are tips on how to balance helping your spouse with getting the help you need.

Trust God to Take Care of Your Spouse

Your dependence on God to take care of your spouse will present itself in various ways. One is prayer; if you believe God is actively working in your spouse's life, you will continue to pray for them.

Another is to take a Sabbath rest from whatever work you do to help your spouse or work you must now do because of what your spouse is going through. If your spouse is sick or otherwise stressed, so that a greater share of the work falls on you, make sure that you take one day each week to rest.

The Old Testament command to take a Sabbath rest one day in seven and to let the land lay fallow every seventh year was an act of faith on the part of Hebrew people. It showed that they trusted God to pick up the slack when they took time off as He commanded. God knows you need the rest; so take it. The people of Israel failed to take off every seventh year, as God commanded, for 490 years. However, God made sure the land got its Sabbath rest. When the people of Israel were taken captive to Babylon they were away for 70 years. That's one year for every seven, just as God commanded in the first place. If we don't take the rest God prescribes up front as an act of faith we may end up having to take the time off. When your marriage is under severe stress you need enough rest. Trust that God can take care of your needs while you take a break one day a week.

Let Your Spouse Be Strong for You Whenever They Can

If your spouse is weighted down with problems or disabled physically in some way, they may not be able to meet your needs like they used to, but your spouse can always meet some of your needs. Surely, they can get a sense of satisfaction from meeting what needs they can for you. Let your spouse offer you support sometimes when you need it. That upholds your spouse's rightful place in your life and strengthens their self-esteem when it may be lagging. If you always take on the role of the "strong one," it can undermine your spouse's sense of self-esteem. There are ways your spouse can still be strong for you, no matter what your marriage is going through; accept that gratefully.

Find or Create a Support Group to Help You Deal with What YOU are Going Through

Regardless of whether or not your spouse gets involved in a support group, get support for yourself. Your spouse's issues and marital issues impact your life. You will need to get help to deal with your issues. It's best if your support group keeps the discussions confidential. There are many groups set up for spouses of those with particular problems. Check local churches or counselors to see what kinds of recovery groups exist. If you can't find a support group that meets your needs, ask a friend to help you set one up yourself.

Get Whatever Medical or Professional Help You Need

Irene was in a touchy situation. She and her husband were actively involved in their church in positions of leadership. When he was diagnosed with stomach cancer, all the attention went to him. Everyone would ask what his prognosis was, but few seemed to notice that Irene wasn't doing so well herself. The long ordeal of medically trying to rid her husband of the cancer, combined with the fear of losing him and the spiritual questions it raised, wore Irene out. She began forgetting things at work, exhibiting signs of depression, and having nightmares and panic attacks. She decided that she needed to get professional help to deal with the effects of the stress she was under.

Now for the touchy part: Her husband had an aversion to getting professional psychological or medical help for what he considered spiritual or emotional problems such as depression. Irene knew that she needed help. She knew her symptoms were physical, emotional, psychological, and spiritual, so she wanted help for the whole package. She was at our focus group, and we all urged her to talk to her physician. She did, but she did so in a way that was sensitive to her husband's hesitations. She didn't challenge his stance on getting professional psychological help. She went to her general physician and had a general check-up. She prayed for the doctor to have wisdom and for the wisdom to share with her husband what the doctor said. The doctor diagnosed anxiety/depression and prescribed medication temporarily. When she explained this to her husband, and the way the stress had been taking its toll on her, he didn't object.

It's not enough to identify that you may be depressed or have a stress-related condition. If the emotional stress has taken its toll on your physical health and well-being, you need to get professional help. A physician you trust can diagnose the problem and help you find a solution, but you have to reach out to get the help. Getting the help you need makes you better able to improve your marriage or deal with your spouse's problems.

Let Your Friends Be a Help to You

Your friends probably want to do something to help if they know about your situation. If they do and they ask you how they can help, don't miss that opportunity. You will want to do all you can to help your spouse, care for your children, do your work, and maintain your home during troubled times. Remember, your friends want to help too. Let them. At least, let them know where you need the help.

Delegate!

Don't berate yourself because you can't do everything perfectly. Instead, step back to assess all that you are doing and all that needs to be done. Consider what you are doing for others that they could do for themselves. Consider everyone's needs you are trying to meet, and then delegate. Get an objective and supportive friend to sit down with you and help you figure out a manageable work load that you can handle for the long haul. Have your friend help you think of others who can help with your home life, work, child care, meals, transportation, and whatever is stressing you beyond your limits. Then ask for help. You may not feel comfortable asking, but family and friends probably wish they could help. If you give them a list of several specific tasks that would help you out, they will probably respond positively.

Get Help for Your Children

When your spouse is going through difficulty, it will have an impact on the children. They may miss time they used to spend with dad or mom; they may worry over any health issues; they will notice mood swings—and probably blame themselves; they may harbor resentment or unforgiveness if you or your spouse has done something wrong that hurt the entire family. Not only should you remain aware of how your children are processing your difficulties, but you should also get them help if you can see they need it.

It's easy to get caught up in dealing with your spouse and marital problems. Make sure you stay alert to signs that your kids may be hurting too. If your spouse is not functioning well as a parent, you may need to compensate in the lives of your children. That may mean taking them to visit relatives, where they are the center of attention, or arranging for a "big brother" or "big sister" who can take up some of the slack in their lives.

Make sure you protect your children. If you and your spouse are too preoccupied with the crisis, get help watching and caring for the children. If they show signs of withdrawal, festering resentment, or depression, get them diagnosed by a competent counselor who specializes in the needs of children. If your marriage is going through hell, your children need help to process what is going on. You don't have to give them all the help they need personally, just get it for them.

Tell Friends and Relatives Where You Stand and How They Can Help

Depending on the kind of crisis or trouble your marriage or spouse is going through, you may find your friends and relatives more or less supportive. There are basically two kinds of situations in this regard: one where people blame your spouse for bringing on whatever you're going through and another where your spouse is in no way to blame for what you're going through in your marriage. If your marriage is going through something they have brought on, say through wrongdoing or perhaps an ongoing addiction, your friends and relatives may not be inclined to help you help your spouse. However, it will help everyone involved in such a situation if you tell them where you stand and how they can help — or at least not cause more problems.

What to Do in Cases Where Your Spouse is to Blame

I can speak from experience in this regard. My family had plenty of reason to be angry with my husband, especially because at the heart of his troubles was his betrayal of me and his marriage vows to me. I was very afraid that my mother and other relatives who lived near us would show him how much they disapproved. I decided that I would stay with him and get whatever help we needed to restore our marriage if we could. I went to my mother and sister and said something like this:

"I know you are angry at how he has hurt me; and that's OK. However, I have decided to stay in this marriage and work through these problems. He needs my help now, and anything you do that would hurt him will be hurting me indirectly. Once we get through this crisis, you can tell him whatever you like, but for my sake, please, support me by not tearing him down. I'm going to need all the support I can get from my family. If you can find it in your hearts to welcome Pat and me together, I can come here to find that support. If you can't, I'll have to find it somewhere else."

They were angry with him, and rightfully so; but they appreciated me telling them exactly where I stood. They agreed to welcome both Patrick and me into their homes, and they never said a negative word to him throughout the entire crisis. By the time the crisis had passed and they saw how truly repentant he was and how much he suffered the consequences of his own wrongdoing, their anger dissipated. In fact, it was replaced by admiration. Tell your relatives and friends what you need from them. Tell them what will happen if they are not willing to give you the support you need. And ask them to help you. In most cases, they will. If they will not, find support elsewhere.

What to Do in Cases Where Your Spouse is Not to Blame for the Troubles

In this case, people won't know what to say or do. They may feel uncomfortable because it seems unfair that something bad happened to someone who didn't "deserve" it. You can help them know how to help you by telling them that they don't have to say anything, or say the right thing. If you can think of something specific they could do that would help a little, tell them. People want to help. If they know what to do, they will feel more at ease around you.

BALANCE STRENGTH FOR TODAY WITH HOPE FOR THE FUTURE
Laugh!

Humor is essential, especially when times are tough. But you probably need someone to tell you that it is perfectly fine to laugh a little. So, I'm telling you! Every one of us felt a twinge of guilt at the thought of doing something that would make us laugh when our spouse or our marriage was going through such hard times. But every one of us in my focus group for this book found that laughter truly was good medicine. If your spouse is up to it, find things to make you both laugh. Watch old episodes of **I Love Lucy** or **Bill Cosby;** read funny books, tell each other jokes, watch funny movies or remember happier times. These bouts of laughter will help you balance out the sadness and release pent up stress.

Don't Stop Being Happy Just Because Your Spouse May Not Be Able to Share That Happiness

Annette, whose husband was in jail for child molestation, had to spend Christmas without him. She was unsure of what she should do. Should she mourn or play down the usually festive holiday just because he was in jail? She decided that the joyful celebration of Christ's birth shouldn't stop just because as part of his punishment for wrongdoing her husband was unable to celebrate with them. So she had a Christmas party. Some of her friends refused to come and thought she was terrible for having fun without him. But I think she did the right thing. She and her children were being punished enough — they needed a celebration. The people who attended had a wonderful time, although there was one awkward moment when her husband called from jail during the festivities. But Annette broke the ice when she said, *"Hi, Honey! We're having a wonderful time! Wish you were here."* They all cracked up, including her husband. He was sad not to be having fun with them, but he was glad his wife was able to help his children enjoy the holidays. In that way, her good humor spared them the loss of the joy of the season. Every once in a while, you need to lighten up!

Use Music to Lift Your Spirits

Ephesians 5:19-20 says,

> *Speak to one another with psalms, hymns and spiritual songs. Sing and make music in your heart to the Lord, always giving thanks to God the Father for everything, in the name of our Lord Jesus Christ.*

Do it; you'll be amazed at the difference it makes. Listen to music that soothes your soul and lifts your spirit.

LOOKING FORWARD
Make Long-Range Plans

Don't fool yourself into thinking things are going to be back to normal next month. Be realistic. If possible, talk to others who have been through similar struggles. Once you can see your way clear, consider the big picture. Think past survival to stabilizing, and past stabilizing to rebuilding your lives. This will help you help your spouse by preparing your heart to be patient.

If Appropriate, Go on with Your Life

If your spouse's crisis or problem is outside your shared domain — such as a problem at work that you really cannot help with — don't feel obligated to bring your life to a standstill. My friend Rayna's husband has been wrestling with problems at work for years. She is a great help to him, but she has no way to help solve the problems that are his to solve at work. She has made sure she gives him the support he needs; but she also went back to college and completed her degree to become a therapist. By going on with her life, she has helped herself, and equipped herself to be more helpful financially in case he should want to change careers. By moving on with her life at times he felt stuck she reminded her husband that there is life, hope, and a future apart from the company for which he works.

Smile at the Days to Come

Proverbs 31:25 says this of the excellent wife: *"She is clothed with strength and dignity; she can laugh at the days to come."* You can smile and laugh at the days to come. If things are really bad, you can be sure that things are bound to get better — especially if you are holding on to heaven. Remember, God knows the plans he has for you, and they are plans for good and not for evil to give you a future and a hope (see Jeremiah 29:11-13). You have good reason to smile at the days to come. Dare to hope, pray, and work toward a better future because that is what God has planned for you both.

I hope that you will prayerfully review these tips and take action to do whatever is necessary to balance your life. In that way, you will be able to continue helping your spouse and your marriage without exhausting yourself. This also shows your ongoing dependence on God. He is the One who will flow through you to fulfill your marital role to your spouse. As you remain continually dependent on God, He will continually flow through you to help you through, and strengthen you to bless your spouse and loved ones without utterly depleting you.

CHAPTER ELEVEN: Do You Take This Man? Do You Take This Woman?

Lord, I Said, "For Better or for Worse," But How Far Does That Promise Go?

Do you take this man (woman), to have and to hold,

for better or for worse, for richer or for poorer,

in sickness and in health, forsaking all others,

keeping yourself only unto him (her),

to love and to cherish, until death do you part?

Whether or not this is the exact wording of the vows you said at your wedding, these questions are at the heart of Christian marriage. The Bible doesn't spell out all the negative and positive ways your vows may be tested. These came by way of tradition; as if those who'd gone before wanted to impress on those about to take solemn vows before God to stop and think about what life might bring. Whatever the exact words, some way or another, a minister asked you, *"Do you take this man or woman . . . ?"* And you said, *"Yes."* You agreed to have God join your life to your spouse's life, a union that God decrees in the Bible, can only be dissolved by means of sexual infidelity, abandonment by a non-Christian spouse, or death. (See Matthew 5:32 & 1 Corinthians 7)

Given the unexpected turns that life can bring, we understand why these are solemn vows. Oh, but none of us knew, nor does any bride or groom getting married next Saturday know, how those vows might be tested. Our feelings of love, our optimistic hopes for the future carry most of us into marriage with little thought to the "worse" that might come along.

At our wedding when we were both twenty-one, Patrick sang these lyrics to me:

> **I will make you queen of our home,**
>
> **Under the glory of the King**
>
> **We'll raise our family in a castle full of love,**
>
> **And thank the Lord in everything.**

"Oh, yes!" I thought, *"That's the life I want! Thanking the Lord in everything!"*

I cherished the words of that first verse. In my starry-eyed idealism and romanticized love for him, I did not focus on the words he sang in the next verse:

> **In times of trial, when things are hard to see,**
>
> **Will you stand by me? With love, it can heal the pain,**
>
> **So let it rain, on the roof of my soul;**
>
> **There is no hole that love can't fill.**
>
> **So, let us climb the hill together . . .**
>
> —"Let Us Climb the Hill Together" by Paul Clark

God knows, love is an uphill climb. The path may lead through times when we cannot hold our spouse close for some reason, when things get worse instead of better, when you are poorer not richer, when there is sickness rather than health, when your love has grown cold and you no longer cherish your spouse or the prospect of being together. And yet, God's will is clearly stated in the Bible. We are to continue the uphill climb called love, together, until death parts us (except in cases with scriptural grounds for divorce).

The key point of this chapter is that there will be times in marriage when your will and God's will do not agree — perhaps even on the issue of whether you will stay in your marriage; I hope to convince you to choose God's will over your own at those times, no matter how hard it gets.

I know that choosing to remain true to your vows and obeying God in marriage can be overwhelming at times. As I write this, I bear in mind one woman whose husband was stricken with cancer this past year, a woman who had to separate from her husband because he repeatedly beat her, my friend whose husband still struggles with homosexual inclinations although he has renounced that lifestyle, and another friend whose husband has been impotent for years. I also remember the gut-wrenching pain I went through by staying with my husband when our marriage was going through such hell life was nearly unbearable. I didn't want you to close your ears to the truth because you might think I don't care or understand the depth of the pain you may be facing. So, I prayed that God would show me how to speak the truth in love and with compassion.

God answered that prayer through something that happened at a church service. A woman with whom I have friendly acquaintance sat next to Patrick and me. I knew her to be a dedicated Christian who diligently studied the Bible, upheld God's word to her children, and earnestly sought God's guidance for her life and her family. I also knew that her husband had been going through something intensely difficult. This morning she looked radiant, happier than I had seen her in quite some time. The pensive aspect was gone from her face. She dressed in bright colors, which seemed to match her mood.

The pastor's teaching amazed me because it coincided with the material I had already prepared for this chapter. Several times Patrick and I looked at each other in wonder at how clearly God was confirming what he had shown me through the message being taught from the pulpit.

The pastor spoke of times when life gets so complicated that we don't know what to do. At these times, he said, it is imperative that we have God's guidance. He warned us away from taking the popular approach that says, *"Follow your heart!"* because our hearts will lead us astray; as Jeremiah 17:9 says, *"The heart is deceitful above all things and beyond cure. Who can understand it?"* The King James Version makes it sound even worse, *"The heart is deceitful above all things, and desperately wicked: who can know it?"* Therefore, the pastor concluded that we need God's guidance, especially when we are going through difficult times. However, he stressed that in order to receive and benefit from God's guidance, we must be willing to do God's will.

The pastor noted that some people say, *"God is more concerned with your holiness than your happiness."* But he countered, *"No! God is deeply concerned with your ultimate happiness, but God knows that true happiness only comes through holiness. And the pathway of holiness requires us to yield our own will to do the will of the Father."*

I quickly finished writing my notes from the sermon in time to stand for the benediction. Then I greeted my friend who was standing next to me. I told her how great she looked and asked if things were getting better (since she had told me about her troubled marriage).

"Oh, haven't you heard?" she asked. "We're separated, and I haven't felt this great in years. I feel like a new woman, like a heavy weight has been lifted from me." She went on to describe her husband's problems, his unwillingness to do what needed to be done to correct them, and her exasperation.

"This is just a separation though, right?" I asked. "You're not planning to divorce, are you?"

"No, we just needed to separate. I'm in counseling. He's in counseling. I'm hoping and praying that he will make the changes necessary." She assured me — somewhat defensively, "We've talked to the pastor, and our separation is in keeping with what Scripture allows in First Corinthians, chapter seven."

She went on to explain how she had done the best she could, but his problems had become overwhelming to her and their children. She told me how her Christian relatives were condemning her decision to separate but that she felt she had to do this. Then she asked, *"Would they rather I end up in a mental hospital or commit suicide?—which is what I was coming to if I stayed with him."*

My heart went out to her. I'd been around her husband enough to see that she was dealing remarkably with profound problems, and I had only seen the tip of the iceberg. I could only imagine the intensity of the stress she was under. It seemed to me that a separation in her situation was both wise and in agreement with God's word.

I told her, *"I definitely support you in this decision. You're not saying that you're separating as a preliminary to divorce, you're separating to reconcile on better terms, right?"*

"Well, yes. I hope he will change; but I can't make him change and I can't fix him and I can't go on like this. So I hope and pray he does change, but eventually I suppose I would divorce him."

I was shocked at this coming from her. *"Let me get this clear,"* I began. *"Do you have scriptural grounds for divorce? Has he committed adultery?"* (I didn't even ask about abandonment since her husband is a professing Christian and has been for many years.)

"No, he hasn't committed adultery. I just can't live this way anymore. And if I have to choose between staying with him as things are and going crazy or divorcing him, I would divorce him. That is not what I want, but I want a marriage with someone who will be a partner in the marriage. He doesn't want to be a partner in this marriage. He doesn't want relationship. I sincerely hope he will wake up and change, but if he doesn't..."

Her eyes flashed a defensive warning, but I was genuinely alarmed and wanted to make sure I had not misunderstood her.

"If he doesn't; then what...?" I pressed, asking, *"You would wait until he violated his vows by being with someone else sexually?"*

"No," she said, *"I don't think he would be unfaithful to me in that way."*

"Wait," I said, *"let me get this straight. You are saying that if things don't change you are looking forward to a time when you would knowingly go against Scripture and divorce your husband? Isn't that exactly what the pastor just described as following your heart instead of God's command? Isn't that what he warned us about?"* And I thought to myself, *Isn't this precisely the kind of decision God led me to warn against in this chapter that I was writing at that time?* And this was my friend! At this point the intensity of our conversation increased noticeably and Patrick arrived.

"No!" She assured me that she had counseled with the pastor and that he was being very supportive and understood her situation. (I later spoke to the pastor myself and – while supportive of her

personally – he did not approve of this course of action.) I tried to convince her that I, too, was supportive and understood her current separation as within the moral bounds of Scripture. What I could not condone was projecting forward to a crossroads where she had to choose between her will or God's will and saying, *"Father, not your will, but mine be done."* I tried to make it clear that I took this position because I care about her and her long-term happiness; but her demeanor indicated that she didn't accept that.

She countered, *"Well, my friends all understand; they're being supportive, and so is the pastor."*

I couldn't let that pass. So I replied, *"I am your friend too. And I want to be supportive, but — as a friend and a Christian — I feel compelled to support you by urging you not to fall into this trap. It is not that I'm saying, I don't care if you are miserable, as long as you do what the Bible says. That's not it at all!"* I tried to impress on her that any lure toward relief or happiness that would get her to turn away from God's will is a trick. The sign pointing toward the path of self-will may read *"Happiness this way!"* but it's a signpost set up by Satan to lead unwary travelers into dangerous territory.

In trying to convince her, I told her about a similar conversation I had with another friend over fifteen years before. I explained that the reason I had grown so intense with her immediately was that what she was saying was an echo of that previous conversation. And I had lived to see where that path led for this other friend. She too had been in a marriage where she and her husband were having problems; he too was not actively involved in their marriage and was causing her emotional turmoil; he too was a Christian and had not given her any scriptural grounds for divorce. And yet this other friend took the view *"Well, I know God wants me to be happy because he loves me. God knows how miserable I am with this man and that I've waited for him to change and have done all I can to help him. God knows I can't stay with him and continue living like this! There is no way God could love me and really expect me to stay in this marriage."*

I had asked that friend fifteen years before the same series of questions I asked my friend at church and received similar answers that boiled down to this: *There is only so much I can take, and if things don't change, God's commands regarding marriage are not going to stand in the way of my relief from this intense pain and my pursuit of happiness.*

My friend with whom I had this conversation more than fifteen years before found a new church and a pastor who did not know her husband. This pastor did not require her to have scriptural grounds for divorce. Instead, he counseled her to seek God's help to make a new life. As she had tried to explain her course to me, she swept those passages of Scripture (regarding the rare exceptions in which divorce is sanctioned by God) aside. She acted as if they didn't really matter or weren't quite clear. Besides, during her separation she had fallen in love with another man who was a more dedicated Christian than her first husband. Everyone seemed supportive and excited at the prospects of their marriage because they were going to go into ministry together.

They did marry, and Patrick and I became friends with her and her new husband. We have kept in touch over the years, and I am sobered by the devastation that has come to them. The second marriage ended in disaster and disgrace. This woman's life, her second husband's life, and the lives of their children have been shattered. The pain and heartbreak she endured and — in part — caused in her second marriage far outweighed that which she sought to escape in the first. She has now gone on to her third marriage with another Christian man, still seeking happiness. I truly pray she finds it, but I cannot help but wonder how her disregard for the inviolability of her marriage vows opened the door for this ongoing heartbreak and confusion.

As I finished conveying this sad turn of events to my friend in church, I could tell she hadn't received my words in the way I'd hoped. We said cordial good-byes, but I could tell she didn't think I was on her side. Patrick and I discussed this and prayed about it. The more we discussed my friend's reaction to what I had tried to communicate, the more agitated I became.

Patrick asked, *"What's all this anger about? Shouldn't your emotions be more those of sadness or deep concern?"*

I struggled to explain the depth of my feeling — what looked to him like anger. *"It may look like anger,"* I said, *"but it's the same reaction I had when our son, Taylor, was eight-years-old and would roller-blade down the driveway and into the street without noticing the car that was rounding the corner. He was only thinking of the fun he was having; I only saw the imminent danger. So I grabbed him; and my reaction came out looking like anger. Under the surface of that immediate and intense reaction was deep love, fear of what could happen to him, concern that he not get hurt, and a sincere desire to protect him. After I calmed down, I took Taylor aside and showed him the danger I saw that he did not. I explained to him that I'm sorry my reaction came across as anger but that I only reacted so strongly because I care so deeply. Then I calmly explained to him why he must choose not to zip out into the street so close to a corner."* The careful explanation shows that my apparent anger was motivated by deep and loving concern.

I didn't have the time after church to carefully lay out my concerns for my friend. So all she saw was my immediate reaction, which — I admit — came out as being harsh. My reaction was: *"STOP!!! Whatever you do, please don't turn aside from God's will to do your own!"* I was alarmed that she might deceive herself into thinking that God's word doesn't mean what it says or that what it says doesn't really matter.

257

Now I want to explain to you the reasons and concern that underlie my passionate response. Here I can give the calm explanation as to why it is imperative that you remain firmly committed to choosing God's will over your own whenever you cannot reconcile the two. You can apply this in general terms throughout your Christian walk and specifically within your marriage — especially when times are tough.

AT THE CROSSROADS BETWEEN YOUR WILL AND GOD'S WILL

When we come to the crossroads between our will and the will of the Father, it matters which path we choose! Everything I explain and encourage you to do throughout this book only works when you are willing to do God's will. You don't have to be able to do it — because no one is able to apart from the power of God. What God requires is that we are **WILLING** to do His will, even when it opposes what we want. That is where we take the path of God's will for us.

Isaiah described a path he called the "highway of holiness." I see this as the path we take when we choose to follow Jesus in yielding to the Father's will for us. Isaiah wrote of this path:

> *No lion will be there, nor will any ferocious beast get up on it; they will not be found there. But only the redeemed will walk there, and the ransomed of the LORD will return. They will enter Zion with singing; everlasting joy will crown their heads. Gladness and joy will overtake them, and sorrow and sighing will flee away. (Isaiah 35:9-10)*

Those who stay on the "highway of holiness" will find "everlasting joy"; they will know times of "sorrow and sighing," but those will flee away. Instead of a ferocious beast overtaking them to destroy them, they will be overtaken by gladness and joy as they continue to follow God's path to the end.

Those who walk on this way of holiness are specifically protected from the "ferocious beasts", who cannot assault them there. This imagery should be familiar. Peter warned all Christians,

> Be self-controlled and alert. Your enemy the devil prowls around like a roaring lion looking for someone to devour. Resist him, standing firm in the faith, because you know that your brothers throughout the world are undergoing the same kind of sufferings. (1 Peter 5:8-9)

I see choosing to turn aside from God's will to follow our own as stepping off the highway of holiness, stepping away from the spiritual protection of God's clear moral boundaries. Wandering off the path of God's will leaves us open to the influence and evil power of Satan. And — make no mistake about this — he comes only to kill, steal, and destroy (See John 10:10).

The movie **The Ghost and The Darkness** tells the true story of a British officer who went to Africa in the late 1800s to oversee construction of a bridge. He left behind his beloved wife, who was pregnant with their first child. Construction was interrupted because of attacks by two man-eating lions that devoured over one hundred thirty men. These man-eaters did not act like ordinary lions that killed for food. They seemed demonic and unnaturally bloodthirsty: terrorizing and attacking by day or night, undeterred by fires. They carried the human remains back to their lair, where skulls and scattered bones were piled up like trophies. The natives called the two lions **The Ghost** and **The Darkness**, fearing the malevolent supernatural forces they seemed to embody.

The officer enlisted the help of a renowned game hunter and sought to kill the lions so the bridge could be completed. He saw the vicious attacks first hand; in scenes too gruesome to describe, he saw men eaten alive. The delays, caused by the lions, made him unable to finish the bridge in time to return home for the birth of his firstborn. One scene in the movie depicts a dream he has while the lions are still on the prowl (but you don't know it's a dream until he awakes at the end of the scene):

His wife and baby arrive unexpectedly to visit him in Africa. As the train pulls in, our view sweeps across the waving fields of golden grass. Therein, you can see the form of a lion moving speedily toward the train platform. A beautiful woman emerges, cradling an infant in her arms, both dressed in pure white Victorian gowns. Crowds are running away from the station in fear of the lion. The officer is running against the crowds, toward his wife and child, yelling, *"Go back! Go back!"* She does not understand his urgency. She cannot hear his words distinctly above the noise of the running crowds. She smiles, expectantly, waving to him and holding the baby out for him to see.

The view shifts to the lion, gathering speed and hurdling through the grass, then to the officer. *"Go back!"* he shouts desperately to his wife as she smiles and hurries toward him. The lion bounds out of the grass, crushing mother and child to the ground and lustily devouring them before he can reach them or turn them back. Suddenly, he wakes up. It was only a dream, in a movie. But to me it vividly portrayed what the Bible says Satan would love to do to you and your family — to any Christian he finds outside the will of God — if given half the chance. Peter tells us that our enemy, the devil, *"prowls around like a roaring lion looking for someone to devour"* (1 Peter 5:8).

When I see anyone stepping off the way of holiness, smiling because they think they are going to find relief from their pain, ease from their suffering, and the happiness that they think God's will has kept them from, I am like that man, crying out desperately to his wife, *"Go back! Go back! Can't you see the lion?"* If I had the chance, I would implore them to go back to the crossroads and turn onto the highway of holiness. Stay in the protection of God's will. You may have sorrow and suffering for a while, but the road will lead you to joy. If you are lured off that highway to do your will instead of the Father's will, the lion who is seeking someone to devour will rush to pounce on you to devour you and your family.

Two Paths at the Spiritual Crossroads of Self-will and God's Will

There are only two paths leaving the spiritual crossroads where self-will crosses God's will. Jesus said, *"If anyone would come after me, he must deny himself and take up his cross and follow me. For whoever wants to save his life will lose it, but whoever loses his life for me will find it" (Matthew 16:24-25).* This tells us which path we are to follow but also something about what the signs will look like at the crossroads. Taking the path Jesus took will look and feel like you are losing your life, but you will really be saving it. Taking the other path will look like you are saving your life, but you will really be losing it.

Let's look at how Jesus made his choice that night in the garden of Gethsemane when he was arrested. Jesus never lost sight of his purpose, which he clearly stated when he said, *"For I have come down from heaven not to do my will but to do the will of him who sent me" (John 6:38).* Jesus remained intent on doing the will of the Father. Throughout life, Jesus' will was the same as that of the Father; he wanted what the Father wanted. But there came a moment, in the garden of Gethsemane, as Jesus approached the cross, when he was pressed beyond the point of having what he wanted agree with what his Father wanted. As a man, facing death, he could not make himself want to endure the shame and suffering he knew awaited him on the cross. At that point he came to a crossroads where he had to choose one or the other, his will or his Father's will.

This was not some dispassionate intellectual decision where Jesus simply knew what Scripture said and just did it. He agonized over yielding his human will to the Father. And yet Jesus' decision to choose the will of the Father over his own — despite the agony — led to his resurrection, his glory, and eternal joy for himself and his disciples. Matthew writes that he was *"sorrowful and troubled."* He needed his friends near him for support, telling his three closest friends, *"My soul is overwhelmed with sorrow to the point of death. Stay here and keep watch with me."* He wasn't kneeling beautifully with his face gazing upward into heavenly light as we see depicted in stained-glass windows. The Bible says, *"He fell with his face to the ground and prayed, 'My Father, if it is possible, may this cup be taken from me. Yet not as I will, but as you will.'"* He didn't pray just once; he prayed the same thing three times.

Mark records that he called his Father "Abba," which translates as the most intimate way a small child addresses his father. He said, *"Abba, Father, everything is possible for you. Take this cup from me. Yet not what I will, but what you will."* Luke tells us that he was in such distress, *'An angel from heaven appeared to him and strengthened him. And being in anguish, he prayed more earnestly, and his sweat was like drops of blood falling to the ground"* (Luke 22:43-44).

When Jesus Christ had to choose either his will or the Father's will, he was in agony. But once he made his decision and God handed him the cup of suffering he had feared, he didn't seek another path. He got up and willingly surrendered to those God allowed to arrest him. When one of his companions reached for his sword, Jesus rebuked him and said,

> *Do you think I cannot call on my Father, and he will at once put at my disposal more than twelve legions of angels? But how then would the Scriptures be fulfilled that say it must happen in this way? (Matthew 26:53-54)*

His agony was incomprehensible, and yet his choice was clear. He chose to abide by the Holy Scripture.

How could Jesus make such a choice? Scripture tells us,

> Let us fix our eyes on Jesus, the author and finisher of our faith, who **for the joy set before him** endured the cross, scorning its shame, and sat down at the right hand of the throne of God. Consider him who endured such opposition from sinful men, so that you will not grow weary and lose heart. (Hebrews 12:2-3)

Jesus could make this choice because he knew that although the highway of holiness would wind through the sorrow and sighing it would surely make its way to the everlasting joy that Isaiah prophesied.

Jesus wasn't choosing holiness **instead** of happiness; Jesus demonstrated that he believed true happiness — eternal joy — comes **through** obeying the will of the Father. That is why he didn't take the turnoff to do his own will when the shadow of the cross loomed up ahead. As we understand this, we can follow his good example.

God has given an example of another man, one who took the other path. He also came to the Garden of Gethsemane the night Jesus was arrested. But he didn't come to do God's will. He came to do his own will. He has a lot to teach us.

We dare not make Judas Iscariot such a one-dimensional villain that we lose the benefit of his example. Remember that he gave up all to follow Jesus. He ministered alongside the other disciples for three years. He learned to pray, *"Thy kingdom come! Thy will be done on earth as it is in heaven!"* He had expectations of what Messiah would do when he came. It was only when the plan Jesus laid out made it clear that the way to the kingdom led through the cross that Judas had second thoughts. What Judas wanted and what God's will demanded were on a collision course, and he was not willing to turn aside from his will to do the will of the Father as Jesus had done. Judas chose, *"Not God's will, but mine be done."* Then he went to the chief priests and asked, *"How much will you give me to betray him to you?"* It's as if he figured he couldn't have the kingdom he anticipated so he might as well get some small measure of gain out of a plan that didn't go the way he had hoped.

Judas could not see how Jesus' crucifixion could possibly be the will of God. So he sought his own way to get something worthwhile out of his three-year investment. He gave up holiness to reach for the small measure of happiness he could buy with thirty pieces of silver. When Judas turned off the path of God's will, Satan was waiting. (This is dramatically depicted in the movie, *The Passion of the Christ*). Sure, Judas got the money. But he never got the happiness he thought it would buy him. Once he saw that Jesus was condemned to death, he was seized with remorse. It's as if his eyes were opened and he saw what a fool he had been. He threw down the money at the feet of the Chief Priests, then went out and hanged himself. He was dead before Jesus; but he did not share the joy of the resurrection.

Let us learn from both Jesus and Judas, and the paths each chose. Jesus chose the highway of holiness. He denied himself what he wanted although he went through tremendous agony to do so. When he chose to do the will of his Father, he had to die on the cross. But when he lost his life, he found it. He found eternal life and everlasting joy. Judas followed the highway of holiness for a while — until it conflicted with what he wanted and what he expected of God. When he came to the crossroads where he had to choose **either** his will **or** God's will, he didn't deny himself. He sought to save his life; but when he tried to save his life by going against God's will, he lost it.

In marriage, there will be many times when we will have to choose whether to stay on the path of God's will or turn aside. You may face circumstances in your marriage that seem too difficult, too traumatic, to possibly be the will of our loving heavenly Father. That is when you may be tempted to turn aside from God's will to find some small measure of relief or pursue happiness down some other path. Your heart and human reason may say, *"Happiness this way!"* That is when you must remember that your heart is deceitful and desperately wicked. At these times you must walk by faith and not by sight. You must trust the One who set up the signs in His Word for your protection and eternal happiness.

The signpost saying *"God's Will"* appear to wind down into the valley of the shadow of death, through a dark night, and up a rugged hill to a place of torturous self-sacrifice. But just over that hill dawns a bright new life that cannot be seen until one crests the hill. This is the path to everlasting life. It leads to fullness of joy, in this life and the one to come. This path is guarded by God Himself, your Father in heaven who loves you. The signpost saying *"My Will Be Done!"* appears to take you away from the cross and out into a lovely golden meadow where the winds of happiness beckon to you. But what you do not see is the shining figure concealed in the golden grass of self-will. Your enemy lurks there, the evil one who roams about seeking someone to devour.

Dear friend, please don't be fooled. You may not be at this point yet, or maybe you are, or maybe you've passed the test and other tests will come in the future. But if your marriage is going through hell, you will have times when facing your situation, and whatever your spouse may be putting you through, may drive you to want to escape down paths that are at cross-purposes with God's will as revealed in the Bible. It may be the desire to get out of your marriage altogether; or the temptation to just get drunk and forget it all; or a longing to have an affair with someone who appreciates you; or the urge to treat your spouse as poorly as he or she treats you. There's no shortage of ways you can do your will when the Father's will seems too hard a road to walk. The fields of life are wide open with options for disobedience. That's why you need to settle this issue up front: Are you willing to do the will of our Father in heaven? Remember that **IS** the path to happiness and joy, even though all you can see ahead is a cross.

Jesus had a good reason to want his disciples to obey his commands, as he obeyed the Father's commands. He said, *"I have told you this so that my joy may be in you and that your joy may be complete" (John 15:11).* The joy we find by remaining true to God's commands regarding our marriage relationship will make the experience of the cross — in whatever form we encounter it — worthwhile.

Jesus compared his death and resurrection to a woman going through childbirth. She has pain, but the pain is forgotten with the joy that a child has come into the world. The pain Patrick and I went through when our marriage was going through hell was intense. Had I known how intense it would get, I don't think I would have gone that far. But it was like contractions; the pain was always measured out so that I could bear each episode. It was the joy that was set before me that gave me the endurance I needed to get through it. Today, when I consider our marriage and the actual joy we share, the pain is forgotten. Sure, I can recall how bad it was — sort of, just like I can almost recall what a contraction was like. But why go there? All that pain was part of the process of birthing the joy God intended all along. That's what we have today. That's what I pray you will have. That's why I urge you, this very moment, to affirm before the Lord that you do take your spouse — to have and to hold, for better or for worse, for richer or for poorer, in sickness and in health, forsaking all others, keeping yourself only unto him or her, to love and to cherish, until death do you part. And pray, *"Father — no matter what happens — not my will, but yours be done."*

CHAPTER TWELVE: PUTTING THE PAST BEHIND YOU

LORD, WILL WE EVER REALLY GET OVER WHAT HAPPENED AND WHAT IT DID TO US?

In 1997 I had the pleasure of helping Lyndi McCartney craft her insights and reflections on thirty-four years of marriage to her husband, Bill, the founder of Promise Keepers (a world-wide ministry to Christian men founded in 1990). Bill was finishing his book **SOLD OUT,** in which he reflects on his entire life in view of what God had done. I was surprised to find that Bill and Lyndi weathered many crises throughout their marriage and that Bill had been an alcoholic for many years. I guess we all tend to think that people God uses greatly are somehow different from the rest of us.

In talking with Lyndi, I was reminded again of the truth Jesus taught about the storms of life in his parable of the wise and foolish builders. No one is exempt from the storms; what makes the difference in the outcome is whether or not our lives are built on the firm foundation of obedience to God's word. The storms come to all, and even those who are "sold out" to Jesus sustain damage to their lives when the storms hit. Bill and Lyndi were no different.

At the end of Bill and Lyndi's book, we approached the subject of putting the past behind and pressing on toward the upward call of God for our lives. That's when Lyndi asked me, *"Can we ever really put the past behind us? I've heard that verse quoted so many times, but I don't seem to be able to get past the past. It seems like I drag it along with me."* Lyndi brings up a significant point. Some people never seem to get over what happened in their lives. It is possible not only to live in the past but also to let the past ruin your future. This is never God's intention. God's purpose is to bring you through the stormy crisis and out of it, into a brighter and happier future. This isn't something that just happens, though. You have to actively cooperate with God's plan to put the past behind you and press on to the good life He intends for your future.

Let me share with you what I shared with Lyndi as to how we do this. Let's stay with the imagery of a storm. When you watch a newscast showing the devastation brought on by a violent storm, the newscasts follow a pattern. There are storm warnings. Then the dramatic footage of when the storm hits, showing the powerful winds, flooding, crashing waves, and the destruction they bring. Then there are the images of blue skies overhead and a ravaged landscape of uprooted trees, houses that have been destroyed, and mud-filled cars and streets. These are used as a backdrop for reports of how many people were killed or injured in the storm. This is usually followed by images of people working to clean up the debris, shoveling mud out of roadways, clearing away the splintered wood, and hauling away the uprooted trees. These are usually accompanied with uplifting personal interest stories about the resilience of the human spirit. And several months or years later you will see that same city shown in the news for some reason other than the storm, but they will show the beautiful new buildings that were built after the "big storm" for which that city will always be remembered. The news story usually doesn't cover the individual lives of all the people who were hurt and have since died or recovered from their injuries.

This seems to be the way it goes. When a big storm has passed, people don't just live in the muck and debris. They don't leave the injured in the streets untended; they get them to the hospital. They don't stop using the roads just because they are filled with mud. After the storm has passed, the effects of the storm have become part of the present. But it's only common sense that people don't just accept their mud-filled streets as part of life and live with them.

This imagery works for me personally as a metaphor for the kinds of difficulties we've looked at in this book. I think it does so because the worst time in our marriage and my adult life was pictured for me emotionally with the dream I described as the opening scene of this book. My marriage went through the big storm of 1988-1989; you know when yours came or maybe you're weathering it now. Just as people pick up, clean up, and rebuild their towns after a hurricane; so too, you are not supposed to just live with the damage of what happened while your marriage was going through hell. You must look up, deal with the debris, and press on toward the future. You are supposed to take action to remedy the damage that has happened in the past. That means cleaning up, rebuilding, and making sure those who were hurt are tended to and given the chance to heal. This is what must be done with the emotional, spiritual, and practical aftermath of life's storms.

Christians sometimes misapply Paul's admonition to the Philippian church, which says,

> *I press on to take hold of that for which Christ Jesus took hold of me. Brothers, I do not consider myself yet to have taken hold of it. But one thing I do: Forgetting what is behind and straining toward what is ahead, I press on toward the goal to win the prize for which God has called me heavenward in Christ Jesus. (Philippians 3:12b-14)*

They act as though we are to simply pick up after one of life's storms and go on without looking back or dealing with the damage.

I agree with Paul that we are to press on toward what is ahead, but the best way to move forward after a storm is to clean up the debris, rebuild our lives according to God's design, and tend to the wounds of those who have been hurt. When you do this, you will truly be able to forget the past because its effects will not be left cluttering up the streets of your present life or impeding your way to the future God has planned for you and your family.

Your crisis will pass. When it does, you and your spouse will need to assess the damage and come up with a plan to clean up the mess that has been made. You'll have to cooperate and put in some good old-fashioned work on your relationship, finances, family life, and whatever else has been messed up.

The clean-up may require hard work, but you will be able to see what needs to be done. Clean-up tends to be self-explanatory because we recognize a mess when we see it. Problems usually suggest the kind of solution they require. Then it's just a matter of finding the resources and energy to tackle the job.

Rebuilding after the storm is a bit more of a challenge than the initial clean-up, especially if the life you knew before the storm has been wrecked. Ours was; there was no going back to the jobs we had, there was no way to pick up in the same town once our good names were no longer good, and many of those we called our friends had deserted us (while those who stood by us became far more dear). There was simply no way we could just repair the life we had known before; that life was wrecked beyond repair.

At first the realization that our lives could not be mended was terribly unsettling. Then one of our counselors gave that view a different spin. He said that perhaps one reason God had allowed life as we knew it to be blown away was that it wasn't built right in the first place. He encouraged us to stop thinking in terms of getting back to normal and start thinking of designing a whole new life on the foundation of our devotion to Jesus Christ and our devotion to each other. That was a freeing paradigm shift. It helped us look at our lives before the storm and assess it for faults in design — like being far too busy doing good things for God to have a close relationship with each other. After we had taken stock of our previous design flaws, we prayed that God would give us a new set of plans to design a whole new lifestyle in keeping with what He envisioned for us. That process of reassessing the faults in our lifestyle and relationship was like sweeping the debris into a pile. Choosing to throw that away and start fresh was like taking that debris to the dump where it belonged.

Then we began to dream again, unhampered by our past mistakes. We stopped trying to get back to where we had been and started looking forward to getting to the life God meant for us to have all along. We sketched out our dreams and prayed for God to help us make them come true. We kept working to maintain our basic necessities of life, even taking jobs that were not our ideal, but we were now aiming for the good life God's word promised us — a life where we lived free and forgiven, a life where our mistakes could help others, a life where our trust would be restored, where our love would regain the passion we once enjoyed, where our children would grow up safe and secure knowing that their mom and dad loved them and each other.

God has made those dreams come true! We had to do the work to build that new life, but God gave us the blueprints and the resources to build it. Our new life is so much better than the one that was destroyed that there is no comparison. If it took that storm to get us to start all over again and build this new life, I thank God even for the storm!

You will get past the crisis. When you do, don't automatically think in terms of repairing the damage to your lives. Prayerfully ask God to show you if it would be better to repair or to rebuild. Ask God to help you see your life in terms of it becoming what He always intended it to be instead of limiting yourself to the framework of what you have known in the past. God had so much more for us than we understood at the time. He has more for you than you can possibly imagine on your own. Ask God to give you His vision. Don't hesitate just because you feel you don't have what it takes to create that kind of new life and relationship with your spouse. God has it all, and He likes nothing better than to help His loved ones enter into the kind of abundant life He intends for them. Pray for the wisdom, resources, practical help, and opportunities you need to build that better life for yourselves and your family. That is a prayer God delights to answer, *"Yes!"*

HEALING THOSE WHO WERE HURT

Clean-up and rebuilding deal with the material damage, but a storm also affects people. Not only will you have to deal with the material damage to your life in terms of practical ramifications, but you must also tend to the people who were hurt. Depending on the kind of crisis your marriage has endured, those affected may or may not have physical injuries. But — no doubt — people were hurt in other ways. It's just that the emotional, relational, psychological, and spiritual wounds can be hidden or ignored more easily than physical wounds. Just as it would be ludicrous to clean up the damage done to the physical structure of a town and leave the wounded untended, it is foolish and dangerous to put your life back in order but neglect the hurts caused to people because of what happened.

This is the mistake that causes the pain of the past to keep recurring in the present. It keeps people from making unimpeded progress toward the future. This may happen because you or your spouse may be afraid to face how the crisis has hurt the people you love most. It may happen because you do not want your spouse to realize how badly you've been hurt, thinking that your spouse has already been through too much. So you hide your wounds, smile, and say you are fine, when you definitely are not.

I had a conversation with an old friend where this was the case. She and her husband were always very active in church and seemed the ideal couple. She told me how her husband had grown lethargic and could hardly do anything anymore. He'd been to doctors who couldn't find any physical cause. She concluded it was spiritual or psychological, but he refused to go to a counselor. As she poured out her heart to me, she told me, *"Life is just not what it used to be. Now everything is an imposition to him. Everything is out of his way. And it bothers me because he is not living according to God's word. It bothers me because he is in the word. Every year since I've been married to him, he has read that Bible all the way through. He says things are new to him all the time. I've been told I'm in his life to rock his boat. I say, I'm rocking it. I've tossed him clear out of the cotton-pickin' boat. I think he's out there drowning because of me.' So I pull back and don't let him know how I'm really feeling. I just live as his roommate. I clean his house. I do all that. But there is something terribly lacking. And it breaks my heart."*

She continued, *"So I go to the Lord and I say, 'I don't know what more to do.' I'm going to counseling. I'm doing everything I know to do, but it's not all my fault. I don't know what more to do. I don't feel free to share my hurts, my aches, and my pains with him. There's always a solution. He's got the Band-Aid for it. 'If you would just do it this way . . .' he says. And I want to tell him that I'm not him and I don't do things the way he does. I do them my way. But I don't say anything. I've gotten to the point where I don't want to talk to him anymore."*

I asked her, *"What are you praying for specifically? Or do you know?"*

With tears in her eyes, she replied, *"I don't even pray for him anymore. I used to pray that God would show him what it is, that he would give the doctors wisdom, and that somebody would walk down the aisle at church and say, 'This is what the Lord is wanting you to know' But it seems like it is always my problem. He's standing at church, and his hands are raised. He's praising the Lord! When the song says I bow my knee, he bows his knees. And I'm thinking everyone around me is thinking, 'What a godly man!' And here I am a basket case. I'm getting counseling. I'm spending money like there's no tomorrow. I'm involved in ministries. It's like, 'How can you be involved in ministries when your life is falling apart? But look at your husband.'"*

So I asked her, *"Does your husband know any of this?"* I knew her husband to be a caring man who surely would have responded to the depth of the pain and frustration she was sharing with me.

She said, *"No, I can't share it with him because it would hurt him. I can't hurt him. I don't want to hurt him. I don't want to see the disappointment on his face. I don't want to see the hurt. I don't want him to feel like he's a failure. So I don't share it. I keep it. I hold it in. Then I see counselors and I yell at my co-workers."*

This dear friend is wounded. She is still hurting. The pain of past wounds has mucked up the main street of her heart. Her inner life is filled with emotional splinters that are causing her to become completely numb to her husband. I suggested to her that in this situation she and her husband were definitely not experiencing the kind of fulfilling marriage and love relationship God says they are to enjoy. But she doesn't want to hurt him.

Sometimes sharing how you have been wounded by your spouse will be painful for him or her to bear. Yes, the truth sometimes hurts, but it's also the truth that sets us free from the pain of the past that ruins our present and threatens our future!

I asked Patrick once, *"What did I do that helped you get your life turned around?"*

He surprised me by saying that one of the best things I did to help him was to open up my heart in counseling to let him see the depth of how he had wounded me. He said that broke his heart. But Scripture says that godly sorrow works repentance. Patrick said, *"If I had been spared seeing the truth of what my sin was doing to the woman I loved, I could have rationalized. I could have gotten around it. But seeing the wounds inflicted in your heart brought godly sorrow, and godly sorrow brought the repentance that made me change."*

I know it may be painful to tend the wounds, especially when your spouse may experience pain and sorrow in the process. But it's worth it. Either or both of you may also be afraid to hear how your children have been hurt by what happened. I know it is scary; I also know it is absolutely necessary to deal with the wounds that were inflicted during the crisis so that they can heal. That is true no matter who was hurt.

BIND UP THE WOUNDS

Hosea 6:1-3 speaks to the necessity of healing those who are wounded as a prerequisite for pressing on to know the Lord. Hosea writes:

> *Come, let us return to the LORD.*
>
> *He has torn us to pieces but he will heal us;*
>
> *he has injured us but he will bind up our wounds.*
>
> *After two days he will revive us;*
>
> *on the third day he will restore us,*
>
> *that we may live in his presence.*

> *Let us acknowledge the LORD;*
>
> *let us press on to acknowledge him.*

When you've been through whatever storms hit your marriage, you may feel like God has torn you to pieces. Whatever your perceived source of the wounds, God is committed to healing, but you must present them to Him. You must allow Him to guide you to get the cleansing and tending that are necessary for the healing to take place.

Time alone does not heal all wounds. A wound left untended will get worse, not better, over the course of time. It will become infected. So, too, your inner wounds. Don't leave them untended. If anyone in your family is hurting, take that as a sign of a wound. Don't argue about whether or not you know how that wound occurred, or who is to blame, or whether it should have happened. If someone is hurting, get help. Love each other; listen to each other; forgive each other and give each other time. While time alone does not heal a wound, even a wound that has been tended and cleansed does need time to heal. Do not demand that others snap out of it; give each other attention, care, and time to heal.

Spiritual Splinters

There is another kind of injury that can happen during a crisis — especially a prolonged crisis — that I call spiritual splinters. These are the small things that happened that wounded someone initially but were not dealt with right away. These may be things that seemed too small to deal with at the time because of the pressing nature of your spouse's condition or marital situation, or things someone did while drunk or under the influence of drugs that hurt others and the offending person may not even remember clearly. These are the kinds of things that are ignored temporarily. You seem to forget about them — but they are still there. That's why I call them splinters.

I hate getting splinters! When I was a kid I had a really bad splinter that was painful to remove, but my dad removed it with a needle. After that, I would always hide my splinters. They weren't a big deal, and I learned that if I kept my splinter hidden for a few days, I would forget about it. During the initial phase of having the splinter, I would favor that hand, avoid using it, and definitely hide it from my dad. Then it disappeared, and if I ever noticed it again it didn't seem to hurt. So my policy on splinters became: Hide it, and if it ever comes up again, deal with it then when it won't hurt.

When it comes to splinters, my husband is a *"Get the needle, tweezers, and peroxide!"* kind of guy. So when my daughter, Casey, showed me a nasty splinter in her hand — when she was about eight years old — we conspired together not to let her dad see it. I assured her that these things have a way of working themselves out. I poured some peroxide on it, covered it with a Band-Aid strip, and forgot about it. The Band-Aid eventually fell off, the pain was gone, and Patrick was none the wiser. The tweezers never came out of the medicine cabinet. Mission accomplished! Or so I thought.

Several weeks — maybe even months — later, Casey showed me a strange white circle that appeared on the palm of her hand. It was entirely numb but had a strange appearance. We kept an eye on it over the course of the next few days as it turned from white to having a pink ring near the center to having a dark dot appear in the center. Neither she nor I associated it with the long-forgotten splinter, but we were curious as to the cause of this strange spot. Then it dawned on me that this unidentified black dot was appearing in precisely the same location where the splinter had gone in.

A few days later the mysterious black dot raised itself up slightly above the numbed skin, and Casey agreed to let me touch it. She felt nothing. So she agreed to let me touch the black dot with a needle. I put the needle into the raised black dot and lifted. A splinter almost one-half inch long came out without so much as a squeal from Casey, who had her eyes closed. After I removed the splinter, her hand healed completely and the numbness went away.

I saw in this experience a similarity to something that happened in the aftermath of our crisis. When Patrick and I were in the process of getting counseling for the wounds we had suffered, I discovered areas of my life where I was completely numb. There were episodes from my past that should have been painful — things from my childhood particularly — over which I felt nothing. These were things that had happened to me when I was young that I had never revisited. When I had been hurt in these ways, I had no remedy, so I just hid the pain. After a while I didn't hurt when I thought about the incidents that had hurt me. But I was also numb emotionally and cut off from that part of my life. The counselors helped me revisit the events that had wounded me but had never been dealt with. This didn't hurt, but it did bring a deep healing that has caused me to regain feeling where I was formerly numb emotionally. With regard to coming out of a crisis, there are spiritual splinters that are still apparent. These are the things you know have wounded you but about which you say *"Oh, I don't want to bring that up. It would hurt me or my spouse too much."* Or, *"I don't need to mention that; it would just start an argument."* I beg to differ. If you ignore the hurts you've endured (this goes for your spouse and children dealing with their hurts too), you will become numb to the people you love. The numbness may protect you from the pain that comes from the process of dealing with these hurts while they are still fresh, but the numbness can bring the danger of numbing you not only to the pain but to feelings of love as well. It is better to deal with the temporary pain of bringing up the sensitive issues and dealing with them currently than to add them to the splinter collection and risk losing all feeling for your spouse. You can let them be while the worst is going on, but as soon as you can bear to deal with them – when they arise in your mind again – deal with them completely.

I chose to thoroughly examine our lives and marital relationship — with the help of counselors — to remove all the past hurts, to forgive, to make amends when necessary, to listen to how I had hurt others, and to give every wound and every splinter the attention each deserved. Yes, it hurt initially. But the healing didn't take nearly as long as I feared; and the healthy relationship we now enjoy made it all worthwhile. The wonderful thing about tending the wounds and splinters in the lives of everyone in our family was that we did heal. Once the splinters were removed and the wounds were healed, there was nothing more to do in that regard. It has now been over twenty years since we decided to work through and remove the splinters of that most difficult time in our marriage. Just as I could not show you where any physical splinters that I got in my hands or feet during childhood were, I cannot now even recall where the specific emotional splinters were from the time when our marriage went through hell.

Binding up our wounds and tending to the emotional and relational splinters has paid off. We were able to rebuild our lives and get on with life. We were finally able to forget all those things that were behind and press on together toward a better future. The Lord was even gracious enough to allow me to return to youth ministry for two years while I was getting my Master's degree. The Lord also called Patrick back into full-time ministry (after 16 years of being in secular work) as a worship leader at a large church where he has served for seven years before moving on to music ministry at another church. The Lord has done such a superb job of restoration, rebuilding, and healing that his congregation had no idea what we'd been through.

Our three children are now 27, 22, and 21. Their lives have been shaped by the open, loving, supporting family relationships that were forged in the fires of hell our marriage went through from

1988-1992. While Casey has a few vague memories of something being amiss, the other two have no personal recollection of the pain and suffering our family endured. Our youngest wasn't even born yet. However, all three of them have reaped the benefits of how we learned to deal with difficulties together because of what we suffered and because we suffered it in the way God prescribes.

Without giving away too much personal information about my adult children's lives, I will share a story that points out the benefits of having worked through the pain of the past. Recently one of our kids was upset by a personal situation in her life. She called her brother and discussed it with him, receiving his acceptance, support, and advice. Then she came home and talked it out with her dad and I. Her sister, overhearing that she was upset, came out to show her support as well. We listened. We cared. We let her vent. Her sister made a pallet on the floor next to her so she could sleep nearby just in case she woke up and wanted someone there. The next day, our son texted me about something and I thanked him for supporting his sister.

He texted back, *"Yeah, I was glad she called me."*

I told him how we had banded together to help her when she got home.

To this he texted back, *"Good, I'm glad we are a stable loving family."*

I replied, *"Thanks be to God."*

They do not realize that we would not and could not have become that stable loving family in which they grew up if we had not dealt with the spiritual and emotional splinters that we got while our marriage was going through hell. So, remember that what you are willing to go through now will become the basis of the stable loving family that will make life better for your children (or extended family if you don't yet have children) and even future generations.

Scars

Wounds and splinters require action on your part, but there comes a time when you have to stop going back to where the injury occurred. This is what I call a spiritual scar. A scar is a reminder of a wound that once occurred. But there is nothing left to be done about it. It's healed. If you touch it, the tissue is not numb, nor does it hurt. It's just a visible reminder that you were once hurt in that place. You probably know exactly how you got every scar on your body. I can even tell you which of my own stretch marks were created by which pregnancy! These physical scars bear silent testimony to what happened, but there is nothing left to be done other than to recall what happened and hold on to lessons learned. Some of the wounds inflicted during your storm will leave scars. That's OK; scars can be a reminder of what you survived as well as what you suffered.

This relates back to Lyndi McCartney's question *"Can we ever really leave the past in the past?"* Can we press on toward the future without dragging the past along with us? My answer is a hearty, *"Yes!"* This is not to say that you or anyone else who went through this storm with you will ever forget what happened. This is not to say that your life will ever be the same as it was before — but then perhaps it wasn't meant to be! But you can get to a place where you will be able to think about it and talk about it without crying, or growing fearful, or flying into a rage, or being consumed with jealousy, or whatever emotions you may now be feeling because of it. You can get to a place where your fortunes are restored and your family is at peace again. You can get to the place where you can talk about it in the past tense and with a sense of joyous understanding as to what God did through it — even if you never understand exactly why it happened.

I know this may sound hard to believe, because there was a long time when I could not believe this would be possible. I was consumed by the pain of the crisis, the battles we had to fight, the enormous toll it took on every facet of our lives. This went on for several years, but we got through it. And you can too! I can speak with confidence, because we have gone on. The problems that once looked like insurmountable peaks that we could not scale have now faded into a misty landscape in the background of our history. Sure, we can still look back and see what happened. But when seen from this distance, in the light of what God has done since, the view of all we have overcome it has become a beautiful sight on the far-off horizon of our shared lives.

God does not want us to waste our pain, but to comfort others with the comfort we have received from Him. Therefore, I chose to go into the archives of our past pain to encourage those of you who are going through something similar. The wonderful thing about that is that I had to delve! I had to go back through journals and consciously recall what it was like. What happened to us in the past is not the center of our lives. God's love and plan of redemption is that Jesus Christ is the One around whom we center our lives. Even though going through this hellish experience in our marriage was the most trying experience of my life, I came through it. He came through it. And we have both moved forward toward the glorious future we believe God has for us. We are not stuck in the past; and you don't have to be either.

You will get through this, not only because you are holding on to heaven, but because God in heaven is holding on to you. He tells us,

> *So do not fear, for I am with you; do not be dismayed, for I am your God. I will strengthen you and help you; I will uphold you with my righteous right hand.(Isaiah 41:10).*

When God is fighting for you and upholding you in this way, you can be assured that the rest of this passage will also apply to you. It says,

> *Though you search for your enemies, you will not find them. Those who wage war against you will be as nothing at all. For I am the LORD, your God, who takes hold of your right hand and says to you, Do not fear; I will help you* (Isaiah 41:11-13).

I know this must be an extremely challenging time of your life. I know that you may be wounded and bewildered. You may feel like you're stuck in the trenches, fighting the same battles continually without gaining ground. You may be tempted to straggle away from your faith, exhausted and afraid. But I urge you to hold on and to stand your ground. I don't know what problems or suffering you're going through that caused you to pick up this book. I do know that God is faithful, regardless of what you and your spouse are facing. I do not know what is at stake in your life or the wounds you have already suffered. I do know that every wound hurts, that every battle for your marriage will be hard-fought, and that every threat to your family and your God-inspired dreams is worth fighting to the death. I also know that God does not intend for you to be defeated. Stand firm in your faith. While you will not come out of the battle unscathed, God can use even your scars for his glory. God knows, there are battles to be fought. And battles to be won! After Patrick and I had come through our most difficult time and I had healed enough to reach out to others, I was invited to speak at a women's retreat. I shared how God had brought us through. I wasn't sure whether the women would be able to relate or if it would help anyone. I was stunned at their overwhelming response. One woman wrote this in a note she gave me. The note said:

> *"Many marriages have suffered much less and fallen apart. People treat marriage like children going steady. God is willing to invest in marriages in pain, but it seems people aren't. We need you. I don't want to hear from the general in the office. I want to hear from the soldier who is seasoned, who has survived, standing next to me with scars from battles won."*

I have seen battle. I have survived. And I have the scars. But I also have the victory! And I am not alone. You've heard the stories of others who've held on to heaven while their marriages went through hell. They, too, have come through stronger, happier, more confident in God, vibrant, and full of encouragement for others — and so can you! There is a camaraderie among these veterans that rings with joy, laughter, and triumphant praise of God. When we show each other our scars, it is not an exercise in shared pity but in tribute to what God has brought us through.

Not every marriage I shared with you in this book made it, but the marriage partners who followed God's will in dealing with their marital hell were protected. Irene, whose husband had stomach cancer, was a widow for several years after her husband died before getting married again. Annette (who stayed with her (pastor) husband while he went to jail for having sex with a teen) tried her very best to make their marriage work. After he got released and she urged him to start working on dealing with the debris of their lives, he refused and divorced her. So, she had no power over keeping their marriage together at that point. However, she could go on with her life assured she had done her best to save their relationship. All the others, Sue and Rusty who were burnt in the motor home fire, Dave and Jan Dravecky who dealt with his cancer, amputation and loss of his baseball career, Roy and Cindy who prayed him out of prison, and the others have experienced a deeper, richer, and more loving marriage relationship as a result of holding on to heaven while their marriage went through hell. You can too.

One day, the spiritual battles you are fighting on behalf of your marriage will be done. God will cause you to triumph as you follow His commands. When you join the ranks of those with scars from battles won, I pray that you become a source of strong encouragement to others, as others have been to me, and I pray I have been to you.

Do you know someone who might need this book?

If so, please pass it along so that it can help as many people as possible. Thanks! Comfort others with the comfort you have received from God.

Acknowledgments

The lion's share of gratitude for this book goes to my husband, Patrick. He first suggested the idea and resurrected the proposal after I had put it aside for several years. He served as my inspiration by affording me the trials which gave me the opportunity to practice what I write about here. He responded to God in an exemplary way so that our marriage and lives today bear witness to the redemptive power of God. He faithfully prayed for me as I wrote, threw out that which didn't ring true, and rewrote. He read and edited each chapter as I wrote it, prayed with me, offered his insight, reviewed, and revised each chapter. He fended off disruptions — which were intense and numerous — ran our home and business, and took care of anything that threatened to interfere with the timely completion of this book — which he considers my most important work to date.

Thanks to the husbands and wives who shared their lives, advice, and hope with me and the readers. Due to the delicate nature of some of their situations, I cannot list all of them by name, but they know who they are — and God knows. They took the time to consider their experience, meet with me, and share what they had been through and what they had learned in the process. Although I did not use all the stories in the text, each couple I interviewed contributed to my thinking and therefore to the overall direction of this book. To each one of you — named and unnamed — I offer my sincere thanks. Those I can name are Larry and Rayna Bertolucci, Janice Bird, Roy and Cindy Davis, Dave and Jan Dravecky, Sharon Grooms, Margaret Dunn, Nan Durst, Gene and Jan Ebel, Amy Krohn, Rusty and Susan Lugli, Bill and Lyndi McCartney, Rick and Chi Mejia. Thanks to Today's Christian Woman magazine for allowing me to use Sue Lugli's story, which was originally written for their publication. Thanks for practical help goes to: Sue Lugli for opening up her home for our focus group meeting. Thanks to my daughter, Casey, for the cover design.

Notes

Chapter 2

1. Paul Clark, <u>Let Us Climb the Hill Together</u>, Songs for the Savior, vol. 2.

Chapter 3

1. For the full story, read Jan's book, <u>A Joy I'd Never Known</u>, (Grand Rapids: Zondervan 1996).

Chapter 4

1. Hannah Whitall Smith, <u>A Christian's Secret of a Happy Life</u>, (New York: Ballantine, 1986).

Chapter 6

1. C. S. Lewis, <u>The Horse and His Boy</u>, Book 5 in <u>The Chronicles of Narnia</u> (New York: MacMiilan, 1954), 138-39.

2. Ibid., 170.

Holding on to Heaven While Your Marriage Goes Through Hell

OTHER BOOKS BY CONNIE NEAL:

Dancing in the Arms of God: Finding Intimacy and Fulfillment by Following His Lead (Zondervan)

The Emotional Freedom Workbook (co-authored with Steve Arterburn)

A Joy I'd Never Known (co-authored with Jan Dravecky)

Walking Tall in Babylon: Raising Children to be Godly and Wise in a Perilous World (WaterBrook Press)

Sold-Out Two-Gether, Co-Authored with Bill and Lyndi McCartney (Word)

The Gospel According to Harry Potter: The Spiritual Journey of the World's Greatest Seeker (Westminster John Knox Press)

What's a Christian to Do with Harry Potter? (WaterBrook Press)

Holding on to Heaven While Your Friend Goes Through Hell (Word Books)

Wizards, Wardrobes, and Wookiees: Navigating Good and Evil in Harry Potter, Narnia, and Star Wars (InterVarsity Press)

MySpace for Moms and Dads: A Guide to Understanding the Risks and the Rewards (Zondervan)

See her Author Page on Amazon.com

www.ConnieNeal.com

Holding on to Heaven While Your Marriage Goes Through Hell

Speaking Engagements

Connie Neal is available for a limited number of speaking engagements. For details contact Connie through www.ConnieNeal.com.

About the Author

Connie Neal is the author of numerous books and contributed significantly to five major Bible projects. She earned her BA in Communication from Pepperdine University and a MS in Education, specializing in Instructional Design for Online Learning from Capella University. She toured as a guest speaker with *Women of Faith* and currently works as a freelance Instructional Designer. Connie and her husband, Patrick, have been married since 1979 and joyfully raised their three children together in a loving intact family by the grace of God. They reside in California.

Made in the USA
Las Vegas, NV
08 December 2022